David Martin is a Fellow of the Bri
of Sociology at the London Sch
Professor at Liverpool Hope Unive
assistant priest at Guildford Cathed

H d ang . Lsd Cand
Jun Dwrel .
Nov, 2013..

THE EDUCATION OF DAVID MARTIN

The making of an unlikely sociologist

David Martin

First published in Great Britain in 2013

Society for Promoting Christian Knowledge
36 Causton Street
London SW1P 4ST
www.spckpublishing.co.uk

British Library Cataloguing-in-Publication Data
A catalogue record for this book is available from the British Library

ISBN 978–0–281–07118–0
eBook ISBN 978–0–281–07119–7

Typeset by Caroline Waldron, Wirral, Cheshire
First printed in Great Britain by Ashford Colour Press
Subsequently digitally printed in Great Britain

eBook by Graphicraft Ltd, Hong Kong

To my parents, Frederick Martin and Rhoda Miriam Martin
and
*For our grandchildren on the occasion of our fiftieth wedding
anniversary, 30 June 2012*

'This autobiography is not meant to be a precise intellectual history, which I doubt if anyone can write about himself, without fudging the facts. Ideas, even if they come from books, are modified by experience in ways too indirect to be assessed at the time, or recalled accurately afterwards.'

Clive James, *May Week Was In June: More Unreliable Memoirs*

'We do not content ourselves with the life we have in ourselves and in our own being; we desire to live an imaginary life in the minds of others, and for this purpose we endeavour to shine. We labour unceasingly to adorn and preserve this imaginary existence and neglect the real. And if we possess calmness, or generosity or truthfulness, we are eager to make it known, so as to attach these virtues to that imaginary existence.'

Blaise Pascal, *Pensées*

'Nature to be commanded must be obeyed. The imagination must be given not wings but weights.'

Henry Adams, *The Education of Henry Adams*

Contents

———◆———

Part 4
EXPLORATIONS IN SECULARIZATION
AND PENTECOSTALISM

Illustrations

Acknowledgements

I am most grateful to Jonathan and Bernice for their many suggestions and amendments, and to Francis, Jessica and Graham for their careful reading of the text.

Introduction: my education in prospect

In my eightieth year, 2009, I was working with my friend Otto Kallscheuer for the European Commission, and he asked me how I became a sociologist. I explained that in 1947 I had been refused university entrance to study English Literature and failed a scholarship to the Royal Academy of Music. I had spent 1952 to 1959 as a primary school teacher in West London and Somerset. I stumbled on sociology by accident when a colleague in the Somerset school showed me his correspondence course for an external London University degree. From 1956, when my first marriage broke up, to 1959, I followed that course in my spare time. To my astonishment I won the annual university scholarship in sociology and entered the university as a postgraduate. Between 1959 and 1971, as I moved from primary school teaching in SW14 to an LSE chair, I was besieged by neurasthenia and a chronic fear I was an interloper with no right of entry. The aftershocks never fully dissipated. Otto thought the story worth telling, though he can have had no idea of the travail of telling it or the re-examination of self it might require.

My religious, moral and intellectual education was an inchoate groping, shaped by apparent accidents and driven by the helpful problems of a revivalist childhood. I had to find a way out of fundamentalism without causing my father terrible pain. The story of my education can be regarded as an act of witness, a conversion narrative that begins with successive losses of faith and continues with unexpected recoveries. The losses and recoveries are social, political and religious, all tied together.

What Evangelicals believe about God will always affect what they believe about politics and society. I began by taking for granted the assumptions of my Evangelical childhood. I graduated in adolescence to a pacifist liberal socialism, until in mid-life I accepted an Augustinian realism about the glory and the wretchedness of the human condition. That final shift began in late adolescence when I read Pascal's *Pensées*. Sociology for me has been about the social incarnation

1

of religious and political visions of human betterment and their refraction and frustration by social realities. If my story makes sense it comes from that project.

Helpful problems of a revivalist childhood

My father was a chauffeur who in his early fifties became a taxi driver, and in his spare time preached in London's Hyde Park. He waited patiently for me to 'give my heart to Jesus'. If he had pressured me I could have rebelled. As it was, I found it impossible to explore the maddening maze of things without undermining what was most precious to him. Decency required dissimulation, and dissimulation was not recommended at home or in the New Testament. You don't hear sermons in the Christian pulpit about the virtues of hypocrisy, so I have had to preach and practise them myself. Our Christianity was upfront and did not provide advice for everyday dilemmas or rules of thumb for negotiating imperfect solutions. There was a gap where most families have proverbial wisdom for morally and practically just about getting by. My moral education swung between hell and heaven with few negotiated settlements. Catholics have casuistry to help them, but we didn't know we could do with a casuistry. Much later in academic life I fastened on the problem of sincerity in politics and the need for judicious hypocrisy for the sake of the greater good or simple charity.

Apart from tactics of avoidance and retirement into bemused apathy, I was equipped with two speeds: forgiveness and outrage, especially outrage over injustice. Though I was inclined to forgive and found it difficult to keep outrage going, my forgiveness could not be relied on. Once I had run out of forgiveness I floundered. Just as Christianity makes no provision for negotiated compromise, it lacks a code of honour specifying predictable responses to predators. That's fine if you are good at just saying 'No', but I had a knack of ignoring the click of the safety catch. Nobody warned me the gospel was hyperbolic about forgiving people up to 'seventy times seven'. When I dealt with estate agents I either allowed myself to be swindled or broke out in uncontrollable anger. In practice, of course, our family looked after its reputation as keenly as anybody else, because faith demanded we keep our noses clean. My parents had lived in a harsh school and knew what was required. My father was canny, and my mother practised a subversive line in sardonic comment. But I was a dreamy and unworldly romantic shielded by the goodness of my parents.

There was another difficulty. My father wanted me to do something useful and likely to guarantee a secure job, which meant (say) £7 a week in the bank. Unfortunately the bracing necessity of work, work and yet more work, literally enjoyed by my father, became for me a sheltered infirmity of purpose. For the first time in history necessity had receded enough to accommodate lackadaisical aestheticism. Even though my school had a scientific bias and most of its pupils left at 16 for careers in the executive civil service or business, it introduced me to life as enriched experience of the humanities. Most pupils at East Sheen Grammar School evaded the humane element and did well. I evaded its scientific provision and did badly. In any case humane study was my sole default mode because I was cack-handed. At home my Meccano set lay strewn around unloved, and at school woodwork stayed an artisan mystery. My shoe laces and ties got into knots or unravelled. I would arrive home from school wearing two caps one on top of the other. As for tying knots as a tenderfoot in the Cubs, I never achieved a single badge. 'Scouting for boys' was not for me, apart from mooning after Akela when she read from *The Jungle Book*.

My mother edged me away from my father's world without wanting to disrupt the faith at its heart. Although a very practical person, from the very start, and before my ineptitude was fully achieved, she did not want me held back by hands messy with engine oil and creosote. Apart from bedtime prayers she left religion to my father, and we only once had conversation about faith. I questioned her about some Old Testament miracle and she said that if God could create the rainbow, nothing else was beyond him. I had no wish to question further. The rainbow was not the kind of miracle I had in mind.

Wherever my father went, people cherished him as a lovable mixture of the canny and the transparent. Though delighted to secure a bargain, he was not at all a lean and hungry Puritan and he loved the groaning table of wholesome food my mother provided even in wartime. What Evangelicals give up in not drinking they make up in eating. My problem had nothing to do with absence of love at home or my father's absence from the domestic scene. He was around a lot. My mother deferred to him as the ultimate authority and his belt was mentioned as a sanction of last resort. Yet I never saw him so much as move to take it off. I was, however, quite often boxed sharply around the ears by my mother, and once hurled under the sideboard when I spoilt a new coat playing on the muddy banks of Beverley Brook in Richmond Park. My mother performed all the male roles (as then understood) apart from mending bicycle punctures and looking after the car. She conducted all business transactions and was responsible for house repairs and house painting. Though a model of domesticity, I recollect the admiration she attracted from male passers-by painting the roof gutters on a high ladder.

This was a pattern of female practicality and initiative reproduced in my second marriage. I preferred and expected domestic arrangements based on informal matriarchy. My father's role was to earn our daily bread, though he sometimes played cricket with my mother and enjoyed playing draughts. That was it: mending punctures, cranking up the car, helping with the paraffin stove and putting up the tent on holiday, washing up and cleaning, always cleaning, either the car or domestic surfaces. His cars and (later) his taxis were polished till they 'shone as the sun in its strength'. What pertained to him *alone* was what Carlyle called the role of 'The Speaking Man', the charismatic preacher. It was as preacher he set my educational agenda. I had a Victorian childhood some three decades after the death of Victoria in 1901. That meant politics and power posed problems once I abandoned the idea the world could be saved if there were more Evangelicals like Wilberforce around.

I have only gradually realized the advantage conferred by problems. My academic colleagues might well be very sharp, but they sometimes lacked focus. I was focused. I just had to make sense of the role of religion in society and the nature of power and politics, especially sincerity and violence. I looked to sociology for clues to the problems set by a simple faith, only to find the problem might solve itself because sociology expected religion to wane rather than to wax. So I was engaged by the secularization thesis as well as by violence in religion. That became my academic vocation. I abjured complaint in favour of understanding. A desire to get the issue right displaced the waning pleasures of indignation.

Pentecostalism: my father born again in Latin America

Peace, war and violence, and the taken-for-granted secularization thesis were more than enough to provide the agenda of a lifetime. But then, as an extension of my critique of secularization, I stumbled on the remarkable growth of Pentecostalism in the 'Global South'. Here was my father's faith realized in a parallel world. One standard sociological reaction to Pentecostalism, supposing it even showed up on the radar, was to dismiss it as blocking the proper path of modernization. To begin with I was sufficiently misled by my discipline to suppose Pentecostalism a form of back-street abortion not likely to

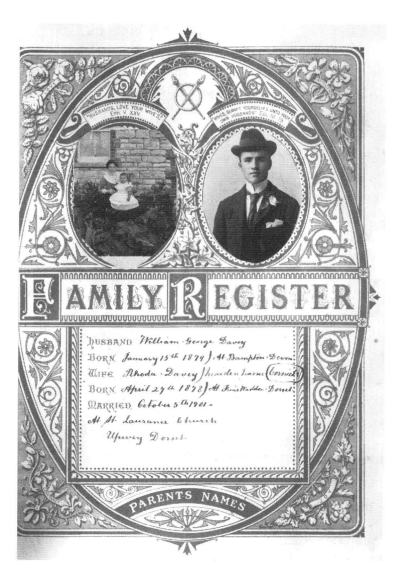

Register in the family Bible:
maternal grandparents William George and Rhoda Davey, 1903

take off in the modern world. It took time to recognize it as one of the main forms of modernization. Hence a wry little book I wrote entitled *Forbidden Revolutions* (1993) on the Pentecostal revolution in Latin America and the (partly) religious revolutions of 1989 in Eastern Europe.

The events of 1989, and the global revitalization of both Christianity and Islam, exposed how shaky and restricted was the Enlightenment's vision of the approved path of progress. Pentecostalism replayed my childhood faith on a global scale. That childhood faith had always nourished a tendency to dissent, and I disliked the censorship many sociologists exercised against people not socialized in their version of the Enlightenment. I rejected any account of history as the supersession of religion by abstract reason and rationalization. I was now engaged by cultural revolutions in the majority world that contradicted everything some of my sociological colleagues at the LSE believed about the proper course of history. The cultural revolution of Pentecostalism was not the kind of revolution they believed in, or thought possible. As for the revolution some of them did expect, neither they nor I imagined the demise of the Soviet Union and the whole Marxist project.

It was only because my American colleague Peter Berger intuited Pentecostalism was my subject, and in the mid-1980s offered me the facilities to pursue it, that I came to track the largest shift in the contemporary religious landscape. It took me some while to realize I was early on the trail of a global revolution fully comparable to the revival of Islam, but unnoticed because not setting the West a problem. The moment I saw the Encyclopaedia and the Dictionary next to the Bible in the homes of Latin American Pentecostals I knew where I was. This was my childhood, my father's house and my mother's father's house, but far, far away, and much later. The moment I met Pentecostal street preachers in Latin America I recognized my father born again in places he could never have imagined. An Evangelical faith now marginal in England, though still massive in the States, was fast advancing all over the 'Global South'. When my wife and I visited Maronite Catholics in Lebanon they asked me whether I could envisage a Christian revival like the Islamic revival. I fumbled, oblivious to the obvious. Once I saw the light I was like a Jew who finds the covenant faith of his fathers implausible, especially after all that has happened to his people, only to observe the covenant seems not entirely abandoned.

Insider and outsider

My childhood was normal if you leave out all the churchgoing and lusty singing of revivalist choruses. Much of it was spent in competitive displays on bicycles, fighting toy gun battles between cowboys and Indians, a game like hopscotch called Box, skipping, and rituals, pursued under cover in tents, beginning with the phrase 'Doctor, doctor' and a request for an investigation of some intimate ailment. Yet Evangelicalism gave me the confidence to be an outsider, because itinerancy in search of the gospel ensures you never quite belong. Except for my mother, who stayed at home on Sunday morning preparing Sunday roast, we might attend Barnes Methodist Church, but we were still set apart and dubious about the religion propagated there.

This status of outsider, always semi-detached, affected my approach to everything. I was not properly integrated into my grammar school and pursued my own idiosyncratic paths; I went to teacher training college as a day student who rarely mixed with other students; I read theology without any scheme of study apart from a brief period in which I took local preachers' exams; I read sociology in the evenings, persistently dubious about what it took for granted; and when I joined the LSE as a lecturer I felt under sufferance as a peripheral attachment. Once when I gave a lecture in a minor institution of the university, somebody commented in amazement, 'You still think you're an outsider.' When I was made a Fellow of the British Academy, my son-in-law felt it was time to tell me, 'Listen David, this *is* the inside.'

Like almost everybody else during the Second World War, I was patriotic. Then in mid-adolescence I began to distinguish between attachment to a culture and chauvinism. I was attached to an *idea* of an England somewhere between Piers Plowman and Vaughan Williams' *Fantasia on a Theme of Thomas Tallis*, but opposed to heel-clicking patriotism. When a church parade was held in the middle of the war in Barnes Methodist Church I felt irritated by the intrusive clatter of soldiers forced to attend a service. So I wandered round Barnes Common with the score of the Ninth Symphony chanting 'Alle Menschen werden Brüder', 'All men shall be brothers'. Romantic naïveté already had me in thrall.

As for the Church of England, I felt it was common property and had profound affection for my *idea* of it. But even after I was confirmed about the age of 50, and in 1983–4 ordained deacon then priest, I remained a commentator from the sidelines, and was sometimes treated as such. What had been dissent *outside*, became dissent *inside* the Church. I loved the Church as a musical and architectural presence not at all confined to the Church of England, and I believed that outward form and inner substance, beauty and holiness, were more closely bound together than some liturgical reformers allowed. That belief energized my protest against any attempt to consign the Prayer Book and the 1611 Bible to the museum. I did not want to be sent into internal exile where I felt most at home.

I was happy for others to explore new forms of expression and experimented with them myself, but I disliked engineered forgetfulness and imposed amnesia. After all, the Bible *was* my father's education, and it was thumbed, worn, and read every day. If my father could read it daily to the point where it informed his everyday speech, I did not understand how the Secretary of the Anglican General Synod, Sir Derek Pattinson, could claim to find it difficult.

Taken for granted: security and the independence of the mobile outsider

My sociological colleagues might explain my outsider status in terms of family origins 'in service', but that was not how my parents saw things. They calibrated the world in moral categories. Once I started wandering from home, intellectually and morally, I was never entirely at home again, anywhere. At the same time my home in SW14 had given me an inner confidence wherever I went, except that mine was derivative and I could not pass it on to our children. My father was supported by a doctrine of 'blessed assurance' and I borrowed my inward security from that unquestioned faith and the unruffled stability of my childhood. Vicarious confidence bore me forward even in the LSE. The LSE was populated by assertive and often anxious refugees, who had good reason to take nothing for granted except what they secured for themselves. No wonder some of them stuck so tenaciously to the secular and secularizing myths of Marxism and Freudianism. The LSE was their spiritual home even while they remained fearful for the future. I was besieged by fear because jettisoned into an alien environment far from home, but still sustained by a vicarious 'blessed assurance'. For an outsider and a dreamer I was remarkably sure-footed.

So much in my background was unquestioned that I was ready to question and challenge where others watched to see which way the wind blew, or kept their own counsel. Unthinking security led me to act in a way that often paid off, but was much more dangerous than I realized. I possessed incidental courage. The same security carried our family through the war, never doubting the 'everlasting arms' lay 'round about and underneath'. The Lord had 'the whole world in His hands'. When my father cried 'Jesus, help us' as the bombs came ever nearer, he had no doubt help was at hand. He remembered the words of the American Civil War hymn 'Hold the fort for I am coming, Jesus signals still'. When petrol ran out or the car broke down, help was always available from a garage providentially parked nearby. As the revivalist chorus puts it, 'Jesus saves'.

We lived on a different timescale from other people, one that could feel like the present but was actually continuous with a past that might be the first Liberal government of 1906, but equally might be the Methodist revival and John Wesley, or the Reformation martyrs, or the disciples in first-century Palestine. I realized my father lived in a continuous present when my aunt Megan's radicalized husband came back from the war in 1945 and brusquely informed him the Labour Party was about to nationalize 'all the means of production and exchange'. My father replied that 'They didn't do that last time', meaning 1924. The Pentecostals I met in Chile also lived in a continuous present, looking back to their conversion and forward to the Lord's return. Meanwhile they were contemporaries of people in the New Testament and talked to the Lord and his disciples 'as a man speaks to his familiar friend'. No matter how humble, they knew if God were for them 'none could be against them'. They took Jesus at his word: 'Al que cree todo es posible' (*Biblia Reina*, Mark 9.23). Everything was possible to the believer. The Baroque statues had walked out of their niches in historic time to become warm-blooded and contemporary. The Virgin Mary and the *animitas* to whom they had in unregenerate times made urgent supplication had become Sophia, the Holy Spirit within them. It was the same Spirit who had empowered my father to speak his heart in public.

Sheer unlikelihoods

What cannot now be imagined is the sheer unlikelihood of everything that happened to me. People forget just how few could expect to go to a university before the Robbins Report in 1963, even if they had attended a grammar school. 'University' was remote and irrelevant, and many parents with no experience of education beyond 14 feared their 'scholarship children' might be cut off from their origins. When I suddenly found myself transported by a postgraduate scholarship from teaching in a local primary school to the LSE my mother murmured, 'I always knew it,' as if addressing an unseen sceptical audience, but she had no idea what 'it' implied. One of my father's friends wondered what special mission in enemy territory the Lord had in store when, like Naaman the Syrian, I 'bowed my head in the temple of Rimmon'. Not that my father failed to be proud of 'it' or omitted to mention 'it' to his regular customers. When Mrs Lawson felt obliged to tell him *her* son was Chancellor of the Exchequer, he felt well up to the competition.

The gap was not just religious, though that provided the most salient marker. The gap emerged in space as well as time. My mother's early 'holidays' were no more than a eight-mile trip by cart from Upwey in rural south Dorset to Abbotsbury on the coast. My father had once driven an employer to Paris with an unforgettable overnight stop in Abbeville, but otherwise Scotland lay at the limit of his imagination. He started with horses and died in the era of jet travel. Even after the war my parents left England only twice, once to visit my sister's pen friends in Holland, and once to visit all of us when Bernice and I took a sabbatical in 1969 near Steckborn on the south side of the Bodensee. When I drove them up a mountain road in Lichtenstein my father was terrified by landscape on a scale he could not take in, and could only mutter, 'This is worse than Hindhead'. For those who do not know Hindhead, it is a very modest Surrey slope of a few hundred feet which in the 1930s could prove problematic for an Austin Seven.

I shared some of this confinement, in space if not in time, merely by being born in 1929, because from 1939 to 1945 the Channel was impassable and 'the Continent' an unknown region full of mortal danger. I even wondered whether I ought to risk crossing the Channel by steamer once normal service resumed. The generation that grew up in those years had an experience unlike what went before or came after. One advantage we did have: we were not cut off by education from our children as some of our parents feared they were cut off from us. The sheer speed of social mobility through education, which was the only mobility we understood, explained why I was so disbelieving when my head of department at LSE, with roots in the Jewry of Central Europe, asked whether I patronized the Algonquin when in New York. I had not yet travelled by plane. When I received my scholarship for postgraduate study at London University I travelled 'deck' to Athens on a wild celebratory journey even my more travelled friends thought adventurous.

From languorous somnambulism to a lifetime's project

My languorous somnambulism was certainly a problem. But something else was even more important, and it has to come first because it is the heart muscle that drives the circulation of my blood, and I find it less easy to identify. Up to the time I was conscripted into the army I experienced a natural accord with the world, a contented sense of self whatever my incidental disappointments, and an expectation of some burgeoning miracle. That expectation was fed by an experience of poetry, music and something I shall call 'the Romanesque', which allowed me distance from my Evangelical home without breaking with it. All these things were fed by my love of the language of hymnody, the Bible and the liturgy. In poetry I was drawn to Gerard Manley Hopkins through my remarkable English master, W. H. Gardner. My own inclination led me to Donne and the luminous lyricism of the seventeenth century, and to Eliot's *Four Quartets*, only recently published. Musically I was drawn to Bach, Handel and Brahms, each of them channelling intensity within formal constraint. 'The Romanesque' meant Abelard and Heloise, medieval Latin lyrics, Henry Adams on *Mont-Saint-Michel and Chartres*, sacred spaces and places like Moissac, Souillac, Vézelay and Saint Martin du Canigou.

Yet the poetry I read was full of intimations of some fall from the 'sweet security' of faith. There comes, and maybe there has to come, the loss of any secure footing you find in Hopkins: 'cliffs of fall/Frightful, sheer, no-man-fathomed'. Only after *that* can you come fully to know what Francis Quarles meant by:

> He's firmly mine by oath; I his by vow.
> He's mine by faith; and I am his by love.
> He's mine by water: I am his by wine.
> Thus I my best beloved's am and he is mine.

Without a precipitous fall no redemption; without a departure into 'a far country' no ring placed again on your finger.

In times of difficulty and joy alike music has remained for my wife and me the pacemaker of troubled hearts. Music, with poetry, exerted an apodictic authority over me and evoked a yearning to possess it and be possessed by it. Yet to discover all music meant and to make music my daily bread would have required more effort than I was ready to give and a much better balance between sensitivity and technique. Aged 18 I had read about many more kinds of music than I had actually heard, because I was restricted to what

I could play on the piano, hear on the BBC or overhear in church. Unfortunately music and poetry alike were dismissed as impractical indulgences and as private passions dangerous to male identity. I was on a haphazard expedition to a secret homeland. I found my way to that homeland by exploring new vistas adjacent to territory already mapped. In the wilderness of the army I heard Vaughan Williams' Fifth Symphony in the education hut like horns blowing from a world already hinted at in church. Matthew Arnold's definition and defence of culture engaged and puzzled me because the Evangelical and Hebraic world he dismissed as philistine was for me full of intimations of entry. My church provided a protected entry point to what was elsewhere dismissed as peripheral entertainment or feared, disliked and disallowed. Those few contemporaries who shared my yearnings found their way by different paths, through opera or the central European orchestral repertory. I had the viols, harpsichords and trumpets to myself until I met my second wife.

Had I known more musical history I might have understood the difference between continental Europe and Anglo-America and realized that in the north Atlantic, the nineteenth-century Evangelical spirit had fostered the pursuit of beauty as a channel to the divine, in spite of its reservations about the aesthetic. I took that pursuit for granted and was outraged when access to the arts was decried and denied as 'elitist', merely because middle-class people enjoyed by inheritance what I devoutly wished to enjoy by choice. I was also outraged by the suggestion that the rites and ceremonies of making music offended against equality and informality. I knew, from observation of the body language of serious musicians, that performance demands deliberate composure and obeisance, followed by acts of address not unlike the gestures of a priest as he goes in to the altar of God. This was what Francis Quarles called my 'Holy Place'. This was my inviolate space.

Conscription exposed me to violation and to sheer arbitrary sadism. It expelled me from my inner Eden. On leaving the army I might have gone to university and my future would have been entirely different. However, I was refused entry because the only subject I wanted to study was English literature, and for that I needed Latin. Had I not spent so much time ecstatically preoccupied with music, or just playing the piano as part of the social life of the church, I just might have bestirred myself to work at Latin. I didn't, and so I stayed in the world of the church youth club even after going as a day student to Westminster teacher training college.

I lost the chance to find a new circle of friends at university. There was a kind of sponsored pairing at the youth club, and a sexual ethic that decreed that once you were seriously involved, in my case with a 17-year-old, you were committed. I had no resources to review what was happening to us, or to negotiate the incompatible models subconsciously lodged in our heads about what we wanted from life or from each other. The sad mess of my first marriage completed what the army had begun. I was by now prone to dissociation, liable to back away from commitment, and from decisions. Dreaminess became somnambulism. I walked into trouble without grasping what I was doing or exercising the will power to change direction. Having got so 'behind' I struggled more violently to catch up, and the struggle created wave on wave of breathtaking anxiety. I had to run faster than other people to stand still. I was driven and dangerous, to myself and others.

If I was badly dissociated by my exit from Eden, my mother's expectations and the expectations of my wider maternal family ensured I easily smooched into situations on automatic pilot. Her family was very close and centred on my grandmother, and my father and I were both inducted into it. My mother's adored elder brother had betrayed family hopes by marrying an older divorced woman and having no children. The lot now fell on me. My mother and aunts cosseted me as the first child of a new generation who would carry the family forward into unexplored regions. I became 'the boy' who preferred to evoke the protective and preferably unconditional devotion of females rather than engage in crude assertion. These unfocused expectations felt burdensome, and when I encountered women who wanted reciprocity rather than surrogate motherhood, the burden grew intolerable. I felt trapped and my withdrawals sparked disappointment, extreme behaviour and a strong desire to kick the automatic pilot into consciousness.

From my mother I derived an anticipated future as a sensitive dreamer and from my father the calling of a charismatic preacher. The one corresponded to my mother's mythic origins in the numinous county of Dorset, and the other to mundane Mortlake, where my father worked and we actually lived. When my father heard I had decided to become a local preacher he said, 'With the Holy Spirit behind you there is no limit to what you can do.' When I sat beside the hospital bed as my mother lay dying she said, 'Do *they* know who you are?' With this dual inheritance the languorous somnambulism was only apparent. Underneath I was driven whither I knew not, and when I ended up at the LSE I overworked to reach an ever-receding goal.

The odds were heavily stacked against my having opportunity to pursue the questions that bothered me in any serious way. Only a series of accidents converted them from background noise into the project of a lifetime able to sustain commitment into old age and make retirement irrelevant. I was working towards something tantalizingly unspecific, but was under-qualified for anything immediate and tangible. It was as though I had been preparing myself for any number of futures, as a journalist, a musician, even a poet or a priest, with no notion of the appropriate track-ways, and lacking the power to follow them through to a desired end as well as prone to accidents in every sense of the word.

If my first marriage had not broken up I might have become headmaster of the little primary school in Bradford Abbas, Dorset. If I had not become friends with a radical socialist while we were teaching together in Wincanton, Somerset, I would never have known there was a subject like sociology tailored to my concerns. For years I read like an intermittent undergraduate in English literature, who never took the course or sat the examination. Having dreamed myself out of a university place and failed to win a scholarship to the Royal Academy of Music, teaching looked like the least unpleasant option available, and at least better than the civil service. I was glad to go to a teacher training college, because it seemed like a partial substitute for a university. Yet the impossible dreams of adolescence came to modest fruition: the music when I realized I could practise the craft of piano accompaniment to solo voice, and the poetry when I became ordained in 1983 and practised the craft of sermon making at Guildford Cathedral; the poetry could slip out sideways in the course of my struggle to express ideas.

One 'accident' more fortuitous than most occurred in 1965 when Arthur Crook, editor of the *Times Literary Supplement* (*TLS*), responded to my complaint about an unfair review of my first book, by offering me the chance to become a regular reviewer. So began a minor career in journalism which took me into territory I would never have explored without the stimulus of yet another book to review. The *TLS* represented quite a shift of genre from my first excursion into journalism as a columnist for *Joyful News* (renamed *Advance*), published by the Evangelical Cliff College in Calver, Derbyshire. People who hanker after writing have to adapt to what turns up.

In spite of the frustrations of my impeded ambition and the seeming limitations on our possibilities, my generation was lucky. But unlike the sixties generation, we knew it. My sense of privilege in finally arriving at a university was only matched by their sense of entitlement, aggravated by injury over the imperfections of the university, as well as the continued existence of a world unfit for them to live in. The contrast between my experience and theirs energized my protest against their protest, especially when I realized they reincarnated my former self. What I had imbibed about the liberated self from the literature of the 1890s and 1930s and from the attitudes of Bloomsbury they reincarnated in the 1960s. Some of my animus against them derived from a contradiction still present in me. I regarded their ideology as like a faulty nuclear reactor, liable to break down and turn emotional landscapes into howling wildernesses, but inside me the nuclear waste remained a subterranean source of leaking radiation.

The despised 1950s were times of hope. Had I not messed up my education in the 1940s by writing too much bad imagist poetry, perversely reading what was not prescribed, and leading a lively social life, especially at church, I might have gone to university at the 'right time' to study English literature. If that had happened I would have studied the wrong subject at the wrong time. Sociology spoke to my interests and concerns when I was mature enough to address them, as it does for many mature students, including those like myself forced to reconsider their lives by marital breakdown.

These chapters are mainly chronological up to my fortieth year. By that time what had been intellectually inchoate had acquired some conscious profile. In any case my fortieth year coincided with the student revolution and that convulsion firmed up my own views with astonishing speed. I wrote and spoke furiously in the long wake of the revolution. My inaugural lecture at the LSE in 1972 was a pivot for this furious writing and speaking which included a critique of parallel 'revolutions' in state education suffered by our children and in the Church, notably the deposition of the twin pillars of English religion, the Authorized (or King James) Version of the Bible and the Prayer Book. Here I partly abandon a chronology in favour of themes. The major theme is Pentecostalism and realizing that the street preachers and self-employed workers in the informal economy of Latin America were reincarnations of my father preaching in Hyde Park and standing proud and independent beside his immaculate taxi.

I hope there is little here damaging or painful to others, or even to myself. My Song of Myself may be an unconscious giveaway, but it is not a form of public confessional or some revelation of life's intimacies and shames. I only tell as much about my first marriage and its fallout as is needed to show that without that difficult episode I could never have moved, aged 30, from primary school to the LSE. I have little to say about *the* most important things in my life: my second marriage, the travails and triumphs of children, holidays, my sister, the death of parents, intellectual interlocutors, professional co-operations and friendships. Cutting the text for publication has reduced the personal stuff even further.

The events of a single day in 1991, when I gave an impromptu sermon to displaced agricultural labourers in Chile, provide a kind of ending. When my father imagined me in my cot preaching at the Albert Hall like the evangelists 'Gypsy' Smith and Aimee McPherson, he could never have imagined me 60 years later having to preach to the rural poor in the company of researchers from the Pontifical University of Santiago about his story and his conversion experience, and its relation to my own story. Of course, life did not end with interim closure in 1991, but enough is already too much.

Part 1
PRELUDES

1

Numinous Dorset and
mundane Mortlake SW14

━━━◆•◆•◆━━━

I really do not know how much time I spent in Dorset but my earliest memories seem more about that county and my maternal grandmother than about our real home at 25 Ripley Gardens, Mortlake. My memories of Dorset begin in the early 1930s, and end when my grandmother died in 1936. My grandfather, George Davey, was in charge of the Portland and Weymouth Waterworks, which had two pumping stations. The main one was in the tiny village of Friar Waddon. The other was used as a reserve when 'the fleet' was in and nestled halfway up a secluded valley above the village of Upwey, famous for its Wishing Well. My grandparents' house lay in the valley at the end of a gated driveway off the climbing road to Martinstown, and was one of two houses built close to the pumping station for its custodians. I remember all the dials showing the different pressures as the big machines clanked and revolved. I also remember going out with my grandfather to check the maximum and minimum outside temperatures and the amounts in the rain gauge for the meteorological office.

The house was screened by hedges and looked onto a grass tennis court, below which was a secret garden buzzing with bees and butterflies and full of sweet peas and honeysuckle. My most vivid memory is of going nervously upstairs to bed in the dark, past a small window looking onto the mysterious shapes of lowing cows. I held a blue oil lamp with a wick to show me the way to a tiny bedroom overlooking the secret garden and itself overlooked by trees full of cawing rooks. Every morning I woke up to the sound of these cawing birds, full of childlike ecstasy. 'My knowledge was divine.'

My grandparents' bedroom was close by my own and over their bed was a picture of the deposition of Christ from his cross. Next to the bed there was a commode, a marble table with a large washing bowl, and a china beaker with cold water to wash with. The alternative to the commode was an outside privy next to a washhouse, with a wooden seat and a hole over a bucket. At night I was reluctant to visit the privy and contented myself with a drain outside the back door.

In the kitchen-dining room there was a huge burnished oil lamp that could be lowered to create a pool of light, and over the cooking range a wooden plaque announcing 'Christ is the head of this house, The Unseen Guest at every meal'. Even then I wondered what the Lord made of the conversations when my aunts got together under the lamplight. My favourite meal was the huge breakfast, with eggs my grandmother called 'toppers' and bacon. My favourite sensation was my grandmother putting me in a tin bath and rubbing me with carbolic soap to relieve the bites of the 'harvesters' I picked up in the garden. My favourite event was the arrival of the milkman with vast churns of foaming milk which he ladled into my grandmother's jug, and my most unpleasant memory is of the corpses of rabbits hanging above the table after they had been flushed out by ferrets and shot.

On Sunday I would set off with my parents down the hill to the village, and hop, skip and dance by a tiny roadside stream to the Ridgeway Wesleyan Methodist chapel where my grandfather sometimes preached when not cycling to preach in distant villages. This idyllic walk went past the garden of the Wishing Well and the single-room village school my mother attended till age 12, and the mill (supposedly) featured in Thomas Hardy's *The Trumpet Major*. My grandfather belonged to the Salvation Army in Portland as well as the Methodist Church, and there was also a photo of him in his Masonic robes. I think he moved from the Liberal Party to the Labour Party, and in autumn 1934 he introduced me to George Lansbury on the front at Weymouth at the Trades Union Congress on War and Peace. Lansbury played a major role in the controversy within the Labour Party over how to respond to the rise of the dictators in the thirties that provided the centrepiece of my first book, on pacifism.

George Davey was born in 1879 in Bampton in North Devon.[1] I found out much later that his brother Edwin became a Mormon and left England for Utah. From Mormon genealogical records I discovered the Daveys lived in Bampton from the eighteenth century. More recent family details, including a written account of a cousin's adventures as a soldier in some late Victorian campaign in Egypt, were recorded in the embossed family Bible. This Bible had large engraved pictures and an impressive clasp, but there was nothing about Edwin. My beautiful cousin Diana followed Edwin's trail by becoming a Jehovah's Witness.

Rummaging in old papers I found some touching poems and a sermon my grandfather wrote for my mother, praying for her welfare when she left her job at Upwey Manor to go 'into service' in Kensington in the dangerous city of London. An early picture of my grandparents showed my grandmother as a beautiful young woman with enormous lashes, not the lady with her hair in a severe bun I knew as a child. When she died at the age of 59 the whole extended family was stricken and I believe my grandfather died of grief or severe depression in a mental hospital called Herrison House. I never went there, nor was I told why he was there.

During the Second World War, especially during the bombing, these early memories of Upwey became a personal Arcadia, and they merged with recollections of another idealized village, Cerne Abbas, in the hills of central Dorset. Both villages were defined by their church towers, and in the case of Upwey by a view from the road above the church. That view included a graveyard where my grandparents now lie buried on the slopes of a protective mound, known as the Windsbatch, with Iron Age remains such as one finds all over Dorset. Whenever I climbed the hill above my grandparents' house I overlooked this mound and had sight of the sea at Weymouth and the Isle of Portland. The coast was prohibited territory in the war, cut off by barbed wire 'for the duration', and the church tower in a hollow represented a place safe from violation. Wartime posters and paintings reassure me this sense of inviolate place was not just my peculiar experience.

Even now part of this marvellous coast is closed off as firing ranges. It runs from the strange and contorted rock formations of Worbarrow Bay and Lulworth Cove to the 20-mile-long shingle beach of Chesil, which I could contemplate from St Catherine's Chapel on the conical hill above Abbotsbury.

Gradually Dorset acquired several layers of meaning. One was of the young women of the thirties like my mother's sisters, enjoying freedoms unknown to any previous generation and riding pillion on motorbikes. A generation earlier, at the turn of the century, the world of my grandfather must have been one where young men were no longer born to be socially placed in the hierarchy of squire, clergy and farmer, and everything he did, including his Methodism, confirmed that new independence of status and spirit. Then there was an eighteenth-century Dorset made up of a patchwork of farms, inns and cottages and, a little later, neat and charming chapels like the one at Bridport. Apart from quarries, net making and boats, Dorset remained untouched by industry, except where it was magically traversed by a railway that burrowed through a tunnel beneath the nearby Ridgeway, with its Neolithic barrows, Roman road, and a modern road with a hairpin bend. Then it burst out again into the landscape of Victorian villas and modern bungalows that formed the hinterland of Weymouth. It left the tunnel at Upwey and Thomas Hardy wrote poems about an incident at Upwey station and about the exhilaration of riding down the Ridgeway.

There was a much earlier Dorset, ruined castles on mounds like Corfe, half-hidden manor houses and quite small churches at the centre of scattered nuclei of habitation, and finally the primal presence of tumuli, Bronze Age remains, Iron Age grass forts and multivallate circles, overlooking the geological forms that had created the Jurassic coast. That was the coast I overlooked westward standing on the high point of Admiral Thomas Hardy's Monument five miles further up the road from my grandparents' house. This landscape created the base line for my sense of human beings in historic and prehistoric time, just as it did for Thomas Hardy and the dialect poet William Barnes, as well as the atheist mystic Llewellyn Powys. I remember reading aloud the medieval poem with the refrain 'Timor mortis conturbat me' on the cliffs near White Nothe and above the abandoned Viking settlement of Ringstead. I also recollect chanting the creed in Latin by the bare walls of St Catherine's Chapel, overlooking the ruined monastery of Abbotsbury and the bright sliver of inland sea between Chesil Beach and Portland. I cycled all over Dorset, enumerating its beauties as though they were mine, and tracing its borders as though they demarcated purity from danger. I walked along Hardy's hairline tracks over the tops of rounded chalk downs or beside small streams to tiny half-enclosed villages, as when I made my way through the water meadows for Morning Prayer in Stinsford church, where Hardy's heart is buried.

This landscape created my knowledge of Paradise Lost, of good and evil, and of the melancholia of mortality, so that years later the simple act of opening the gate of the church of Upwey St Lawrence caused me to break down in a prolonged paroxysm of grief. Personal and public history fused for me in the history of a landscape and I read the Victoria County History of Dorset to grasp the universal in the local: the little Roman temple on Maiden Castle Iron Age fort, the straight street lines and exposed mosaic floors of the new first-century county capital of Dorchester, the founding of the diocese of Sherborne in AD 705, the sad remains of Bincombe Abbey, the suppression of the Monmouth Rebellion in 1685 by Judge Jeffreys at the Bloody Assize,[2] the tiny church in the hamlet of Winterbourne

Came where William Barnes ministered, the grand fleet assembled at Portland.

My father came from rural Hertfordshire near Cuffley, only some 40 miles north of London, but in 1891, the year of his birth, it was thoroughly rural. It held none of the aura of Dorset for me, partly because my paternal grandmother now lived with a daughter in Barnham, Sussex. She was born about 1853, she dressed in black and signed her name with a cross. Her husband was long dead, killed by the kick of a horse. It seems he was once a drunkard who abused my grandmother but he became a convert and preached at street corners, singing hymns as he played his accordion.

My father left school at the age of 11, his hands permanently marked by the weals inflicted by canings, and he worked in the stables of a newly reconstructed mansion on the (Cardinal) Pole estate belonging to a well-known local family called Hanbury. Then he left, like my mother, to go 'into service' in London, at Lambeth Palace during the time of Archbishop Davidson, and became (in 1912 maybe) the chauffeur of a Delaunay-Belleville. As the romance of my mother centred on place, any romance surrounding my father centred on cars, and the Delaunay-Belleville was a French creation of the early twentieth century, very much the king of cars and the car of kings.

Later I became used to admiring the magnificent vehicles my father drove, and even to riding in them when some rich lady wanted to pet a small boy or stoke my imagination with books of Norse tales. Our own cars were at the other end of the price range, for example the Austin Seven my father bought for £5. When my father left the employ of the Archbishop Mrs Davidson gave him a New Testament.

After that he drove the crime novelist Edgar Wallace, the Liberal MP Walter Runciman, then President at the Board of Trade, and for some months in the autumn of 1913 he was one of chauffeurs of Mr Asquith at 10 Downing Street, with memories of taking the Prime Minister to play golf in Scotland at Lossiemouth. He also remembered taking Runciman to his country estate at Doxford in Northumberland, and recalled feeling guilty that on one occasion he used Runciman's car to spend a weekend at home in Hertfordshire. Such was his sense of obligation to his employer.

My father became 'soundly converted' under the preaching of a famous itinerant evangelist called 'Gypsy' Smith. Gypsy Smith was born near Epping Forest and grew up 'wild', with not even a day's education. The death of his mother had something to do with his conversion and perhaps the death of my father's father had a similar effect. Certainly my father idolized 'the Gypsy', seeking him out to

The author's father, Frederick Martin, with horses, aged 12,
Poles, near Ware, Herts, c. 1903

The author's father, Frederick Martin, aged 21, with Delaunay-Belleville
when chauffeur at Lambeth Palace, 1913

offer his services as a driver, and on one occasion (so my aunts told me disapprovingly) he contemplated his young son in his cot and prayed that one day he too might 'be used mightily of the Lord' in bringing many souls to glory. Maybe he imagined his son preaching to some great concourse in the Albert Hall, which to my father was the height of ambition. I too imagined myself in the Albert Hall, not preaching but stirring a vast audience with some stunning performance, like Eileen Joyce playing Grieg's Piano Concerto on the sound track of *The Seventh Veil* or José Iturbi playing Chopin's A flat Polonaise in *A Song to Remember*. I had internalized a 'burden' of expectation, then fused it with absurd notions of genius, and transposed it into a different key.

At some point in the late twenties both my parents were employed in personal service in Kensington, my mother in Cornwall Gardens. This was a very grand area developed in the late nineteenth century, with pillared entrances, and I remember visiting some of my mother's friends still 'in service' in basement rooms. My mother had been a 'tweeny', a between maid, and she worked for Ellen, a 'superior' lady, to use my mother's description, in charge of all the domestics for an almost impossibly remote employer, Mrs Laurie. Here my mother acquired her knowledge of gentility and good manners. My mother's friends in this 'downstairs' world were unmarried women who dandled me on their laps and encouraged me to play with their necklaces.

One was called Maisie, an orphan brought up by a church adoption society. She went to the same church as her employer, the society church of St Mary Abbot, and her attitudes and demeanour taught me just how deep deference could run. She could not imagine anyone downstairs ever walking directly into the upstairs by the front portico. That came out when my mother told her I had recently done just that. Yvonne, my LSE secretary, had asked me whether I knew a Mr Nixon from the United States because he was in town and perhaps I might care to meet him. I was puzzled by this mysterious Mr Nixon, until Yvonne added the message came from William Waldegrave. Mr Nixon would be at home with him on Friday, and several other government ministers would be there as well. Naturally I went and was rewarded by hearing Mr Nixon pronounce the word Watergate in person, and assure us that Ronald Reagan had good advisers and would not make a hash of the presidency if elected. But Maisie was unmoved: 'Ah well, you see, Miriam, those Kensington houses have gone downhill a lot since our day.'

My father was also deferential, but he had an inner core that was almost brashly self-confident, something I noticed among

Pentecostals in Latin America half a century later. 'Blessed Assurance' was one of his favourite hymns, and it had an everyday translation as an inward certainty that the criteria of this world were as nothing in the light of the world to come, when Jesus should return in glory to claim his own.

That came out when I was invited in 1976 to a private lunch with the Queen. My father simply wanted to know whether Her Majesty had said grace before we began to eat. She might be the head of state but that paled into insignificance should she not be among those caught up to meet the Lord in the air as promised by Paul in 1 Thessalonians. I transposed my father's attitude into an obdurate independence towards whatever my academic colleagues took to be agreed truth.[3]

My parents met at the Central Hall, Westminster, a famous preaching auditorium built in Edwardian Baroque by the Wesleyans that announced their presence at the heart of London opposite Westminster Abbey. There must have been many recent arrivals in London for whom this was a friendly home from home as well as a place that spoke of arrival and respectability. I was christened there in 1929 by the Reverend Dr Dinsdale T. Young, a great figure of the time whom I just about remember, resplendent in his ministerial frock coat. This is where my mother had been in the choir, had made recordings with it and even sung solo.

As a small child I was taken to the Central Hall on Sunday evenings and the moment a service began there was a great clattering of seats as two thousand full-throated voices sang 'O for a thousand tongues to sing my great Redeemer's praise'. The 'long prayer' was an endurance test, especially if you contorted yourself in a crouching position, but the sermon, though it might last 45 minutes, was exciting. This was 'preaching for a decision'. While Dr Young spoke of the horror of sin and the greatness of God's mercy, I would lie on my mother's lap and play games in my head with the Central Hall's intricate ceiling. After the service, the organist Arthur Meale might even play his own famous composition *The Storm*, though maybe I never knowingly heard him play it because he died in 1932 when I was three.

I now realize how many of my father's most cherished beliefs chimed with those of Dr Young, or perhaps derived directly from them. My father would say the Bible was 'true from cover to cover'. He also expected the Second Coming of Christ. His favourite hymns were 'There is a fountain filled with blood/Drawn from Immanuel's veins' and 'Just as I am without one plea/Save that thy blood was shed for me'. My father spoke lovingly of the precious blood of the Saviour and passionately declared that 'There is power, power, wonder-working power, in the blood'. Then there were hymns like 'Will your anchor hold in the storms of life', 'Draw me nearer, nearer, nearer, Blessed Lord, to thy precious bleeding side', 'I will sing the wondrous story/Of the Christ who died for me', and 'The Old Rugged Cross'. I played the piano while he sang, conducting himself as though encouraging invisible choirs to join in.

So long as 'the Doctor' was at 'the Hall' we went there to 'feed on' the gospel, though we also went to prayer meetings in parts of South London, until maybe my mother had had her fill of peripatetic piety. Indeed I suspect my mother occasionally curbed my father's enthusiasms in the interests of normality, especially when he preached and sang in our street accompanied by his friend Mr Chatfield on the ocarina. Street preaching was all very well in Hyde Park, where my father worked with the minuscule Society for Evangelizing London, but it could come too close to home. Often when my father came in from work my mother would ask him whether he had 'been in the park', which embarrassed him because he could not lie. I am sure my mother passed on to me her own embarrassment at loss of self-control and immersion in the egalitarian ocean of religious ecstasy.

When Dinsdale Young died in 1936 we entered a further period of itinerancy. We 'sat under' Alan Redpath at Richmond Baptist Church, a preacher whose name I forget at the Hammersmith Rivercourt Methodist Church, Dr Campbell Morgan at Westminster Congregational Chapel and his successor Dr Martyn Lloyd Jones, and later we returned to the Central Hall under Dr William Sangster. Sangster was so winning and powerful, in spite of a very unattractive voice, that one of his sermons on the love of God persuaded me for at least 15 minutes that I should give myself to God's service. But my father interrupted my reverie with something so irritating that the love of God and my burgeoning vocation were completely dispelled. We did *not* go to hear Dr Donald Soper, because he was suspected of a purely 'social gospel', nor did we contemplate sitting under Dr Leslie Weatherhead at the City Temple, because he preached psychology. My father's heroes were the great Evangelical preachers of an earlier generation, like Billy Bray, Dwight L. Moody and Charles Haddon Spurgeon. Occasionally he would call out 'Amen' when the preacher reached some particularly moving climax. He also loved extempore prayer meetings, and engaged Jesus in long and passionate prayer with sighs on his knees most mornings.

There was little opportunity for his religious enthusiasm at our nearest Methodist church in Barnes, though he was once allowed to 'conduct' choruses before the service, and also allowed to preach in one or two tiny Methodist 'causes' as an auxiliary. One minister at Barnes, the Revd Professor Eric S. Waterhouse, was 'empty' of 'real gospel' or desire to convince of sin or even to warm our hearts. Properly converted people desirous of 'being fed' heard him with studied disapproval. A 'strong' Evangelical Yorkshireman at Barnes named William Cartwright ostentatiously read the Bible during sermons by Waterhouse and once recruited me as a gangly youth to open-air witness outside the Hammersmith Rivercourt Church, to my acute embarrassment. To this day I feel pity, sympathy and admiration for people who stand in busy thoroughfares to preach or declaim Scripture, like a black woman I heard in a New York street pouring out long passages of Isaiah by heart or a preacher offering salvation to indifferent multitudes opposite Victoria Station as they crossed the road by Little Ben.

As a man whose life centred on cars my father judged the success of a church by the number and opulence of the cars outside. Physical and social mobility were connected, though we had no interest in social mobility. Washing and polishing the car, or burnishing anything else shiny like shoes or plates, was my father's most satisfying activity. Being washed in the blood of the Lamb meant being washed behind the ears. In 1937 and 1938 our regularly burnished Austin Seven took us on grand tours of Scotland, attracting mild ridicule because the car sported a Bluebird in the back window. Whenever we reached a serious mountain road like the one-in-three gradient of the Devil's Elbow in the Grampians, we had to walk to give the car a better chance. For me and my sister this journey to Inverness was an epic adventure, and we pitched our tent each evening like the intrepid travellers we felt ourselves to be.

Our home at 25 Ripley Gardens, Mortlake was built in the late twenties as part of a building boom. Like Woking, where I eventually fetched up, it was mainly a creation of the railway age beginning in the 1840s. Yet it still had some of the buildings and atmosphere of an eighteenth-century village and was tucked away on a gracious bend in the Thames between better known eighteenth-century haunts like Barnes and Richmond, with their commons and parks. I took these bosky spaces for granted and had no idea this was the most salubrious area of London apart from the heights of Wimbledon, Hampstead and Greenwich. Handel had lived nearby at Barn Elms when he first came to England, and Gustav Holst had lived in one of the elegant riverside houses less than half a mile away on the number 9 bus route that ran across the river to Hammersmith – a place Holst evoked in a work of menacing modernity. Hammersmith Bridge marked the real beginning of London and Hammersmith Broadway was London's pulsating western artery, leading directly to its heart by way of Earls Court, Kensington and Hyde Park. Initially the buses had curving outside stairs to the upper deck and their route began at the Avondale Road bus station flanking Tinderbox Alley and backing onto our modest No Through Road to the east.

Mortlake lay conveniently close to a transport system that included buses along the Upper Richmond Road to Richmond one way and to Barnes, Putney and Wandsworth the other. The Upper Richmond Road was our busiest local thoroughfare and a main route for the famous Green Line buses. From Mortlake station the railway took its passengers in only 20 minutes to Clapham Junction and Waterloo. The Southern Railway had once been the London and South Western Railway, and its small intimate carriages displayed attractive pastel watercolours of the English countryside by Rowland Hilder. Walking west along the Thames towpath I could easily reach Chiswick with its Palladian villa and mysterious gardens, or press on to Kew and Richmond. At Richmond you could take the river steamers

David Martin, aged 4, with his mother outside 25 Ripley Gardens, 1933

The author's mother, Miriam Martin, aged 22

up river through the locks to Teddington and Hampton Court. Mortlake might be mundane compared to Dorset, but I realize now it had atmosphere, and it was marvellously placed for my excursions into London proper or into the nearby parks and commons, the Thames Valley and the Surrey countryside.

The railway at Mortlake was accompanied on either side by the snaking narrow roads of North and South Worple Way, and it cut us off to the south within a narrow rectangle of roads 250 yards by half a mile. On its northern boundary we were cut off by Mortlake High Street and the Thames towpath between Watney's Brewery and the White Hart riverside pub. The Oxford and Cambridge boat race finished at Mortlake, and every child identified with one or other crew much as they do now with Premier League football teams. The other boundaries, east and west, were Sheen Lane and White Hart Lane, and there was a sharp division between the part behind the White Hart Lane boundary, which was as regular as New York with First Avenue and Second Avenue, and the irregular patterns in the part behind Sheen Lane. My life was lived in the alleyways and twisty paths of a crazy warren lying behind the little shops, grocers, greengrocers, shoemakers and ironmongers, off Mortlake High Street. Its Victorian and Edwardian dwellings had steps up to porticoes, but the area was mostly made up of charming cottages with small neat gardens fronting the winding pathways, like Mullins Path by the side of my school.

Little remained of an earlier Mortlake, except the parish church with its graveyard, belfry, quaint cupola, and tower inscribed *Vivat R.H.8 1543*, and a short alleyway from the High Street to the towpath, close to what had been the home of the alchemist Dr John Dee, and to buildings connected with the seventeenth-century tapestry factory that produced the famous Raphael cartoons. Near the church, down a sheltered pathway, was a tall nineteenth-century schoolroom on the site of an earlier 'charity school', and some 1905 buildings making up the rest of the Church of England ('National') school. The Catholic church, with its own small school, was on the railway side, off North Worple Way, and was famous for its Arab tent mausoleum to the explorer Richard Burton. What had been a handsome Dissenting ('British') School from the 1840s still stood in South Worple Way.

Between Ripley Gardens and the adjacent churches lay Worple Street, a single row of older houses whose lower physical and social elevation and grey brick contrasted with the bright red newness of Ripley Gardens, though these despised houses are now transformed as 'period cottages', and snapped up by childless executives. Here was our most obvious social boundary and a high fence separated Worple Street people from resented newcomers now obliterating what had once been allotments. Our own modest garden had a concrete yard, shed and coal hole, and a trellis beyond which lay a pathway flanked by grass, flowers, small trees and fruit bushes. The railway to the south marked our wider social boundary before you arrived at the spacious middle-class dwellings of Sheen, although just the other side of the tiny 'Spur' railway bridge for pedestrians there were mean-looking houses (as we thought) like those in Worple Street, and a disreputable pub. Social status and size of house increased southward between the railway and the Upper Richmond Road, and rose even more sharply with the large houses and mansions on the tree-lined slopes up to Palewell Common, Sheen Common and Richmond Park. This urban ecology was barely implicit in my consciousness then. We were modestly 'respectable' in our new house with its two main bedrooms and one small one upstairs (with lavatory), and its two main downstairs living rooms (with hallway and kitchen).

Our 'front room' was sacred space for receiving visitors, with its mostly unused fireplace, its piano, one large picture of a rustic cottage and a smaller one of the temple at Taormina, and its family photos. At some point we acquired a green ceramic figure of a putto holding a cornucopia thanks to my father's habit of rescuing objects binned by his West End employers. The back room with fireplace, small bookcase and sideboard was for more formal meals, relaxing to snooze or read or listen to the wireless, while the kitchen with gas stove, table, dresser, sink, Ascot burner, mangle and washing tub was the centre of domestic industry and ordinary eating. The street was our play area and regularly visited by the lamplighter, the ice cream man on his bicycle ('Stop me and buy one'), the coalman on his cart pulled by a horse dropping steaming ordure useful for the garden, and the rag and bone man crying his wares.

My father mixed more with 'sound Christians' than neighbours, whereas my mother made sure to stay on good terms with them. I enjoyed the street life and spent time with the Tappin boys at number ten. Minus my father we went out as two families for car rides to beauty spots like Friday Street or Burnham Beeches, and I realized wide-eyed that Mr Tappin cherished a *tendresse* for my mother in spite of her not completely successful attempts to keep his advances at bay. It was Mrs Tappin who gave me volumes of Southey, Longfellow and Milton to read, making an incomprehensible remark about Milton's unfortunate politics. The Pearces at number 27 were 'funny' and 'did not speak' or throw balls back, while Mrs O'Brien at number 23 did speak and throw balls back. She was a Catholic and we pitied her because the priest said she was 'living in sin' for marrying a Protestant. The lady living opposite us attracted criticism for being 'constantly at her front gate', though I saw no other signs of immorality. Our house was on a mortgage from the Abbey Road Building Society. Its initial price was £500 and 80 years later it had multiplied a thousand-fold. My parents saved and worked very hard to keep up the payments and had any number of little insurances and accounts with friendly societies. In the early years my mother went out to work to make a little money by personal service and we took lodgers as well.

Apart from the *Daily Mail* cartoon strip 'Teddy Tail', I read *The Methodist Recorder*, *The Fundamentalist*, *The Christian Herald* and *The Herald of His Coming*. I liked *The Christian Herald* because it ran stories for the moral instruction of children. Apart from *Psychic News*, *The Herald of His Coming* must have been the only paper primarily devoted to events in the future. There were several Bibles, including Weymouth's (unread) modern translation, as well as Bunyan's *Pilgrim's Progress* and *Grace Abounding to the Chief of Sinners*, Foxe's *Book of Martyrs*, a *Life of David Livingstone*, sermons by Charles Haddon Spurgeon, *Wycliffe: Morning Star of the Reformation*, a *Life of Wesley* and a book on *Christian Holiness*. A vividly illustrated book called *Our Paradise Home* featured volcanic apocalyptic imagery taken from Revelation. We had a *Chambers Dictionary* and Cyril Alington's *Encyclopedia*. Bible, dictionary and encyclopedia went together just as they do today among Pentecostals in Latin America. The entry on 'The Earth' was emended in my childish hand to conform to the chronology of Genesis. Once I had acquired Milton from Mrs Tappin, I declaimed the opening of *Paradise Lost* from the top of the stairs, though I had scant idea of what the leaves that fell in Vallombrosa could possibly be about.

Then there were my mother's Edwardian Sunday School prizes, *The Old Torn Bible* and *Maggie's Mistake* which I read with great moral profit, *Oliver Twist*, *David Copperfield*, *Robinson Crusoe*, *Treasure Island*, *Uncle Tom's Cabin* and *Westward Ho!*. My mother often spent part of the afternoon reading classic English novels, especially Scott, Dickens and Hardy, when not listening to 'the cricket' on the wireless, above all England playing Australia. (Almost her last words before she died in late August 1981 were about the Test match: 'I hope England don't let Australia get away with it.') On hot afternoons in 1938 I remember the great Hedley Verity bowling Bradman, and

Hutton scoring centuries, including the highest score so far in Test cricket of 364. I expanded the number of books with Jules Verne and the gung-ho imperialist tales of G. A. Henty, as well as boys' stories by W. H. G. Kingston, Fenimore Cooper and R. M. Ballantyne, all three celebrated in a poem by R. L. Stevenson. Some of these books I bought for a few pence from the Chain Library in the Upper Richmond Road, until I too moved on to Dickens and Hardy. If you begin by reading the Bible you can end up just reading almost anything. When a taxi driver in Mexico City told me of his Evangelical background he asked me what I thought of Baudelaire.

Apart from home, school, cycling and the pleasures of playing in the street, the education of David Martin was continued by Barnes Methodist Sunday School. I have another early memory about how this happened. My mother would sometimes go to Barnes Common to watch the cricket or to visit her loquacious Evangelical friend Gertrude Perris, and one sunny afternoon in 1933 or 1934 we passed by the Methodist church and my mother asked some workmen why they were building an extension next to the church. They said it was a new Sunday School, and joked that maybe I would like to go to it one day. For years I did just that, twice a Sunday, as well as Sunday morning service, walking the mile or so with my sister, some five to six years younger. The experience affected her rather differently. She was very musical, a good pianist, interested in English romantic poetry, and in early adolescence painted mysterious landscapes. Eventually she married a Roman Catholic from Ulster and became a Catholic, something my father eventually took surprisingly well, especially when he recognized how like himself my sister's excellent choice turned out to be: sober, reliable, conscientious.

Sunday School began with a trial visit, which so excited me I rushed around out of control, and a teacher wondered whether I ought to wait a bit. All the same, I entered the beginners' department and enjoyed drawing, playing in sand, moulding plasticine, listening to stories and singing. I sang 'Jesus wants me for a sunbeam', 'Hear the pennies dropping/Listen as they fall/Every one for Jesus/He shall have them all', 'Jesus bids us shine with a pure, clear light', 'There's a home for little children/above the bright blue sky' and 'When he cometh, when he cometh/To make up his jewels/All his jewels, precious jewels/His loved and his own'. Albert Midlane's 'There's a Home for Little Children' was a piece of nauseating Victorian necrophilia, but at six I retained immunity from nausea and chirruped merrily. Perhaps the basic children's hymn was 'Jesus loves me! This I know,

/For the Bible tells me so./Little ones to Him belong/They are weak, but He is strong.'

As I moved through the school receiving stars and prizes for attendance and medals for collecting 'missionary money', I sang more advanced songs, like 'Brightly gleams our banner, pointing to the sky/ Waving on Christ's soldiers to their home on high' (tune by Arthur Sullivan) and 'Dare, dare, dare to be good'. I ransacked the little Sunday School library until I had read all Angela Brazil's novels about what went on in private schools for girls. I also read a series produced by (or for) the Juvenile Missionary Association about missionaries in exotic places like the North-West Frontier. Mr John Parsons came to tell us about his experience during the First World War and showed us the breast-pocket Bible that deflected the bullet that would have killed him. We enjoyed Sunday School treats to places like Herne Bay in specially chartered trains, and film shows of Charlie Chaplin and Laurel and Hardy. These shows were my main exposure to film as my parents did not approve of the cinema. I still find it difficult to follow the narrative conventions of film.

Sunday Schools are often run by an atypical group of church members and mine was no exception. I have sometimes wondered whether Mr Balfour, the superintendent, was a British Israelite. Miss Rose Chamberlain was a severe spinster who kindly picked me up so long as I was too young to manage the journey on my own and she explained to me the dangers of the Church of Rome. This supplemented the warnings of Mrs Gertrude Perris, a follower of Mr Kensit of the Protestant Truth Society, who provided me with startling information for a boy of eight about the dangers of confession and ritualism, and the machinations of the Anglo-Catholic peer, Lord Halifax. She passed on her weekly resumé of the views of the Beaverbrook editor of the *Sunday Express*, John Gordon. But these were only incidental oddities. There were so many able unmarried women who encouraged me and found fulfilment in the activities of chapel and church, like Miss Marjorie Elmer, a professional chemist who played the piano for the Sunday School and ran the Juvenile Missionary Association.

Sunday Schools do not today figure as major sources of serious education, as they certainly were in the nineteenth century. But even in the thirties they could widen perspectives on the world, reinforce habits of reading and listening to stories, and provide opportunities to perform set pieces in public. When you were taken into 'the big church' for the opening part of the service there was always a children's address with a story and a moral, and you would often be asked questions and acquire information. I became noxiously good at answering these questions, and when I overheard somebody comment I could not *really* know all that, I tried to ward off criticism with occasional answers that were not quite right, like locating Mount Everest in India. When I used the word 'concomitant' I was told, 'Somebody seems to have swallowed a dictionary.'

The Sunday School Anniversary was an important event in late spring when we all filed onto a special platform in front of the pulpit to perform little anthems, sing solos or recite. At Christmas we were encouraged to sacrifice something we really cared about to less fortunate children, and I still feel the salutary pain of giving up a red aeroplane. The annual prizegiving was a major event with huge piles of instructive books. Occasionally you might take part in a little pageant, and I recollect being dressed for a pageant like a young prince in a seventeenth-century portrait. Gradually, if you stayed the course, you might be invited to do a little teaching and introduced to skills of presentation. Eventually there might be serious sequential Bible study, and my first introduction to exposition came when I was asked to take over a group of young helpers and work out a syllabus for presenting the story of the Book of the Acts. The moral atmosphere was wholesome and supportive, and parents felt happy to offload progeny for Sunday morning or afternoon and give themselves time to snooze or tend the garden.

Sunday School was part of the inexorable rhythm of Sunday, the prescribed day of rest that was a day of constant activity, devoid of profane pursuits, when you were on your best behaviour and dressed in your Sunday best. The Sunday School was the scene of my first rebellion, against Miss Rush, a teacher and disciplinarian who had been very kind to me. Having discovered rebellion I then rebelled against my father, which I found emotionally very costly because I dimly realized he could not understand it. Finally I rebelled against the ultimate and real authority of my mother, which proved much less costly because she understood and I was not trapped in a cycle of incomprehension.

2

Mortlake Church of England Primary School

I went to the infant school at Mortlake reluctantly, with constant glances back home. I read early and enjoyed reading out loud in public, so I was quite put out when a girl received 20 for reading aloud and I received only 19. There was always some girl pushing me for star roles at the things I shone at, though Derek Spratley also worried me by being so good at arithmetic that I started hurrying to keep ahead and got a lot of sums wrong. As I went up higher through the classes I often found myself sharing a top desk with a girl or being selected to do monitoring jobs with Jean Smart, a tap dancer, who counted out the dinner money with me or helped me stack the hymn books after assembly. I liked privilege and difference.

Miss Neill taught me a lesson that I have continued to misapply. We were taking turns to dance around the maypole and she praised me for not pushing and shoving. I concluded that holding back elicited verbal or other rewards, and by the time I had cottoned on to the survival of the fittest this retiring disposition had become a disabling habit. Perhaps that is how I ended up with the triangle instead of the drum in the percussion band. I also overlearnt a lesson in honesty from the upshot of a scuffle in the cloakroom. A boy punched me and I punched him back, but he denied it whereas I admitted it, so the headmaster caned him for lying and commended me for truthfulness.

I soon realized I could not rely on this happy conjunction of morality and immunity. I recognized that success often attended dishonesty and theft, as when somebody purloined my precious piece of Roman pottery from the newly discovered Roman town house at Colliton Park, Dorchester, I decided to try it myself by stealing a book of cigarette cards from a friend in spite of not wanting it. Swearing

36

David Martin, aged 3, 1932

David Martin at Mortlake Church of England Primary School, 1936

blind I hadn't proved such hard work I learnt there were costs to morality and immorality alike.

I loved going to church and the holiday on Ascension Day, the toffee apples sold in the house next to the school, watching the sparks fly in the riverside smithy off Mortlake High Street after school, and drinking school milk through a straw. I loved singing hymns at morning assemblies and singing the prayer 'Now the Day is Over' at the end of the afternoon session, and singing lessons – especially 'Early one morning/Just as the sun was rising'. I also loved Miss Rose Steele. Miss Steele encouraged me to write poems for her, and when I was briefly evacuated to Reading she gave me sixpence for the postage needed to send her more poems. She taught us to speak poems collectively in a very histrionic way. We had to preface Tennyson's 'The Brook' by raising both our arms in the air, and lowering them bit by bit as we moved down the scale, saying, 'Bubble . . . Bubble . . . Bubble . . . I come from haunts of coot and hern', etc. We performed other balletic exercises to accompany Alfred Noyes' 'Come down to Kew in lilac time, in lilac time, in lilac time;/Come down to Kew in lilac time (it isn't far from London)'. Miss Steele went through history, from the sabre-tooth tiger to cavemen and Glastonbury lake village. She also put me next to 'dirty Gerty', a girl who was shunned for smelling. I consented to this with as much grace as I could muster, until urine trickled along the seat and made me nearly as wet as she was, at which point I told Miss Steele I could take no more.

I told Miss Steele I wanted to stay in her class for ever, because the next class was taken by Mrs Boddy, a frightful disciplinarian with a moustache. Mrs Boddy terrified me. Once when she sent me on an errand with a message, I was too frightened to take the message in but dared not ask her to repeat it. So I lingered in the corridor for an age, unable to deliver the message and unable to go back to Mrs Boddy. No wonder she put on my report that I was 'Quiet and rather slow'.

I did not like 'drill', and I disliked country dancing because I was clumsy and could never work out how to thread my way through the twists and turns. I did enough fighting to avoid being put upon, and was ranked seventeenth in the class for who could bash whom, but backed this up by helping a pugnacious boy with his sums if he protected me with his fists. I was a quick calculator and, like most people educated before 1960, could do sums in my head, including such esoteric fractions as one-sixth of a pound equalling three shillings and fourpence. Fractions did not help in the Richmond swimming pool, where I was held under the water by a thug called Reginald Purdy and thereafter hated the smell of chlorine. Nor did it help me when running the gauntlet of the narrow passage past Mortlake Roman Catholic School to Mortlake Church of England School. You could easily be stopped and harassed by rough children from the south side of the 'Spur' railway bridge. When my eldest son Jonathan attended the same school a quarter of a century later he escaped being harassed in the same passage by climbing so high up the Catholic school his persecutors dared not follow him.

Some of my classmates walked in irons, and once the school was told one of our schoolmates had died of scarlet fever, and we were to be quiet passing the house and respect the drawn curtains. When my grandmother died I came to school with a black patch sewn on my coat. There was an organization called The Waifs and Strays to which we were encouraged to give our pennies. Then there was Empire Day, when a military man came and unrolled a map to show us the countries marked red as part of the Empire. We assembled in the playground to salute the Union Jack, also the Australian flag, to acknowledge our connection with Mortlake in Australia.

My mother met the headmaster, Mr Slater, to discuss whether I had a chance of winning 'the scholarship'. This was a rarity at my school, and after that consultation my mother acquired the papers, teaching herself and me what was needed to pass them. I enjoyed this intimacy with my mother and specially enjoyed mastering the angles in different kinds of geometrical shape. Perhaps most crucial were the eight volumes of *Newnes' Pictorial Knowledge* bought by my mother from a doorstep salesman who claimed they would help with 'the scholarship'. I was allowed them volume by volume, beginning with volume 2, 'History'. I read it over and over again and acquired a lasting interest in history, including the history of art and music. I still encounter history pictures, like Walter Raleigh pointing out to sea and *And When Did You Last See Your Father?*, with a stab of pleasurable recognition. Volume 8 was 'General Knowledge', a subject in its own right, and I think my general knowledge fed off it for many years. My cousins in Barnham, Sussex, acquired their information from *The Children's Encyclopedia* compiled by Arthur Mee, and I read that too. The *Pictorial Knowledge* volumes were particularly good for geography, and I received a prize for geography entitled *Lis Sails to Tenerife*, and another prize about gypsies in the Midi and at Tarascon, which led me into a world of southern enchantment I could not anticipate ever entering.

There were other ways of learning. Jigsaw puzzles were often informative, in particular a puzzle that had a fascinating border with pictures of the ships of the main shipping lines, like the Union Castle and Lloyds. Most boys collected cigarette cards, often picked up in the street, and these might include series on the ships of the principal navies, especially the Royal Navy, or the uniforms of different regiments. Pocket diaries included lists of the height of mountains, length of rivers and size of cities, and I can still remember the population of London in 1931 was 8,202,818 and the height of Everest 29,002 feet. London was the biggest city in the world even though the Thames was not the biggest and longest river.

You were allowed two attempts at the scholarship, one at nine and one at ten. I failed the first time and only recollect I was unable to answer a question about who Il Duce was. The second time, I passed and remember that *Newnes' Pictorial Knowledge* provided the background knowledge for a composition on 'Bridges'. At one point my teacher came past and her finger touched a particular sum. I realized it was wrong but felt unable to correct it because my attention had been drawn to it improperly. The teacher came past once more, her finger again moved to the mistake, and this time I suppressed my scruples.

Before I went to the grammar school with 18 other scholarship boys from Richmond and East Sheen, the disruptions of the war meant I attended three schools in one year, either just in the mornings or just in the afternoons. The first school was in Dorchester, Dorset, to which we had gone just before the declaration of war, staying with my mother's sister. This was a shock, because Auntie 'Dick' and Uncle 'Blackie' were more modern than my parents, and they amused themselves 'kidding' me. My parents did not play about with the truth and I was unused to teasing. We went to Dorchester because everybody believed that 'the bombing plane will always get through', which meant that London was scheduled for immediate destruction. We all anxiously gathered around the wireless in 180 Monmouth Road, Dorchester, at mid-morning on 3 September to hear Neville Chamberlain announce, 'consequently we are at war with Germany'. I wandered out down the lane reflecting that 'we beat them last time, so we'll beat them again'. My 'war effort' in Dorchester consisted of collecting silver paper under the direction of the daughter of the prison governor.

I loved walking to the Dorchester school at 'top of town' because the route lay partly along the tree-lined raised 'walks' that had replaced the old walls. My greatest pleasure was to watch the water after rain gushing along the gunnels. The school itself had been evacuated from Acton and my teacher was a mannish woman who wore plus-fours and a brown beret. To begin with I was on the top row but then started to sink, ending up in the third row, next to a boy named Baldwin. One day the teacher started at the front row saying they were all safe bets for the scholarship, and likewise the second row, but when she reached the third she said, 'The scholarship ends here', excluding myself and Baldwin; 'or maybe it stops here', including us both as marginal cases. It was not reassuring. Equally unpleasant were the boxing lessons arranged for the boys in the hall behind All Saints Church in High East Street. I moved stealthily back and back in the line of those to enter the ring, determined not to engage in this wretched sport. The great compensation of each and every day was to walk in a crocodile along the banks of the River Frome, watching the bubbles from the lavatory and the water flushing through dykes, and bending the grasses before it. At the end of our street there was a grassy pre-Roman and Roman amphitheatre to rush up and down, and just south of Dorchester there were the high grass palisades of Maiden Castle to climb, dating from the second millennium BC.

I adopted a Scottish accent as a way of being different in Dorset, while back in Mortlake I adopted a Dorset accent as a way of being different in Surrey. In Dorchester I saw my first real film, *The Lion Has Wings*, about the RAF and was barely able to believe these were genuine pictures of planes in flight. I also played intimate games in a tent on the lawn with Eileen and Kathleen Garner, the evacuees billeted with the next-door neighbour, until my mother forbade 'rolling about on the floor together'. The neighbour was determined to improve the hygiene and discipline of these city waifs, and brushed their hair every morning with moral vigour, using a prickly brush. I would sometimes walk with Eileen Garner along the chalky lane that led into the fields and the woods sheltering the little hamlet of Winterbourne Came – the parish of the parson and dialect poet William Barnes – rubbing ears of corn as we went. This was the path followed by Thomas Hardy when he visited his friend Barnes.

By Christmas there had been very few air raids. London had not been destroyed by the Germans, so we went home and I started at another school, mornings only. Then, at Easter, there was another evacuation scare and this time I became an official evacuee, sent by train to the home of Mrs Tregay in Caversham Heights, a well-off suburb of Reading. She was expecting a Catholic boy, but welcomed me warmly nevertheless. Her son Billy was not so welcoming and constantly knocked over the wooden brick structures I played with in a marvellous garden, full of pleached avenues. The Tregays also had a fine library where I enjoyed browsing for books like *John Halifax Gentleman*, and Billy did not. They had a maid (on whom I had a crush), a cat and a dog, all total novelties to me, though the *Children's Hour* series 'Mompty and Peckham' about that kind of household should have told me what to expect.

Children's Hour, with Uncle Mac, introduced me to the imaginative resources of middle-class life and was as much part of my education as *Newnes' Pictorial Knowledge*. Music like Wolf-Ferrari's *Jewels of the Madonna*, Elgar's *Chanson de Matin* and Victor Hely-Hutchinson's *Carol Symphony* introduced serial dramas, and intimations of magic. Helen Henschel provided an introduction to serious music beginning with the last movement of Brahms' First Symphony, 'Castles of England' was thrilling and instructive, 'Toytown' was amusing, and Commander Stephen King-Hall commented on current affairs. *The Lost World* by Conan Doyle, about an expedition to an Amazon plateau, evoked prehistoric monsters in such a horrifying way I rushed to turn the wireless off, and dreamt about pterodactyls for years.

At school in Caversham I saw another real film about the dangers encountered in the construction of the Canadian Pacific Railway, and was hugely excited. As always I loved singing and happily trilled away, especially when we sang 'Cherry Ripe'. I had another crush on a young supply teacher, who wore a pink sweater, and had a ten-year-old niece called Phoebe. This was a problem because I could not walk beside the loved one after school without walking beside Phoebe, a scrawny girl wearing unattractive glasses. I roundly fended off crude suggestions that I was in love with Phoebe without admitting 'Miss' was the real object of my affections. One day 'Miss' asked which were my favourite songs and I said 'God Save the King' and 'Rule Britannia', both of them (like 'Cherry Ripe') good eighteenth-century melodies. I felt mortified when 'Miss' was too taken aback to reply. Perhaps I should have said 'Smoke Gets In Your Eyes', 'You Are My Sunshine', 'This Is the Army Mr Jones' or 'Any Umberellas'.

Mrs Finch, my class teacher, was another favourite. On one occasion she asked whether I liked the teacher in the next class to hers. I did like her, but I knew she was unpopular, so I shook my head. 'Really,' said Mrs Finch, 'I am surprised because she certainly likes you.' I felt a fraud but could not go back on my lie. One day Mrs Finch pointed to a boy called Tomkins and said he had the brightest future of any of us. I smiled complacently, excepting myself. Mrs Finch noticed and said, 'That applies to you too, David Martin.' True enough, Tomkins turned up in a lower form at the grammar school, and I watched his teenage career with interest in case Mrs Finch was right. But as the Chinese communist leader said of the effects of the French Revolution, it was 'too early to tell'; and *Who's Who* provides no information.

3

East Sheen Grammar School

I arrived at East Sheen Grammar School in September 1940 and, as a scholarship boy, found myself in the A form. I had now entered an unknown region so far as my parents were concerned. Though I had access to books, my new schoolmates, at least the ones with paying parents, had chemistry sets. The years that followed my arrival at Sheen were broken by air raids when we filed out to the long brick shelters built above ground, though in some lessons, especially maths, I was only too glad to have them interrupted. Before the war we had practised filing into trenches, and putting on our gas masks. The barrage balloons going up all over London made a beautiful sight. My father became a war reserve policeman for some three years before taking what was known as The Knowledge, an exacting test you had to pass to work as a cab driver, through cycling around wartime London. Once he became a cabbie our income of £3 a week doubled, even trebled. We stared in disbelief at the pile of notes on the kitchen table.

The bombing of London educated me in high explosives and their varied effects. Most mornings during the Blitz I cycled around collecting shrapnel. I documented where the bombs, incendiaries, Molotov cocktails, or land mines, had destroyed houses, in a blue book in which I also recorded the number of raids, or at any rate alerts, each day. Sometimes there were five sirens a day, and always an air raid alert overnight, at least up to late 1941. It all started up again in 1944, with unmanned flying bombs that came down when their engines cut out, and then with noiseless rockets, the first of which landed close by in Chiswick. One night in the first phase of bombing I noted 45 explosions from nearby bombs. Our house was never hit, and I felt so bereft of stories to tell at school that I asked the dear God to let us suffer some non-fatal incident so I could have something to say. Occasionally I walked to school with my case over my head as the shrapnel rattled down over the roofs.

Apart from being in Swindon with my uncle and aunt when the first bomb fell on 7 June on the county cricket ground, my first raid was on a summer day in September 1940. My mother and I stood in the garden, fascinated by formations in the sky above us like shoals of silver fish, until the whistle of descending high explosives told us these planes were not ours. My mother dragged me into the kitchen, her body arched over me next to the gas stove. Later, in 1944, I remember my mother throwing her body over my sister in the upstairs bed as a flying bomb cut out. Briefly in 1940 we used the concrete Anderson shelter in the garden, with a plug between our teeth to stop us biting ourselves in the blast. But the shelter was dank, the beds were uncomfortable and we felt safer under the stairs. One night my mother, my sister and I were under the stairs, with my father under the kitchen table, and as a stick of bombs came ever closer he called out 'Jesus, help us!' I am sure he hoped destruction would fall on the devil's establishment at Watney's Brewery about a quarter of a mile away. My aunt Alice, who lived in Ewell, also called on divine help, and quoted, 'A thousand shall fall at thy right hand, and ten thousand at thy left hand, yet it shall not come nigh thee,' which even then struck me as hard on my other rather slatternly aunt Rose, who smoked, drank and even swore, and lived just down the road.

I felt real fear for the first time when a land mine destroyed two streets by Barnes Methodist Church and made the church unusable. Nevertheless my sister and I were still sent regularly to the Sunday School. My most stupid escapade was with Colin Slaughter, who lived in the house opposite. An air raid warden had left the door of a hut ajar in the nearby playground of the Mortlake Primary School. We stole in and took six incendiaries back to Ripley Gardens, unscrewing the tops and building up little piles of dark powder. We then noticed parents at their gates shouting at us to stop. The grammar school's chemistry laboratory was bombed, and one day some of us were in the playground by the assembly hall when a Stuka swooped out of the mist, dropped a bomb in the field across the road by the Bank of England building, and we spreadeagled on the ground in a serious fright.

My mother must have been very resourceful in this time of rationing and queues, because we ate well. She kept chickens, which to my horror she strangled and plucked herself. She 'dug for victory' and maintained a ritual sequence of meals beginning with a roast on Sundays, and bread dipped in hot dripping on Mondays, traditionally washing day. She made bread and butter pudding, though butter was very scarce, Queen of bread pudding, and marvellous cakes for which she won prizes. Not for us the terrible fare of the 'British Restaurant'. Some special occasions symbolized the wartime ethos, like the singing of the Coventry Carol by King's College Choir in the famous Christmas Eve service. I went up to the National Gallery to hear Myra Hess play Bach and Mozart, and to see wartime pictures by Paul Nash. These concerts were put on to show what values were at stake in the war. This music represented a better Germany and was the antithesis of Nazism. I attended my first Promenade concert in 1943, the forty-ninth season: a Bach–Handel programme.

I cycled a lot during these school years, round Richmond Park most mornings before breakfast, sometimes up to Piccadilly or out to Guildford. Once I climbed to the outer dome of St Paul's Cathedral and saw nothing but destruction and bombed-out churches all around. I also spent far too much time with Jean Langridge on her sofa or, just once, on Wimbledon Common, which became an initiation into a new range of emotions. I fell out of love with Jean by reading Shaw's Preface to *St Joan* walking to see her one summer evening. It was the sentence about Joan being one of the queerest fish in the Middle Ages that did it. I had never known saints written about in that offhand, anti-Romantic way. My romantic universe collapsed and Jean Langridge lay with Jeanne D'Arc in the ruins. When I arrived at her back alley for the usual cuddle my disenchantment was difficult to explain. Her house was later bombed though no one was hurt. Her father had just decorated it and he showed me the damage. It was the first time I saw a man cry.

The subjects I did well in at school, history in particular, were given fewer marks than science subjects, and I limped along without a single 'commendation' over the whole five years up to the School Certificate. Even in geography, which I enjoyed, I resisted the settled tracks, so that an essay on an imaginary journey across France, meant to end up in the coalfields of Décazeville, ended up in the nearby abbey of Conques, and included such sentences as 'and now we see in front of us the tower of the basilica of St Apollinaire'. Violet Markham's illustrated book *Romanesque France* had made me more interested in Vézelay and Moissac than Décazeville. No wonder I was delighted when the Germans bombed the chemistry laboratory. As I often gained no marks at all in science, some teachers tried unsuccessfully to have me demoted to the B or even the C stream. I flourished briefly when we were taught economics for a couple of terms by a lively and interested young man, who related the subject to public affairs, but then he disappeared, perhaps to the war, and economics disappeared with him. I really enjoyed arguing the toss about the virtues of free trade, but it never entered my head that London University gave degrees in the subject. Or perhaps my head was too full of poetry and literature to imagine a subject able to draw on my Liberal political interests. I had no idea there was a discipline called politics.

One teacher in particular, MacLaren, encouraged me, and I was deeply attached to him. One day he told me I could do anything a boy named Peter Powrie could do, and as Powrie did very well at school and became a well-known geographer, my morale was bolstered enough to avoid collapse. MacLaren was the master whom I subsequently most wanted to know his intervention had borne fruit.

'Mac' sensed I would be distressed more than other pupils if he, of all people, were to 'slipper' me. Once when I committed some minor misdemeanour he came up behind me and murmured, 'You are not immune.' I glowed with gratitude. Another time he asked for English words with French roots and I suggested 'jaundice'. He said I had a good vocabulary and I glowed again. On one occasion a tall and sexually precocious boy named Marshall threatened a supply teacher with violence. Some of us were faintly admiring and Mac reprimanded the whole class, telling us we should think about what we had done during the Lord's Prayer at morning assembly. I crawled with shame. Sometimes I would run into him on the way to school, and I remember shyly showing him an eighteenth-century edition of the *Lettres de Madame de Sévigné* I had bought for sixpence in a Richmond secondhand bookshop.

Apart from getting more and more behind in subjects where you could not make up for lost time, I was confused by divided aims. My parents could not guide me because their only model was one where you left school before your teens and started to earn money. My father's idea of the grammar school was that it would enable me to earn more than twice what he did in a safe clerical job. My idea, in response to a questionnaire given us by Mr Hyde, one of the French masters – was that I would like to be organist of King's College Chapel. Mr Hyde told us not to put 'teacher' unless we were high flyers.

To say I had divided aims is misleading given my total lack of direction. It would be truer to say my time was divided between music, church and school. Most evenings I played the piano at church or attended the church youth club, or went to choir practice, or canoodled on Jean Langridge's sofa, or did preparation to teach in Sunday School. About this time, maybe a little later, I was encouraged at church to visit incapacitated soldiers at the Richmond Star and Garter Home and take them out in their wheelchairs. The reading I did was more off the syllabus than on it, the complete novels of Hardy for example, which had the additional attraction of reminding me of Dorset. Dorset was continually in my thoughts: I imagined myself not really from Mortlake or Surrey at all. I came from where my mother came from. My self-presentation at school, designed to make me distinctive, given I acquired no worthwhile scholastic profile, was of a Dorset lad. I wrote my first essay in the critical first person on Hardy when invited to comment on an author I liked. The teacher responded to my enthusiasm and I realized that I was entitled to my opinion. Hardy was not on the syllabus, and so he was a personally chosen possession, and my very own by the link to family and not to school.

It was bad enough being bottom in science and maths, but for an aspiring poet or writer it was worse being nearly bottom in English. Maybe this was because one of the English masters had perfected his own method of 'clausal analysis', which required sustained attention rather than cultivating my sensibility. My one relief came in poetry lessons. I had to keep my hand down for much of the time, in spite of wanting to respond to questions, in case I might be identified as liking poetry as well as music. If you added being exercised by religious questions, my fellow pupils might think I was no better than a girl in trousers.

John Chalker was an exception, because he had political and literary interests. Night after night we walked between the eyrie in his house where he kept his books and the Lower Mortlake Road, reviewing books and the human condition. Leslie Smith was also an exception: we three 'intellectuals' were serious minded, interested in literature and politically engaged, with 'Smith' a butt of criticism as a Conservative. (For years we referred to each other by surnames not Christian names.)

My saturation in the English Bible gave me instinctive access to some kinds of poetry and prose. Ruskin felt familiar because the writing was so resonant, morally and socially serious and biblical. The grave sentiments of Gray's 'Elegy in a Country Churchyard' also felt familiar, and Milton's 'Ode on the Morning of Christ's Nativity' and Wordsworth's 'Ode: Intimations of Immortality' were my meat and drink.

The rediscovery of the metaphysical poets, especially Donne, was in full flood at the time, and my introduction to Donne revealed a religious and erotic complexity I could revel in. The moment I read the line in 'The Relique', 'A bracelet of bright hair about the bone', I was hooked.

If my home gave me any advantage it was entry into the seventeenth as well as the nineteenth century. I hunted in the hymn book for hymns that were also seventeenth-century poems, like Samuel Crossman's 'My Song is Love Unknown', Henry Vaughan's 'My Soul There is a Country' and John Mason's 'How shall I sing that Majesty that angels do admire?'. There, at least, faith and literature fused, as faith and music fused in Bach, Handel and Mendelssohn.

Then one day our English master, Dr Gardner, told us there was a third great ode alongside the odes by Milton and Wordsworth: Gerard Manley Hopkins's 'The Wreck of the Deutschland'. Dr Gardner had grown tired tramping through analysis of the characters of *Falstaff* and *Hamlet*, but he was the editor of the first complete publication of the poems of Hopkins, and that really engaged him. After recovering from our surprise about this third great ode, a few of us became enthused with Hopkins and this enthusiasm carried over when Gardner taught us in the Arts sixth. He asked us to give our views on certain cruces, like the disputed last line of the poem, 'That Nature is a Heraclitean Fire', and Leslie Smith even checked the proofs of Gardner's edition. Gardner also taught us Chaucer, just a few lines each lesson because he insisted on going into the Anglo-Saxon roots: not for us Nevill Coghill's later modernization of the text.

The headmaster, H. H. Shephard, was a mathematician with literary, religious and musical interests who had intellectually founded the school with hand-picked teachers. Occasionally he took over our class when a teacher was away. Once he read the whole of Wordsworth's pastoral poem 'Michael', about a rugged shepherd, his comely wife Isabel and his son Luke, news of whose prodigal life so afflicts his aged father that thereafter he 'never lifted up a single stone'. We made almost as little of its 'sentiment' of noble simplicity as we had earlier of Richard Jefferies' *Bevis: The Story of a Boy*. It affronted our male self-images, even mine, and Chalker and I compared it very unfavourably with the rich diction of Keats, with Smith standing up for prosaic Wordsworth. Occasionally Shephard took over religious instruction, as it was then called. One period was given over to St John of the Cross, and he asked us to raise our hands if we understood anything of the Dark Night of the Soul. This required a personal exposure even more dangerous than responding to poetry, but I raised my hand all the same. One period was spent on Albert Schweitzer and his biblical criticism, and this provided a faint prelude to the severe shock I sustained a few years later in 1950 on reading Schweitzer's *The Quest of the Historical Jesus*.

For senior boys the headmaster ran the Music Circle, a solemn conclave of the serious-minded held in the library. He supplied the records, which were changed every five minutes by Hodges, the librarian, a bespectacled character, who sometimes invited me home to watch him conduct the 'Emperor' Concerto or the Ninth Symphony. I followed him as librarian, and it was during my watch that Grove's *Dictionary of Music and Musicians*, the generous gift of the headmaster, disappeared. I was suspected of purloining it, a natural supposition given the fate of part of the Loeb Classical Library and the habits of some previous librarians. But it was untrue and to this day I hope the headmaster believed my protestations.

One day in the library Mr Shephard surprised us by telling us we were an intellectual elite. He also surprised me personally by asking me to read out an essay on the renaissance of English music. The essay ended with references to Edward Elgar and the sentence 'We now await the master.' I was very serious and could not imagine why this was greeted with smothered laughter.

The head asked me to play Brahms' D minor Ballade for the parents' Open Day and promised he would make sure they kept quiet. When we were about to leave school he devised a special prize for me, since there was no recognized achievement for which I deserved a prize. It was Albert Einstein's *Mozart*. Perhaps this was partly in acknowledgement of my role as pianist for morning assembly, where I enjoyed

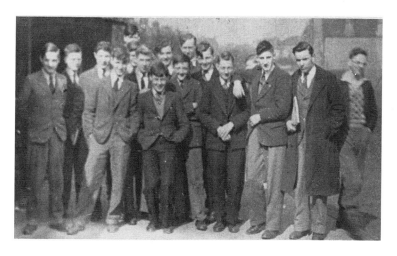

David Martin (second from right) with fifth form,
East Sheen Grammar School, 1945

coaxing reluctant male masses into singing. I also (untypically) enjoyed reading the Bible lessons at morning assembly, especially my favourite from Ecclesiastes about the silver cord being loosed, the golden bowl broken and all the daughters of music brought low. It felt like a precursor of the symbolist and imagist poetry I was starting to write, although I also experimented with sequences of consonants and syllables on the analogy of music with no clear subject matter at all. I must have picked up imagism from anthologies featuring poets like Richard Aldington, H.D. and Laurence Binyon. Dr Gardner took Chalker, Smith and me to the Café Royale, and to Marlowe's *Edward the Second* and Shakespeare's *Henry the Fourth, Part Two*. He also gave John a commentary on the *Four Quartets* and me *Rimsky-Korsakov* by Gerald Abraham. Gardner had gone to the trouble of discovering I did not think much of Ernest Walker's *History of Music in England* to make sure he had the choice right. Walker had blamed Handel for the demise of English music and I was having none of that.

To read English at London University you had to have some Latin, and our Latin master had been away in the army, so Latin lessons only began in 1945 in the sixth form. Initially they were taken by Mrs Seligsohn, a German refugee. Mrs Seligsohn once asked me to read Virgil out aloud and expressed pleasure at the 'beautiful' way I did it. Another sixth former interjected, 'It is just such a pity he doesn't understand it.' She decided to rectify this by inviting me to her apartment near Richmond Hill where she gave me free private tuition. I looked forward to meeting her but not to Caesar's *Gallic Wars*, Virgil's *Georgics* or Cicero's *Pro Sexto Roscio*. Cicero's legal rhetoric interested me, not his grammatical constructions. I deluded myself that I wanted to work in response to her kindness, and even took the *Georgics* with me on a cycle ride deep into the Surrey countryside. But I fell asleep in the warm air over the Georgics and the text slipped into the long grass. One evening Mrs Seligsohn shook her head reprovingly and said that all I wanted was to come and talk to her about Plato. Once she confessed she had been cozened by living in England into thinking the Victorian church of St Matthias, Richmond, an example of genuine Gothic. I was astounded to realize that people like her looked at buildings with an educated sense of their provenance. I wanted to be educated like *that*.[4]

A little earlier, in the upper fifth, Miss Kathleen Holroyd, a blonde teacher in her very early twenties, aroused less intellectual interests. She was the first female teacher in an all-male school, brought in to teach maths because of wartime shortages. Eric Emery and I got into the habit of walking her home, and we became a trio of David, Eric and Kate. We saw ourselves as her intimates and tried to persuade her to come to the Music Circle, but she declined, saying the solemnity of the head's presence was just too oppressive. One day she used Emery's Christian name in class ('Oh, Eric!'), provoking a murmurous buzz of speculation between derision and envy. I was infuriated to think the class did not realize she used my Christian name too, but how could I nudge beloved Kate to stir up the same envy by using my name publicly? O Kate, Kate, why not me?

In 1945 I stood as Liberal candidate in the school's mock election to accompany the national election, and made speeches with a certain flair, having acquired the technique of persuasive public speech from a thousand fiery sermons. Public speaking intoxicated me, just as it did my father in Hyde Park, and I had a good grasp of liberal moral rhetoric, maybe gleaned from Morley's *Life of Gladstone* or the speeches of John Bright. In the general election itself I distributed leaflets for David Ennals, the local Liberal candidate.

I was also editor of the school magazine and habitué of the Senior Literary and Debating Society. The library became a hideout for those not interested in wearisome country runs through Richmond Park or bawling raucous support for local heroes on sports days. The Lit. and Deb. provided me with yet more opportunities for making speeches and devising phrases, though occasionally I was rebuked for being over-forceful, for example deploying the phrase 'a hoary-headed complex of conservative opinion' in a debate on women's rights. I defended an idea picked up from Shaw that 'When Socialism has delivered the leisure there will be time for Liberalism'.

Editing the school magazine gave me the first thrilling sight of proofs and print, including my own poems. One was about seeing lovers one night embracing on Gray's Bridge, Dorchester, another evoked Debussy's 'La Cathédrale engloutie' and another was entitled 'On Hearing the St Matthew Passion from the Dome of St Paul's'. Soon after I destroyed them all and Leslie said this was an unnecessary sacrifice merely to prove I had taste. John Chalker was bemused, or amused, by my use of the phrase 'phallic fronds'. I had lifted this, without understanding what it meant, from *The Well of Loneliness*, a lesbian novel I found discreetly placed on the top shelf of the library.

When I went for interview at King's College London, the Dean, Dr Eric Abbott, commented I had a more impressive CV for activities outside the curriculum than inside it. He rightly turned me down, and my subsequent visits to King's were when Les had become a postgraduate and was performing in plays like *The Duchess of Malfi* and

The Witch of Edmonton. Leslie wrote a thesis on the sub-plot in Jacobean drama which I read. He was also finding himself as a thespian and a gay man, though he did not make that known until much later. In 1991 I was invited to King's College to give the F. D. Maurice Lectures,[5] but forbore to mention the invitation was nearly half a century in arrears.

This educational trajectory is a variant on Richard Hoggart's profile of the Scholarship Boy, in my case a scholarship boy confused by the transition but certainly not full of lower-class resentment. The service class is not resentful but respectable and it picks up elements of style from people my mother called 'superior'. Superiority was more a moral category than a social one, though it did involve not being 'common', as well as a certain self-respect combined with modesty of demeanour, considerate manners and speaking 'properly'. In the same way I treated high culture as high because it was better than low culture. If elites had differential access to it then the answer was to widen access, not to condemn quality as elitist. I never doubted then, or since, that there was a 'western canon'.

My education did not include any biological or indeed practical information about sex. I was unformed and uninformed. I was not told sex was dirty because I was told nothing at all. If the scholarship had tested biology I would certainly have gone to the Central School, not East Sheen Grammar. My notions of the female form were derived from a girl with one exposed breast in *The Glory that was Greece*, a book on Florentine painting, including *Primavera*, a picture of a naked girl looking in the mirror in a 1930s Royal Academy Summer Exhibition, Harry Bates' sculpture of a naked Pandora opening her box, the waif-like model in G. F. Watts' symbolic paintings, Frederick Leighton's *The Bath of Psyche*, and a bust of the Empress Eugénie, wife of Louis Napoleon. Then there was the Anthropology section of the Kensington Exhibition and the sculpture room at the Victoria & Albert Museum. In the V & A I was intrigued by Michelangelo's David and Donatello's David, and realized that naked maleness was more varied than I had thought possible. These intimations of the human form apart, I was confined to a copy of *La Vie Parisienne* stumbled upon in a secondhand bookshop, a magazine called *Lilliput* with very soft-focus pictures circulating at school, and another magazine with much better definition lent me for the night by a fellow pupil. I would have to rely on induction by such kindly females as might provide it, and apart from being asked to explore her blouse by a girl at Sunday School, I was just into my third decade before that element in my education was seriously undertaken. This is not a modern story.

As for the literary accompaniment to this slow erotic development, I moved from 'Drink to me only with thine eyes' to various seventeenth-century invocations of Cynthia, Celia and Anthea, and then to Elizabeth Barrett Browning's *Sonnets from the Portuguese*: 'Shall I tell thee how I love thee?' My novel reading graduated to Moravia, Mauriac and Gide, but I absorbed more atmosphere than information. It was a dangerous imbalance. My early emotional education was as chequered as my intellectual education.

4

A passion for music

My mother sang 'I Have a Song to Sing, O!' and 'Dashing Away with the Smoothing Iron', which for her was a work song, appropriate for washing days and ironing days. She sang 'The Man that Broke the Bank at Monte Carlo', 'Pack Up Your Troubles in Your Old Kit Bag' or 'It's a Long Way to Tipperary', and was a virtuoso whistler.

I sang 'I Dream of Jeannie with the Light Brown Hair' and other songs by Stephen Foster, as well as trying to imitate the voice of Irish tenor John McCormack. I loved 'Keep the Home Fires Burning' and obsessively chanted 'You Are My Sunshine'. In singing lessons at primary school I sat at the front, well away from the reluctant male growlers, and revelled in folk-like songs, 'Barbara Allen', 'Annie Laurie' and 'The Bay of Biscay O'. Late on sunny afternoons Henry Hall's Dance Orchestra provided musical wallpaper: 'Here's to the Next Time' and 'The Teddy Bears' Picnic'. My aunts sang 'Smoke Gets in Your Eyes' and 'The Bells of St Mary's'.

Like my mother I sang in my church choir. At that time Stainer's *Crucifixion* provided a less demanding alternative to *Messiah* at Easter. I enjoyed its famous Palm Sunday chorus, 'Fling wide the gates, for the Saviour waits', as well as Maunder's harvest anthem 'Praise the Lord O Jerusalem'. My saturation in hymns gave me access to tonal and literary worlds that informed how I thought, felt and expressed myself. I ransacked the nine hundred or so hymns in *The Methodist Hymn Book*. The tunes and the words of hymns by Isaac Watts and the Wesleys, including John Wesley's magnificent translations from the German like Zinzendorf's 'Ich habe nun den Grund gefunden', or by George Herbert, John Greenleaf Whittier and Robert Bridges, were my earliest real education. They ensured that I would always respond most intensely to a combination of words and music. I was so in love with sacred music that I came to believe music was itself sacred, which is close to an alternative religion. In 1960 I dumped a woman for not having heard of Schubert's C major Symphony.

My mother did not sing opera, apart from Gilbert and Sullivan, and even 'the great Caruso' was not a name to conjure with. The reasons were social as well as moral. Socially we were a long way from opera and even further from chamber music, though faint intimations of *Lieder* filtered through by way of Richard Tauber, a singer much adored by my mother's youngest sister. I picked up my mother's moral map of music, including *terra incognita* like opera. My mother disapproved of jazz just as people earlier disapproved of the waltz and quadrilles, and later disapproved of Bill Haley, especially when 'Rock Around the Clock' caused a riot in a Hammersmith cinema. By the thirties my mother approved of waltzes, and when female friends were invited on special occasions into 'the front room' I was invited to play 'Tales from the Vienna Woods' as well as 'Wine, Women and Song' on the piano. Jazz had something to do with disorder, violent body language and sex. I do not think my mother was colour prejudiced. We never encountered black people, and we adored spirituals and Paul Robeson. My mother's moral map of music was based on the difference between the decorous and the raucous. Music could be too loud and people could be too loud.

My father only sang hymns and choruses, but some of these were joyfully raucous, with a lot of repetition and quick quavers in dotted rhythms, like 'Whosoever heareth, *shout, shout* the sound/Spread the blessed tidings all the world around . . . Whosoever will may come'.

Whether musically decorous or raucous, home was a place where everybody sang. Methodism was a singing church and it was as important for my musical education as the seven years I spent with a well-known piano teacher. My musical talents were enough to make me an asset to the church and something of a project for my teacher, but I followed too much my own predilections as well as being absorbed by a search for expression and understanding I could not define. As at school, I was inclined to go dangerously off piste, and school and music made competing demands I had no idea how to reconcile. My passion for music made my local Methodist church much more of a second home than it was for my parents, but its round of activities, especially the musical ones, took up more and more of my time to the point where it distracted me from school work. Maybe I wanted to be distracted in this way because school was not going well.

My musical education at church began when I asked the organist and choirmaster, Mr Harrop, to show me how to play the hymn tune 'Arizona'. I picked up 'Arizona' so fast it seems Mr Harrop told my mother I was a genius, which was damaging nonsense because the romantic idea of genius defines music as a virtuoso art when it is a craft, historically a science, you can practise in less glamorous ways.

When I played the piano for the church choir Mr Harrop found my playing too expressive and indulgent. The women of the church and the adolescent girls liked it, but he tried to rein it in, and when he taught me the organ he had me on his own ground. The organ is more of a machine than the piano and as members of a craft guild, organists can be severe taskmasters. Mr Harrop wanted to initiate me into the craft, starting with the Eight Short Preludes and Fugues then attributed to Bach, but once alone in the organ loft I deluged space with sound. I was seduced by lascivious stops like the Tremulant and abandoned the severities proper to Bach to indulge tastes picked up elsewhere. Soon the congregation was making its 'freewill offering' to the Air from *The Water Music*, 'Dove sono', 'Pie Jesu' or 'Softly and gently' from *Gerontius*. I also devised harmonizations of plainchant using examples from a book called *The Singing Church* by C. Henry Phillips, and evoked the sacred with the Sanctus of the G minor Mass by Vaughan Williams, but the good Methodist people seemed not to mind. It sounded religious.

Barnes Methodist Church introduced me to another strain of music through the kindness of a Sunday School teacher, Miss Dorothy Rush, whom I called Tommy Farr, after the heavyweight boxer, because she was forceful and had a very deep contralto voice. She sang the 'Cobbler's Song' in the Wesley Guild production of *Chu Chin Chow* and took some of us to the Albert Hall for acted versions of Coleridge Taylor's *Hiawatha* and Gounod's *Faust*. She also gave me my first chance to hear *Messiah* at the Albert Hall, once she discovered I was desperate to hear it complete. There was always some unmarried lady, at church or school, often active in both, who was willing to oversee, encourage and help.

My first piano teacher was not a serious practitioner and let me wander at will, playing pieces not written for the piano or attempting works that were too difficult, like Beethoven's *Pathétique*. My mother complained I did far too much 'banging' and sought out Mrs Hélène Gipps, a Swiss lady from the Frankfurt Conservatoire who ran a 'school of music' in the Upper Richmond Road, East Sheen. Mrs Gipps charged a guinea a lesson, which was a lot for my parents, but they went further, and scraped together £100 for a grand piano. After a year or two, my mother told Mrs Gipps she could not afford the lessons, whereupon she taught me for nothing.

Mrs Gipps decided I should concentrate on modest works, like the Dussek Sonata movement set for Grade Four of the Royal Schools of Music exams. However, when I only just scraped Grade Four, she immediately put me in for Grade Six, guessing Mozart's Sonata K309 might engage me more than Dussek. I went one better than a scrape at Grade Six, and did very well at Grades Seven and Eight with major works like the Mozart A minor Rondo. I entered for the LRAM and ARCM piano performing diplomas at the same time as I took Higher School Certificate and was comprehensively humiliated. The moment anyone asked me to identify a first or second inversion of a chord or to write down a clapped rhythm, I entered a cloud of unknowing. I had rhythm but a poor sense of time. I could not cope with the way Academy examiners stared out of the window in case I was overwhelmed by their interest, and then told me to stop and 'Pick it up again here.' This destroyed any attempt to build up the architecture of Franck's *Prelude, Chorale and Fugue*, though it was the kind of strenuous and powerful work that suited me very well. I later played it at a concert and its huge tolling conclusion provided the most satisfying moment of my performing life. I also entered for the Ada Lewis Scholarship at the Royal Academy, but Chopin's all-too-famous E major Etude suited neither me nor the examiners. I was going nowhere in music. The only way to stop Mrs Gipps giving me yet more free lessons was to write her a graceless letter, half blaming my failure on her teaching. It worked.

Music mattered to me more than anything else and performing it provided me with far greater satisfactions than I was likely to find elsewhere. It was also a problem. I did not practise properly, because I was intent on expressing my emotional reaction rather than thinking about it technically. I had more sensitivity than technique, and though this took me quite a way it set a limit. With some compositions my sensitivity and flair ensured I did enough serious practice to continue lessons. Alec Rowley, a composer and a well-known festival adjudicator, commented on my 'genuine pianism' and said that whereas other competitors were English my temperament was Italian. I found Bach daunting because there was no way of circumventing the technical difficulties, above all correct fingering, but I was sufficiently engaged by his music to persist and very proud to receive a prize for 'love of Bach'.

I first discovered the pleasure of overhearing the attention of an audience at an informal concert when I lost the inhibitions inculcated by Mrs Gipps and let the drama of the middle movement of Beethoven's early D major Sonata take over. To my amazement she asked why I had never done that before. If that was what she really wanted, I knew how to do it and was ready to do it again. Intensity, drama and expressiveness became my trademark and she said, rather musingly, that people would like it, but was it Brahms or was it me?

Playing Brahms' Rhapsodies and Ballades in public became my forte: they were so expansive, poetic and plangent, and I could exploit all the latent resonance and power in the lower range of the piano. The first movement of the Grieg Piano Concerto provided equal opportunities for high rhetoric, though my maths faltered at seven against nine and eleven against thirteen in the cadenza, carefully articulated by Mrs Gipps on the score in ink. But that was nothing compared to the annual concert when Mrs Gipps hired the Wigmore Hall and I sipped the wine of serious performance. The wonderful nine-foot Bösendorfer piano said 'Play me', and Beethoven's 'Moonlight' Sonata and Ravel's *Sonatine* soared airborne. When four of us played Dvorak's 'New World' Symphony arranged for eight hands we bestrode the world. French music might be second division in the Gipps canon, and I took on Ravel reluctantly, but once fully engaged I was delighted by the subtle colours and atmospherics and the easy way it lay under the hands. I knew instinctively what *ralentissez beaucoup* meant and let the resonances mingle like perfume: decadent maybe, but inviting.

I had other problems with music and Mrs Gipps besides competing demands and reluctance to make technique my first priority. Like my parents, Mrs Gipps had her own moral, religious and aesthetic map of music. She was a Christian Scientist who had broken with the Richmond Christian Science Church to form her own circle, She claimed psychic powers such as the ability to locate lost objects, and dismissed 'the germ theory' as an emanation of 'mortal mind'. Her body was apparently shapeless and swathed in dark claret material, except when she waltzed around conducting us in boisterous frolics for eight hands. I do not think she proselytized her other students, but I seemed interested and she gave me Mrs Eddy's *Science and Health* to read. I kept this at bay saying I preferred St Augustine, which was sheer bravado, since I had read no more of the *Confessions* than the famous sections on the seductions of music and 'boiling loves'.

However, I was intrigued by her musical metaphysics because I wanted to justify intellectually my intuition that music was a 'real presence'. Pascal's 'hidden God' spoke without equivocation in an uncorrupted speech that made manifest the numbers governing the cosmos. It was both 'the still, sad music of humanity' and the trumpets 'sounding from the hid battlements of eternity'. Mrs Gipps gave lectures to her circle on 'Music and Metaphysics' at the old Kensington Imperial Institute. I attended them, and read the published versions. These lectures were idiosyncratic variants on Renaissance theories of music, in particular the Pythagorean mathematics of the harmonic series. She claimed the harmonic series was rooted in the physical world in a way that made atonalism a blind alley.[6] She had renamed the chord structure of music according to her metaphysical system and occasionally used this terminology when teaching. The chord sequence from subdominant to tonic became principal to ground.

I started reading Renaissance musical and architectural theory for myself and linked it up with reading mystical literature, such as Inge on Neo-Platonism and Shelley's 'Adonaïs'. The One and the Many mingled with ideas of the 'Unitive Life'. It was far more interesting than Stewart Macpherson on musical theory and the writings of her admired mentor, Tobias Matthay, on piano technique. Moreover I was beginning to explore a wider historical map of music that had no interest for her. She was typical of musicians in the continental tradition in regarding the church choirs and choral societies as English and provincial, but they provided me with a slipway to European traditions mostly outside the Austro-German canon.

The amateur choral tradition celebrated just the repertoire someone from a revivalist home might gravitate towards. One evening on *Children's Hour* I was hit between the eyes by the Hallelujah Chorus and rushed out of the room to hide my tears. I became a Handelian when Handel's reputation lay in a trough, but the only Handel I ever played for Mrs Gipps was the Prelude and Fugue of the D minor Suite. I intuited the Baroque was just a preparation for the classical, just as 'the divine Mozart' was a Dresden china preparation for Beethoven. Profundity needs a third period pointing forward to the future, and, though I did not then know it, Handel had written some of his greatest music in his early twenties.

I found a musical centre of gravity between 1600 and 1750. When performing I was a natural for the Romantic piano repertoire, above all Brahms, but when listening I was drawn to the Baroque. The moment I heard a sequence, a trill, a harmonic crunch or a trumpet I was away. Handel became an obsession long before his massive revival in association with the oddly named 'early music movement'. My adolescent reading of Bernard Shaw's music criticism alerted me to the failings of Victorian-style performances of choral music and implicitly made me wonder whether the Evangelicalism that had introduced me to Handel was also responsible for his occlusion as one of the great masters of human drama. Victor Schoelcher's pioneering *Life of Handel* (1857) introduced me to the musical gulf created by the Channel, and made me wonder whether Schoelcher's Alsatian background made him more receptive to Handel than his French fellow countrymen. If Elie Halévy was right about Methodism saving England from a French Revolution, maybe Protestant choral music provided yet another reinforcement of social harmony.

Much later, and after a complete change of climate, I wrote about the Baroque revival, and wanted to explain why Handel was for so long confined within the borders of the Reformation and only regained his cosmopolitan universality in the last decades of the twentieth century. Perhaps 'early music' had to wait until new media made possible its dissemination in performances by musicians of the top rank, as well as the social changes that made acceptable the male counter-tenor and the 'magic' mechanics of Baroque libretti. I also explored what I called 'The Sound of England' from the Tudors, Purcell and Handel to the English musical renaissance and Benjamin Britten. I thought I could hear England as well as see it on my bicycle.

When the wartime film *The Great Mr Handel* appeared at the tiny Plaza cinema, Barnes, I sat there, ecstatic in the dark, for fourpence a time. When Handel was the BBC's Composer of the Week I would get up before seven o'clock to listen. In my physics School Certificate exam I played *Messiah* in my head for virtually the whole three hours. My physics teacher once caught me out – as I intended he should – writing down the dates of all Handel's 40 operas, and he asked why I was not allowed to take music instead of physics. In the chemistry exam, I wrote, 'There is no chemistry in this answer book, but if you are interested in the influence of Schopenhauer on Wagner read on.' I read the *Notebooks* of Samuel Butler, who shared my Handelian obsession, and ransacked the music section of Foyle's bookshop for the scores of oratorios and the triennial Handel festivals at the Crystal Palace with choirs of up to four thousand. I tried to imitate massed choral sound on the piano. But where in wartime might I hear this music? I went eagerly on 14 June 1944 to the standard Wednesday Bach–Handel Prom concert, and was thrilled to hear the famous G. D. Cunningham play the Handel G minor Organ Concerto, and again on Wednesday 25 July 1945 to hear Thalben Ball play the B flat Organ Concerto.

It was not only music of the seventeenth and eighteenth centuries that accompanied my passionate explorations, but the siren voices of Rome and Byzantium. I read Egon Wellecz on the relation between Western and Eastern chant. Perhaps it all began with Helen Waddell's *Peter Abelard* and her translations of medieval Latin poems, but there was also Violet Markham on the Romanesque, and an architectural student at church who introduced me to Abbot Suger and the aesthetic theories behind the building of St Denis, as well as Giedion on *Space, Time and Architecture*. Then the minister's son introduced me to the counter-tenor voice of Alfred Deller singing 'In darkness let me dwell'. Good Nonconformists are always being led into by-path meadows by the distractions of Catholic and Anglican music and liturgy and I even imagined being a liturgiologist, conveniently forgetting the state of my Latin grammar.

I enjoyed getting a grip on musical history through studies of Bach, Purcell and Mozart, Donald Tovey's *Essays* and A. L. Bacharach's *The Musical Companion* (1934), and it never occurred to me all this was other than common knowledge among educated people. *The Great Musicians* by Ernest Oldmeadow (1908) showed me that beyond the twin castles of Bach and Handel lay unexplored territories: Monteverdi, Lully, Palestrina, Lassus, Byrd and 'the Eternal Chant'. This was a beckoning world far from home, school and Mrs Gipps. Renaissance polyphony provided relief from the pressures of self-expression, though after prolonged exposure I could scream for the full-blooded assertion of C major. A brief encounter with Maureen, a Catholic girl, introduced me to Palestrina's *Missa Papae Marcelli* at Westminster Cathedral. The smoke of incense rose up from the altar, the sunlight momentarily caught the enormous hanging cross, and the Eternal Chant continued unperturbed. Maureen's devotion to the sanctity of Don Bosco proved less attractive. All this, from Renaissance aesthetics and Handel to Byrd and Palestrina, was the lonely exploration of a private musical passion remote from the worlds of my contemporaries.

I could not have formulated my problem at the time, but I was engaged by the history of music and changes in musical language because it was full of intimations of transcendence, real presence if you prefer, which I experienced quite directly in music between 1600 and 1750. I was motivated to explore back to 1200 and beyond into chant, and forwards more problematically, though the sacred made an unexpected return in modernism. For me the sacred was realized through music and poetry, but especially words set to music, in enclosed places and open spaces, churches and vistas, ceremonies and prospects. Intimations of transcendence came to me in seventeenth-century poets like Donne, Vaughan, Herbert and Traherne, but after them I was at home quite intermittently in Smart or Blake, or Samuel Palmer in painting. Much later I again found myself at home in Hopkins, Eliot and Auden. Benjamin Britten was a marginal Anglican but his choice of poetry to set corresponded very closely with my own predilections: medieval, Elizabethan and Jacobean lyrics, Donne, Smart's 'Rejoice in the Lamb', Auden's 'On this Island'.

My musical education took another, seemingly more promising turn when the conductor Ronald Peck invited me to accompany the Putney Choral Society. He was a great admirer and friend of Nadia Boulanger and the initial programme consisted of Fauré's *Requiem*, before it became well known, as well as Bennet's 'Weep, O Mine Eyes', Howells' 'Here is the Little Door', Parry's 'My Soul, There is a Country' and Bach's Cantata *O Ewiges Feuer*, for Pentecost. Fauré provided my second introduction to French music and after initial hesitation I entered into it as easily as French piano music. Parry's setting of Henry Vaughan and the harmonic world of Herbert Howells belonged to the mystical tradition I was already deeply engaged by through poetry but only intuited in its musical mode. Unfortunately the Bach cantata accompaniment was an awkward piano reduction. I could manage it on my own, but not when eyeing the impatient beat of Ronald Peck. My humiliating experience with the Royal Schools of Music was replayed until I became paralysed with fear. Peck found a ruse to get me out of it all, and my only further foray into choral accompaniment was much later for the LSE Choral Society in works like Britten's *Rejoice in the Lamb*. But playing Britten is not like managing a Bach reduction while eyeing an impatient conductor.

Music did not come right for me until 1970. I became accompanist for my wife Bernice when she had lessons with a former prima donna of the Berlin Staatsoper, Sabine Meyen-Jessel, This was a late and unexpected fulfilment. I could now exploit my affinity for the Romantic repertoire without encountering the technical demands of solo works. Mrs Jessel resembled Mrs Gipps in her devotion to the Austro-German canon, though instead of the three B's it comprised *Lieder* from Schubert to Strauss and opera from Mozart and Weber to works by Germans virtually unknown in England, like Lortzing. Our passion for Handel, Baroque opera and sacred music, Britten and the English tradition, was largely up to us but she was ready to look at what we brought her. The French – Berlioz, Gounod, Fauré, Duparc, Debussy, Ravel, Chausson, Poulenc and Hahn – were allowed a modest place at high table. That was in part because they were allotted a class, alongside the English, in competitive music festivals, which in our experience were too frequently theatres of cruelty and favouritism. Like me, Bernice had been able to study music through someone's kindness: her head teacher at Bury Girls' Grammar School had paid for her singing lessons. I discovered what I could do instead of hankering after what I could not. The craft of accompaniment allowed me to realize my passion for music just as the craft of sermon making allowed me to realize my passion for poetry.

Madame Jessel, as she was known, came from a wealthy Jewish family in Berlin, which had endured the horrors of chronic inflation in the early twenties. When she went on the stage at the Berlin *Staatsoper* she entered a cut-throat world where you needed either to have money or offer sex. She left Germany in 1939 with her husband, Dr Herbert Jessel, after leaving the Berlin opera with the coming of Hitler in 1933. Before that she had recorded with Julius Patzak, and in 1929 had sung the Queen of the Night before President Hindenburg. She settled permanently in Woking and took in two Jewish refugees, Susie and Illa, as wards to bring up with her own daughter, Maussi. She made a corner of York Road, Woking, for ever Berlin, and enunciated the place name with metropolitan distaste. Her pupils were expected to emulate her exacting standards of comportment, and each night she made herself up in case any nocturnal happening exposed her unprepared to her public.

All her pupils were female. They kept together for decades and you could learn a lot from them about the overlap between music, church, charitable disposition and social responsibility. Musical, cultural and educational aspirations went together, and in a later generation they all would have gone to university. I often accompanied these talented women, and realized how many different musical niches people could occupy, even Gilbert and Sullivan, which Mrs Jessel regarded as a private English joke. I happily accompanied *The Daughter of the Regiment* and *The Pearl Fishers*, though they were well off my beat.

We were pushing at the boundaries at a time when new media and concerts by Graham Johnson's Songmakers' Almanac made exploration easier than ever before. The Schubert repertoire known to Mrs Jessel and Elena Gerhardt was only a fraction of what was now accessible. Bernice enjoyed the new freedom to devise and give themed concerts. Walton's *A Song for the Lord Mayor's Table* and Britten's settings of Auden in *On This Island*, and of Donne and Hardy, offered marvellous opportunities for collaboration. Sometimes Bernice pushed at boundaries I found quite testing, the Mozart concert arias, or Strauss's 'Schlechtes Wetter' and Wolf's 'Ich hab' in Penna', both of which involved a lot of hectic scampering. Yet the wild rhythms of De Falla, Granados and Turina posed few problems. I could rely on Bernice totally. An hour's concert of French or Spanish song or a work like Prokofiev's *The Ugly Duckling* would be memorized beyond possibility of a fluff in the travelling times between Woking and Waterloo.

David accompanying Bernice for a singing lesson with
Sabine Meyen-Jessel, York Road, Woking, 1978

With Mrs Jessel as attentive critic I discovered the relation of singer and accompanist was very different from that of repetiteur and conductor. It evolves into a small miracle of mutuality, where expression, volume and speed are conveyed by tiny cues and minute body movements, such as the singer's head and eye movements and intakes of breath, and the disposition of the pianist's shoulders and hands. The singer has to know the music absolutely by heart, and the pianist needs to know it virtually by heart, because only habituation and automatic command of technical difficulties allow freedom of interpretation. I had imagined there were just good singers and bad ones and had little idea about choosing the right kind of voice and musical personality for the appropriate musical vehicle. Nor did I realize that fast coloratura divisions were easy and long drawn out melodies difficult. I knew well enough there were arts of presentation in speaking: how you use pauses, and how and where you stand and throw your voice according to the acoustic. Anyone who has preached or spoken in public has to know such things, so it was naïve of me to suppose singers just stood up and sang.

Mrs Jessel had sung the Woodbird in *Siegfried*, and towards the end of her life we performed Wagner's *Wesendonck Lieder* for her. The last song, 'Traüme', is particularly poignant, and as it died away she put her hand on my knee to say 'Ach, Kinder, es ist genug' – 'it is enough'. When she died, the funeral took place at the North London Jewish cemetery, and a quartet played Mozart. Her adopted daughters were there, of course, Susie with her husband, the Labour Party number two at the Treasury, Edmund Dell. I gave the address, recalling the vanished world of the *Staatsoper* before Hitler and the moment she sang in the presence of Hindenburg. None of her 'girls' could bear to sing Schubert's 'An die Musik' on such an occasion, so I read it, first in English and then in German: Du holde Kunst, in wieviel grauen Stunden . . .

5

The Non-Combatant Corps

I was not always a pacifist, and I doubt if anyone has been a born pacifist unless a member of the historic peace churches. At nine I wrote a composition on the Duke of Wellington for Mr Gibbs at Mortlake Primary School under the title 'Who I would like to be'. Perhaps I acquired this ambition reading Tennyson's 'Ode on the Death of the Duke of Wellington', and novels with titles like G. A. Henty's *With Moore at Corunna*, as well as a poem about Sir John Moore's famous death at Corunna by Charles Wolfe. One of my favourite boys' tales was a typical piece of heroic bombast by D. H. Parry called *Sabre and Spurs: A Tale of the Peninsular War*. According to the 'imperial' novels of the time, history consisted of charging gallantly on horses, beating the French or the Marathas, and acquiring Gibraltar.

I also absorbed semi-historical stories for children that surrounded history, especially English history, with a romantic aura: Captain Marryat's *Children of the New Forest* about the English Civil War, Charlotte Yonge's *The Little Duke* about Richard the Fearless of Normandy, and James Whistler's *The Prince of Cornwall* about the Christianization of Wessex in the time of King Ina. Rudyard Kipling's *Puck of Pook's Hill* proved too subtle, and mostly evaded me. I liked to read about children who were really aristocrats: Frances Hodgson Burnett's *Little Lord Fauntleroy* and Mark Twain's *The Prince and the Pauper*, as well as Anthony Hope's Ruritanian fantasy *The Prisoner of Zenda*.

This reading fed an appetite for real history, but meanwhile provided a misleading image of the male warrior hero. It was no fault of my parents that I absorbed books with titles like *Seven Battles that Changed the World* or read Macaulay's 'Naseby', the poems of Sir Henry Newbolt, like 'Drake's Drum', and the polemical historian J. A. Froude on *English Sea-men in the Sixteenth Century*. This was reinforced by Scott's *Ivanhoe* with its Saxon hero Cedric and his daughter

Rowena, Rider Haggard's celebration of the Viking hero *Eric Bright-eyes*, *Quo Vadis* with its Christian hero Ursus, and the various works of John Buchan, a writer much read in the trenches during the Great War. The warrior hero had his last hurrah with my stunned reaction to Olivier's film of *Henry the Fifth* in 1944.

In the third form at East Sheen Grammar School, for reasons I dare not imagine, I joined the Cadet Corps run by the German master, Major Kirkby. However, playing about with rifles from the Boer War proved not to my taste. When my putties unwound on a route march, putting everyone behind me out of step, and still trailing ridiculously when I was relegated to the end of the column, progress to the leadership of the Corps looked unlikely. By now disliking the whole thing and failing to turn up for parades, I was ambushed after school by Corporals Biddlecombe and Anning. One of them hurled me over his shoulder so maladroitly that when they marched me in before Major Kirkby my nose was still bleeding badly. Of course I had promised not to tell on them but, anyway, the Corps proved very ready to discharge me, no doubt as poor material.

I rapidly moved in a liberal-socialist and pacifist direction, partly under the influence of my fifth-form friend John Chalker. I now read Oscar Wilde's *The Soul of Man under Socialism*, Lytton Strachey's *Eminent Victorians*, and Bernard Shaw. Though I had stood as the Liberal candidate in the school's mock election in 1945, I was delighted with the election of the 1945 Labour government. Above all I was attracted by Tolstoy's Christian pacifism in his essay 'The Kingdom of God is Within You', as well as interested in Gandhi's embrace of *ahimsa* or non-violence. My father's heroes had been preachers like Moody and Spurgeon and mine became Donald Soper and George Macleod of the Iona community. I was so inspired by George Macleod speaking on the wireless about the resurrection I could even imagine joining the Iona community. My favourite hymns now gravitated to the utopian verses of John Addington Symonds' 'These things shall be/A loftier race than e'er the earth has known shall rise', Clifford Bax's 'O brother man fold to thy heart thy brother' and the gentle eloquence of the American Quaker John Greenleaf Whittier. I read the *New Statesman* and (later) *Peace News*, the paper of the pre-war Peace Pledge Union, and I was mildly attracted by Herbert Read's anarchism. A reading of John Bright's speeches against the Crimean War, picked up in a Kensington bookshop, acted as a catalyst.

Conscription in Britain lasted for some 15 years after the war. So, when I was called up as a conscript on leaving school in 1948

I lodged a conscientious objection, and persisted in spite of strenuous attempts to dissuade me by the military personnel in charge of my medical examination. I found myself before the Fulham Tribunal, facing a panel that included the well-known classicist Professor Pickard-Cambridge. The minister of my Methodist church, the Revd Rudland Showell, accompanied me to the tribunal, though he made it clear he thought my formal statement of conscience an indulgent plethora of objections likely to prove counter-productive. He said I should have stuck to the religious objection, and he was right. As the proceedings wound on I noticed that Quakers and Plymouth Brethren went through easily, because they were members of denominations able to point to a historic peace witness, whereas Catholics faced serious probing and political objectors a grilling.

My objections included all varieties, liberal, socialist, anarchist and Christian, as well as a further objection which must have been particularly problematic: an artistic objection based on my commitment to creation rather than destruction. All of these turned up later in my LSE PhD thesis on pacifism between the wars. Of course, there was no necessary connection between holding a classic liberal view against conscription and strict pacifism, but they certainly went together in my mind as part of a suspicion of state compulsion and of the nefarious ways of foreign policy. My reading of Bright and others convinced me that 'Truth is the first casualty of war'.

I told the tribunal I was incapable of bayonet practice, let alone bayonet fighting, and this at least was obviously true. I concluded by quoting the Revd Albert Belden in *Peace News*: 'I object to being a state slave of war.' This was another impolitic mistake, as it sounded aggressive rather than quietist, and had political overtones. I asked sarcastically who had been designated as the likely enemy, and objected to the possibility of fighting our erstwhile allies, the Russians. I did rather better when I argued that military build-ups were a vicious spiral and we needed to break the spiral. Somebody had to start. When pressed for quotations from Scripture I half-remembered the relevant sections of the Sermon on the Mount about not resisting evil but overcoming evil with good, and quoted something from St Paul or the Psalms about 'Vengeance is mine, I will repay'. Under pressure I spoke with desperate conviction.

The tribunal assigned me to the Non-Combatant Corps (NCC). That was always likely because the No Conscription Council had advised me to 'go as far as I could consistent with conscience', and the NCC was a compromise. The explanatory literature said the NCC might be deployed for mine-clearing and medical assistance, and that gave it an attractive humanitarian gloss. In fact it was used as a reserve army of clerks, because its members were more than usually capable of reading and writing. The Army put NCC recruits in with the Pioneer Corps (later designated Royal) – which was an imaginative symbiosis, because Pioneers were less than usually capable of reading and writing. According to army ratings the NCC ranged educationally from 11 (graduate) to 31 and the Pioneers from 61 to 81, the lowest grade.

While waiting to be called up, I worked as a temporary file clerk in the Hammersmith income tax office, and while deep in the files, another temporary file clerk introduced me to Oswald Spengler's *The Decline of the West* and the idea that revolutions rarely end well. On a very hot day, on 6 May 1948, I arrived at the Pioneer Corps camp at Kidderminster, Worcestershire. I was in the Army now and about to undergo 21 months of extremely unpleasant, if sometimes ridiculous, experiences. The camp was made up of rows of huts like slugs lying parallel on a hillside between Kidderminster, Stourport and Bewdley, and looked misleadingly benign in the warm May sun.

I did not get off to a good start. I was assigned to a plum job in the officers' mess serving drinks, but someone from a Methodist teetotal background does not know the names of drinks, let alone the etiquette of ordering and serving them. Drilling also proved a trial and I was gullible enough to suppose the question 'Does anyone here play the piano?' a genuine enquiry rather than a method of selecting soldiers for unpleasant duties. When NCC recruits were asked to respond to an appeal to give blood not one of us responded, which reflected badly on our humane and progressive motivations, but we had concluded it was a version of 'Does anyone here play the piano?' I was also warned not to stand around like the Venus de Milo, a way I had of trying not to be noticed, elegant in her but unmilitary and awkward in me.

One way of convincing soldiers they were totally subject to arbitrary authority was to hold them endlessly in line to receive permission to take weekend leave, and then announce leave had been suspended. The soldiers in charge behaved like this to show they could, and nothing was more calculated to engender undying hatred of the military. Section 40 of the Army Act, 'conduct prejudicial to good order and military discipline', was always held in reserve for any purpose whatsoever, including 'dumb insolence'. Later, as an orderly room clerk, I became used to officers consulting NCOs about what infringement of Section 40 they would use to 'get' this or that soldier on morning parade. Leaving camp was always hazardous because one could always be hauled back for whatever arbitrary reason happened to appeal to the duty corporal.

NCOs in the Pioneers complained that the Kidderminster depot was 'run by the NCC for the NCC'. In fact it was run rather humanely by a 'senior' member of the NCC – we were all officially confined to the rank of private – who was first clarinettist of the London Philharmonic Orchestra. He was envied for his 'cushy' billet, way down the corridor from the open plan section where most of us lived. His clarinet concerto awaited completion on his music stand. Obscene threats were made about his accommodation, his role and his person, but they came to nothing.

Most of the NCC recruits in my hut were Exclusive Brethren, fisher-folk from Peterhead on the north-east coast of Scotland. When NCOs burst unceremoniously into the hut early in the day shouting 'Stand by your beds', they faced ranks of Brethren already by their beds but on their knees in prayer. The Exclusive Brethren took seriously St Paul's injunction not to be 'unequally yoked together with unbelievers'. They never lent money, and read their Bibles even in the coffee break. It was the perfect education for a future sociologist of religion.

Intellectual debate outside the closed circles of the Brethren was lively, and a barrow boy from Erdington demanded to know my opinion of Hume's *Dialogues Concerning Natural Religion*. I had not yet read Hume but he said that didn't really matter. He only needed to know I wasn't a Brother. We would lie on the grass in the evenings watching the sun go down over Bewdley and the Wyre Forest, overhearing distant hymn singing from an NCC hut, and criticizing the Brethren and the world. I shared the marvellous tarts sent by my mother, with him, and only with him, because I recognized a moral problem. Clearly a person of conscience and progressive opinions ought to share with others. On the other hand my mother meant the tarts for my sustenance and I ought not to buy cheap popularity at her expense by sharing them with everybody. Sharing just with him was my compromise, though I occasionally also offered my tart to an Open Brother who wanted to talk providing we kept our friendship secret.

I also became friends with a rosy-cheeked Anglican ordinand. He took me up almost as soon as I arrived. 'Thank God you're not a bloody EB,' he said. He was an Anglo-Catholic and not interested in my views about David Hume. Instead he wanted to know what I thought about the Athanasian Creed. I confessed uncertainty. He invited me to his billet where he read it out to test my orthodoxy. I did very well with 'neither confounding the persons nor dividing the substance', but baulked at 'This is the Catholic Faith which except a man believe faithfully he cannot be saved'. It seemed very restrictive. Happily he didn't believe that either. Like the barrow boy, he said it didn't really matter, and I was enrolled as a temporary acting Catholic.

The successive cohorts of recruits who occupied the beds close to me included a remarkable assortment of people. One was a Pentecostal with plastered-down yellow hair and an obtrusively large watch. He was not worried about the Athanasian Creed but about whether I had received Jesus Christ as my personal Saviour. Finding my replies unsatisfactory, he offered to 'bull' my military boots and make them shiny if I read his tracts. This was a bargain for somebody who preferred reading to bulling. His prayers had a different tonal quality from those of the Exclusive Brethren, high-pitched, warm and veering towards ecstasy, and I was relieved when he went off to 'fellowship' with another Pentecostal in the quartermaster's stores. His place was taken by a product of a Glasgow Socialist Sunday School where he had been taught an ideology of peace and free love. He was going to the Royal Academy of Dramatic Art, and on propitious nights would light candles around his bed before giving performances of Shakespeare sonnets, 'Annabel Lee' and 'The Ballad of Reading Gaol'.

Some soldiers pretended to be mad, and wandered about literally barking or saying 'Bang, bang, you're dead' in the illusory hope of being thrown out of the Army. A Scouse thug threatened us all with a knife, which I felt he might well use if I enquired too intrusively about his conscientious objection to violence. He did, however, speak loudly and often of his intense sense of grievance at being allocated to the Army when he was a merchant seaman and only wanted to be in the Navy. Of course, being allocated to the wrong service is not among the acceptable legal reasons for seeking exemption. He swore horribly and sat sharpening his knife most evenings. Anyone who did not speak with a Scouse accent he accused of being a homosexual.

Another recruit was an autodidact with a classics scholarship to Oxford who promised to teach me Latin by the conversational method. I had not done well by the normal method, so was anxious to try. However, the opportunity disappeared after an unfortunate conversation between him and the Commanding Officer. He refused to put on his uniform and was marched into the CO's presence on a charge. The CO said, 'But my dear chap, don't you believe in democracy?'

When my friend replied, 'No sir,' the CO asked,

'Then what the hell do you believe in?'

'Theocracy, sir,' was the answer.

'And where in God's name has that been practised?' said the CO.

'Among the ancient Israelites,' explained my friend.

The CO exploded. 'And what the hell do you take me for, a bloody Israelite?'

He went to Birmingham gaol.

Another objector was a Zionist who read Rilke. For my part I read Clive Bell on *Civilization* and *Art*, and stuck Corot's painting *The Leaning Tree* over my bed as witness to another and better world.

The nearest other world lay with the Finch family I had made friends with at Bewdley Methodist church, where I became organist. They often invited me to share the quiet and ordered domesticity of their home on the hillside overlooking Bewdley. Arcadia opened up whenever I walked along the banks of the Severn between Stourport and Bewdley. But my real encounter with a transformed world came in October 1948 when I took a bus from Kidderminster to stay with very old friends of my mother at Ashford Carbonel, near Ludlow. I was troubled and exhausted by life in the camp and fell asleep on the bus, with my head banging against an iron knob by the window. When I woke and got out of the bus in Ludlow I found myself in a light-filled, benign and peaceable township, where the inhabitants, young or venerable, appeared like creatures of transparent goodness and beauty. I walked by inevitable inclination into the church of St Lawrence, recognizing it as the temple at the centre of this heavenly city, and also went to the castle where I recollect a notice saying Milton's *Comus* had been first performed there in 1634. Then I set out to walk three miles through the landscape to Ashford Carbonel, touching objects, like grey stone walls, to cherish them and feel their texture.

My host appeared at the door of his house, an unexpectedly old man with hair like white wool, and that evening I found Olive Wyon's *The School of Prayer* (1943) by my bed which introduced me to a new way of thinking about prayer and quotations chiming with the experiences of the day, such as Henry Vaughan's 'The Morning Watch'.

> O Joys! Infinite sweetness! With what flowers,
> And shoots of glory, my soul breaks and buds!

I gradually came to associate all the Welsh marches, from the Wye and the Usk to the Clun Valley, with this particular numen. In my imagination I had a map of sacred geography from Abbotsbury in

Dorset to Huish Episcopi and the Glastonbury Tor in Somerset, from the Malvern Hills to Leominster and Ludlow. Even the names of places were incantations.

I was next posted to a very different world in the Military Police Station, Canning Town, in the slums of East London, as an orderly room clerk, though I had received no training for this. In any case I doubt if training was provided for the kind of meeting for which I was detailed to take the minutes. It began with the announcement by the chairman: 'I am Sergeant Jones, commonly known as the blue-nosed bastard.' There followed detailed accounts of intercourse with local women on the mess dining tables. I kept my pen poised, uncertain whether I was expected to summarize this, but guessing it need not be minuted. The problem was the virtual absence of any other material. I was rapidly relieved of this post and assigned to telephone duty. At this I lasted a little longer until I held the phone at a distance when a caller broke into a particularly ferocious bout of abuse. After that I cleaned lavatories and woke people up. I failed again because I was far too polite. Gently shaking soldiers and informing them it was probably time to stir was ineffective, given the normal methods. I was usually roused in the morning by a broom swung above my head and hitting either side of the billet with loud bangs while Sergeant Jones rasped in my ear, 'Out of that wanking pit, you bastard.'

The military policemen were repulsive sadists who boasted of how they had selected soldiers on duty in the Middle East on minor made-up charges just as they were hoping to go on leave to England. They competed with each other in arbitrary bookings as a form of entertainment. Unlike the Pioneers they knew nothing of the ways of the NCC and leapt at the chance to haze a private with a middle-class accent. One day I was screamed to attention and called a fucking coward. To this I objected 'Sir!', and was immediately bundled into the sergeant's office and told in blazing tones it was a sergeant's prerogative to be addressed as 'Sergeant', not as 'Sir'.

'Spell prerogative,' he bawled.

I complied.

'I can spell it too,' he said, 'and I haven't got my matric neither.'

How I got away with listening to Byrd's four-part Mass on the mess radio I do not know.

Someone must have decided to put me on a charge. There was always some military reason available, in this case an inadequately cleaned belt. I was confined to barracks for the weekend, and my spell of 'jankers' required me to polish all the stairs with red polish and all the windows with paper. As I worked Sergeant Jones would stump past, chuckling 'O be joyful in the Lord, Private Martin.' In our next confrontation he called me to attention in front of a group of corporals and recited an alphabet of sexual intercourse to which I was supposed to respond or mimic letter by letter. I only remember that it ended with Zambuk, then a well-known emollient. As I remained expressionless throughout this perverse catechism, Sergeant Jones took me into his office and pointed to a citation in dispatches signed by Marshal Foch. 'You heard of him?' he asked.

I nodded. 'C. in C. Allied Armies in the First World War.'

He turned triumphantly to his coterie. 'You see, you ignorant bastards, *he* knows who Foch was.' Next time I saw him he took me aside and said 'If anyone tries to fuck you around, just tell me.'

This unexpected patronage was not entirely effective. My blankets were removed and I was ordered to pay for them and their replacement. I had to fight this or in time lose all my equipment. I succeeded because my father sometimes collected me in his taxi, and my tormentors concluded my father was a magnate who sent the taxi, not the taxi-man who drove it. I did not disabuse them. When I threatened my father would complain to the War Office, the blankets instantly reappeared.

The next problem also involved equipment, and resulted in my being sent back to the Kidderminster depot. For a while I helped the Company Quarter Master Sergeant (CQMS) by filling in forms in his stores, and he was accused of malfeasance by the Regimental Sergeant Major. Maybe the RSM had not been let in on the takings. The CQMS begged me to say I had received boots from him when I had done nothing of the kind. Finding myself a witness for a court martial to take place at the Chelsea Barracks, I had to go to Whitehall to make a statement. To my surprise this was written down by an army lawyer with barely any reference to me. He dictated a set of stereotyped phrases I was required to sign. Of course, the CQMS was found guilty and reduced to the rank of sergeant, while I was reassigned to NCC HQ as an awkward nuisance. Like every other recruit I always took the very latest train possible to Kidderminster, leaving at midnight and arriving back at camp at first light, and I think it may have been on this journey I spent the hours reading St John and St Paul.

My next posting was to 522 Pioneer Company, in a camp on a desolate strip, dotted with low black huts, near Donnington, Shropshire. This was a nest of theft, violence, collective sodomy, suicide and every kind of petty fiddle. I was not surprised when a soldier hanged himself. I shared this assignment with two other NCC personnel, one a Jehovah's Witness and the other, Steve, a quiet Anglican full of country lore from Cucklington in Sussex. We were to run the Company Office under a staff sergeant and a corporal. Some of my duties were not detailed in the Army Regulations I updated nearly every day, such as assisting the staff sergeant on his midnight fishing expeditions for eels in the Bridgewater Canal. It was a kind of comradeship and I enjoyed watching the luminous writhing of the eels in the dark. I felt it built up a relationship likely to afford protection against arbitrary interference. Another comradely role was writing letters for Pioneers who had emotional problems with their women friends. I had to find solutions to the problems as well as coining the most winning phrases.

I was detailed to greet recruits arriving from initial training at the Worcestershire depot. They were taken aback to be treated politely with enquiries about their home town and family circumstances. Yet I gradually fell into the expected habit of not immediately making out travel passes on Fridays so soldiers could go on leave as soon as possible. A new Company Sergeant Major upbraided me for this and, somewhat shamefaced, I was glad to comply. Of course, he also expected me to make out free travel passes way beyond his entitlement. I had reluctantly to send out arrest warrants for soldiers AWOL – absent without leave – and here I helped a little with minor but crucial delays in their dispatch. Of course, sometimes it was better to act quickly to minimize the time they eventually spent in Colchester or Shepton Mallet Military Correction Establishments. Soldiers were regularly discharged en masse on account of mental problems, some of them simulated. After demob I encountered a soldier discharged for madness and chronic simplicity and found him remarkably sane and sophisticated.

Once I agreed to act as anonymous letter writer to the lieutenant in charge of welfare about the quality of the food. The Army Catering Corps sergeant had not been selected for culinary competence but on account of his sufferings under the Japanese. Complaints were regularly requested in the Army and regularly punished, and still officers complained that they received far too few complaints to act on them. 'Why don't they say this is not the kind of thing they are used to at home?' mused the CO, Major J. F. C. Harrison. As for my complaint about the food, I was marched in to the lieutenant's office and asked to explain myself. He agreed anonymity was acceptable, but said I was a fool to rely on it, since I was the only person who could write. After that we discussed whether soldiers went to the NAAFI because the official food was really bad or gorged so many delicacies in the

NAAFI they had no appetite for the decent and homely fare provided by the Army.

Some of those who got into trouble were very sad cases. A young man in the bed next to me asked what NCC meant. He suggested I must have objected to armed service because I was a pianist and needed to protect my hands. If a classical pianist had the wit to acquire exemption, a jazz pianist like himself should have done the same. Unhappily our discussions ended when a nasty little group identified him as a homosexual, stripped him naked and blacked his private parts. Another sad case would in earlier times have been labelled a simpleton. He asked for time off to attend church and when an NCO said, 'You don't fucking go to church, mate,' swore back very effectively. He was later assaulted in an act of collective sodomy for which I typed out the evidence before the perpetrators were sent to gaol. In another instance I had the task of telling a soldier his mother had died and made out a railway warrant for him to go home on compassionate leave. The officer in command said he hadn't time to deal with that sort of thing now, which shocked me into saying soldiers had a right to compassionate leave. The officer reluctantly agreed to sign the warrant, grumbling, 'There is far too much talk about rights in this army.'

Everyone longed only for leave and discharge. As I looked after both, I was in a position of power without rank and subject to constant lobbying. Soldiers anxious to state their claims concluded I was at my most vulnerable stuck on the open latrines where we faced each other in mutual squalor. Actually I had plenty of other sources of information about their needs, since they decorated the latrine walls in their own excrement with comments like 'Only another 90 fucking days to go'.

The prospect of a visit of inspection by the general commanding Western Command worried the authorities in 'N' Camp into trying to suppress this habit. The decision to forbid it in daily company orders, read out by corporals every early evening to their little platoons, created a problem of phraseology. The orderly room staff sergeant dictated the following, which I typed obediently: 'Any soldier found writing in his own shit on the walls of the company lavatories will be put on a charge.'

At that point the Company Sergeant Major stormed in and screamed, 'Fucking hell, you can't use a word like "shit" in company orders. There is a proper military bloody word for that – hexcreta.'

I retyped the offending sentence using the proper military bloody word, but the orderly room sergeant was not subdued. 'Which of these fuckers knows what the hell "excreta" means?' he rasped.

The RSM responded, 'Tell all the NCOs to explain it, and, in case there is still a problem, put a hasterisk by it to say that in the event of further uncertainty they may enquire from Private Martin here in the Orderly Room. Let him explain.'

The life world of the military was sealed off as a set of practices that were taken to be obligatory, but recognized as different from the courtesies appropriate in the outside world. When my parents came to visit me they were treated with singular courtesy, invited to eat in the sergeants' mess and closeted with the Commanding Officer. I knew the sergeants boasted of pissing on the floor of their mess after bouts of drinking, but now they offered their better selves for inspection. Eventually I acquired a status slightly aside from the hierarchy. I was even invited by the CO to contribute to a concert by playing my own truncated version of the first movement of the Grieg concerto. As compère, the CO introduced me as an oddly gifted visitor from a far country who had rendered acceptable service.

I had various bolt-holes: visiting the nearby ruined abbey of Much Wenlock by bus, attending one of the three local Methodist churches (originally Wesleyan, Primitive and United), or even walking five miles to church in Wellington. I wrote to my mother about 'lifting up mine eyes unto the hills' and I looked longingly at the small nearby mountain called the Wrekin. Or else I sat and absorbed a landscape criss-crossed by rivulets and canals from a vantage point on a curious knoll near Lilleshall. By the orderly room brazier on winter nights I read the whole of Keats: 'St Agnes Eve – Ah, bitter chill it was! . . . by degrees/Her rich attire crept rustling to her knees'. But not for me. There was also the Education Hut where I first heard Vaughan Williams' Fifth Symphony, and where I was recruited to teach. Occasionally I overshot the mark and was warned: 'You are here, Private Martin, to teach these soldiers to fucking read, not to read fucking Shakespeare.'

My main hideaway was the garrison church, where I became organist. The female choir, a relief to the eyes after relentless maleness, processed in regularly to what was now my favourite introit from the Fauré *Requiem*: 'Tremens, tremens, factus sum ego, et timeo . . .' One officer, Lieutenant David Cox, from the Royal Ordnance Corps, left a lasting impression. He was later to be ordained, and his body language as he knelt to receive the sacrament affected me. Till that moment devout posture had been outside my experience.

The junior chaplain, Mr Lilley, explained he came of a good northern family, and he possessed an expert knowledge, rarely called upon in 522 'N' Pioneer Camp, of the Ethiopian Coptic Church. He did not mind being asked in Chaplain's Half Hour whether he had visited the brothels of Alexandria, but he did mind being disbelieved. When I first encountered him he was writing wearily to 'My Lord Bishop of Norwich', asking 'how much more purgation' was required of him. I usually found him busy with the *Daily Telegraph* crossword and complaining that nowadays people seemed incapable of finding the creative element in work. He did his best to educate me, socially by lending me Osbert Sitwell's autobiography *Left Hand, Right Hand*, and theologically by lending me Oliver Quick's *Doctrines of the Creed*. I made more of Quick than Sitwell. He arranged for me to attend a Moral Leadership course in November 1949 at the chaplains' headquarters in a house in a beautiful park at Bagshot, Surrey. I found the two senior chaplains extraordinarily impressive, and one had a long talk with me about Reinhold Niebuhr's critique of pacifism. During this blessed week I came to love Compline, the concluding service of the day, with its near silence, fluttering candles, short prayers for protection, and the hymn *Te lucis ante terminum*.

The day before I was to leave the Army was 2 February 1950, and the chaplain invited me to the garrison church for the Feast of the Purification of the Blessed Virgin. I was allowed the morning off to receive communion. Something about the name of the feast appealed to me, and I never forgot to connect my release with the Feast of the Purification. Candlemas remains a high point in the liturgical year.

6

Further education: training, teaching, marriage break-up

———————

After the Army I worked briefly at a primary school off Clapham Common in Wix's Lane to gain teaching experience. Of this I remember almost nothing except playing the piano for 'The Ballad of London River', the London County Council children's anthem. Then in September 1950 I went to the Westminster Methodist Teacher Training College in a Victorian Gothic building in the Horseferry Road. My grant as a day student was £36 in the first year and £60 in the second. I suppose Westminster College had long been a route into the teaching profession for young men, particularly Nonconformists, for whom university was not a likely avenue of advancement. I was probably among the last students to follow this route. Not long after, everything opened up. Social mobility through universities became normal, and teaching became a graduate profession.

My two friends Leslie Smith and John Chalker went to London University with county major scholarships to read English, Leslie to King's College, John to Queen Mary. East Sheen Grammar School did not expect to send its pupils to Oxford or Cambridge and John Carey, later Merton Professor, was one of the first. John and Les both took Firsts – John later becoming Professor of English Literature and a vice-principal of Queen Mary – and I picked up some of the ethos of a university education from them, attending intoxicating inter-collegiate lectures at King's on William Blake.

My first essay at Westminster College was 'My Education So Far'. I called it 'Pioneers, oh Pioneers' (after Walt Whitman's poem), recalling my time in the Pioneer Corps, and it began 'I was educated by the Methodist church and the BBC but I did nevertheless go to school.' There was some truth to this, since the Methodist Youth Club, run by a physicist, John Perry, had provided a formative educational experience. And the BBC under Lord Reith had widened my range of cultural reference enormously.

Pretending I was at university rather than teacher training college, and pretending I was reading English with subsidiary music, had its awkward side. I made clear I did not care for so-called lectures in history by Dr Oxley devoted either to his thesis on Barking Abbey or how to spell 'Isaiah', 'exaggeration' and 'accommodation'. He told me not to be arrogant. Dr Oxley refused to mark my papers and I was asked to meet the vice-principal for a little talk about doing what I was asked to do, which he conducted in a kindly way, as though he understood the problem.

In our English course we studied a volume of pallid Georgian poetry, which again reminded me this was not a university. But this time the lecturer, Dr Shepherd, was sympathetic, and invited me to devise my own course in poets of the twentieth century. I enjoyed this and wrote on a sequence of English poets from Hardy to Eliot. He found my references to the Eternal Feminine rather high-flown but continued to encourage me, and suggested I should really be on a degree course. We became friends and he asked me, among others, to read poems to complement the readings of Dame Sybil Thorndike when she gave a recital at the college. This was an important occasion, but he wanted me to speak by heart a Masefield poem called 'Beauty' that enumerated the several gifts of God revealed in her voice, hair and eyes 'and the dear, red curve of her lips'. I said it was unspeakable, and that I would rather not take part than recite it. Tolerantly he turned the choice over to me and I chose Marvell's 'To his Coy Mistress', which was perhaps what I was angling for all along. Perhaps I felt Masefield offered too brief an exposure to an audience.

Another lecturer in English invited us to create social 'characters' along the lines of the Elizabethan author John Earle in his *Microcosmographie* and challenged us to see if we could imitate the style of Charles Lamb. I enjoyed these little exercises and found that Lamblike phrases came rather too easily. Perhaps they did not do that kind of thing in the real university, but it felt more like it. My music thesis on Byzantine hymnography and Western chant also felt more like it, though what the music department made of it I do not know. From time to time I even wore the university scarf.

In the early stages of the course I was so far misled about what was expected that I read as though anticipating an examination at university level, and was startled by initial examination results starry enough to rob me of any such delusion. I had read works like Roger

Ascham's *The Scholemaster* and the whole of Wordsworth's *The Prelude* before realizing I had overshot the mark. Essentially this was an education in teaching practice, except that the practicalities were not well attended to. I suspected some of our teachers had been signal failures at teaching, and in due course I would sympathize. We needed instruction in how to keep order and organize a school day, but this was mostly left to teaching practice, where we sank or swam by our own wits.

Two experiences did feel like university life. The first was in August 1950 when I hitchhiked from Calais to Stuttgart for the Liberal World Congress, with students from the London University Liberal Club, and heard speakers like Salvador de Madariaga. We split into twos at Calais and my companion was Heather from Bedford College. We had various mild adventures, like dossing down together in a school classroom and being fruitlessly advised by a French policeman to make the most of it. I fear I excused our unnatural restraint by telling him we were English. Luckily we were picked up by architectural students who liked the look of her, and they took us in their truck as far as Strasbourg. This was my first encounter with a mysterious 'Continent'. Now I could see the places I had read about, including Laon, Rheims and Strasbourg. So far my sense of architectural beauty had been shaped by the chaste profile of Salisbury Cathedral; now I stood looking at the west front of Strasbourg Cathedral in all its extravagant and assertive verticality. This was Goethe's 'divine tree making for the sky'. I also encountered a more extravagant and tangible piety on Low Sunday when the cathedral celebrated *La Communion Solennelle*. Huge crowds of young people made a profession of faith, processing round the cathedral dressed in white and holding candles, while the choir sang *Ave Verum Corpus*. Two days later I was lost in the Black Forest near Freudenstadt and sleeping toe to toe with others in a vast circular bed in the Naturfreundehaus, Kniebis.

In August 1951 I attended an international student conference on the Lorelei Rock, above the Rhine. An *Evangelisch* service was held in an arena overlooking the river, built as a *Thingplatz* by the Nazis. We were addressed by a Lutheran pastor, translating from German into perfect English as he went along, and when we said the Lord's Prayer I was shaken to hear the word 'kingdom' overlaying the word *Reich*. When we were taken to Pforzheim, we saw destruction far beyond anything in the London Blitz. There was hardly one stone left standing upon another, and nobody said a word. Nearly nine-tenths of the built-up area, including the medieval centre, had been destroyed by the RAF. In one night alone in 1945 one in four of the inhabitants died, whereas in Dresden it was one in 20. Even the bomb damage in Cologne did not compare with the destruction of Pforzheim.

My first three years of teaching, from 1952 to 1955, were at the Old Oak Primary School, near Wormwood Scrubs prison. This was the school for a London County Council estate known as a rough area. The head teacher once warned me not to teach poems with the word 'sod' in them in case parents whose own use of language was much more colourful complained. He also explained why it was inadvisable to use phrases like 'A lovable little rascal with a mastery of local patois' when writing reports. Less helpfully, an inspector suggested I move on from teaching folk songs and the occasional Bach chorale to performing the *St Matthew Passion*. All the same, the school was well run by a devout Roman Catholic head, newly appointed, and the teachers worked together amicably to create a supportive atmosphere. Maybe the march-like section of Beethoven's *Hammerklavier* Sonata was not the normal fare when the children filed out of assembly, but nobody complained.

David Martin (top right), teacher at Old Oak Primary School, East Acton

I married my first wife, Daphne Treherne, in 1953 and we moved to Yeovil, Somerset in 1955, hoping a new place would help us make a new start. Our marriage had been in trouble before it began. I taught for the first year at Wincanton Primary School, and for the first term I lived with local people, on my own except when Daphne came down for the weekend, while we waited for our new house to be available. Daphne was now pregnant but we barely had enough money to eat, and colleagues clubbed together to give us a hamper of food. When our son, Jonathan, was born, it briefly seemed the marriage could be salvaged. I moved to a school closer to our Yeovil home, and deluded myself we were ready for a new start. The delusion should have been obvious. We went through what were then the sordid requirements to secure a divorce, and I was given custody of Jonathan. Daphne had other children by two other marriages and died early and tragically of cancer.

This memoir is not about emotional involvements and debacles apart from the role they played in my subconscious pursuit of my own education and the way that informal education finally caught up with formal education at graduate level. In my six years with Daphne, beginning when she was just 17, things went wrong almost from the start. The outward form of our 'relationship' was traditional and stable. The inner content was subject to all the corrosives of intellectual change as they affected my cohort of scholarship children and Daphne's networks at the girls' grammar school, where she had found the framework of authority irksome.

I never considered finding out what was in her head beyond being uncomfortably aware she wanted to get out of the constrictions of home and school. To my father she was 'a Christian girl', whereas to my mother she was a further inhibition on the things she still hoped I might achieve. The security of my home had been built on age-old inevitabilities enveloped in a great silence. Problems were not there to be negotiated and solutions were never sought. They were immovable mountains to be climbed. Both Daphne and I responded to unfocused intimations of freedom beyond the constrictions of everyday routine, but with different notions of what that might look like. I absorbed it through Romantic literature; she directly, especially in the Richmond 'scene' where she mixed with people, some with serious money, avant-garde artistic connections and 'advanced' opinions. Maybe from her perspective I was the kind of dreamer who might provide an escape route to wider horizons, whatever those might be. Unfortunately the income and intellectual horizon of the primary school teacher does not offer easy entry to intimations of the good life as reflected in the arts pages of the *Observer* and the *Guardian*.

Maybe this vague aspiration to a less constricted existence inspired Daphne's bouts of unaffordable expenditure on clothes, her rejection of household routine and enjoyment of life modelling for a famous art school and Duncan Grant, or her time spent with mildly bohemian company in Richmond. I was not much given to routine chores either, though I took domestic order for granted and felt disturbed by its absence. I too had an unachievable notion of the good life modelled on the academic career and university circle of John Chalker. Only on holidays where the demands of routine were suspended, especially our honeymoon, did our notions of freedom briefly overlap. But even on holiday we had different expectations. She preferred the beach at Perranporth and I wanted to look for the half-buried oratory of St Piran.

Once I realized we were incarcerated together in mutually incompatible ambitions I succumbed to a bondage of the will that for decades blocked the path to emotional maturity and diverted active agency solely into academic pursuits. I was simultaneously conscious of the great inevitabilities and of an unfocused desire for freedom. My first response in the wake of marital disaster was to go into emotional deep freeze and pour all my energies into the pursuit of my education. For decades I remained liable to damaging breakouts which in their turn became constricting and oppressive beyond any active exercise of will or initiative. I lived my life in the passive voice, a virtuoso of the intransitive.

The last thing I wanted to do was work in the garden. Daphne did not wash dishes and I did not dig borders. The state of the front garden in our new house in Yeovil told passers-by everything they needed to know about the untended relationships within. Only when Daphne had left did my parents descend to reduce the garden to an order satisfactory to affronted neighbours. Even then, I swanned off with the lodgers to the coast in my father's car while he in his late sixties toiled away at digging up the garden. People who performed mundane tasks were mostly invisible to me, rather like the gardeners the other side of the ha-ha or silent housekeepers. Daphne and I, brought up in SW14 and SW13, had acquired the attitudes of romantic aristocrats on an income of £30 a month.

Emotional compatibility or shared interests did not loom as major considerations before getting married. There was no notion of a period of experimentation and trial, and in order to 'break up' you needed external authorization and permission. The permissions were not available. What was seemingly secure and recognizable from the outside, at least to my parents, was in practice undermined from within by romantic notions of freedom. These included the wrongness of asserting rights, duties and boundaries, and all the volatility and lability that can emerge if things do not work out and there is emotional mayhem. The contradictions of the sixties were already present in us, but not the escape routes. People in this situation are liable to seek stronger and different stimuli once earlier excitements become dulled by familiarity. The expected domestic duties and sexual mores had lost their definition and the marital package was wide open at the seams. Daphne was in need of the boundaries she fought so violently against, and I was ill equipped and disinclined to provide them or understand what was going on. I knew I wanted to 'get on' with my 'work', even though this remained unspecified. I felt I was getting behind, permanently stuck in this emotional morass, and would some day have to make extreme efforts to catch up. Meanwhile Daphne exerted increasing pressure to make me react and assert a boundary.

Eventually she crossed the boundary in a way bound to arouse a strong reaction, in part because it involved a man outside the range of the kind of people I knew or with whom I could share a community of interest. I felt serious anger, confusion and pain, all of which rapidly subsided into feelings of relief and unexpected release. I could 'get on' with my 'work', which had now acquired the definition of a correspondence course in sociology, on top of my desire to redeem the humiliation of failing the professional performers' diplomas of the Royal Schools of Music.

During the year after she left I taught in the Yeovil primary school. I also preached in the local North Dorset/South Somerset Methodist circuit, cycling hundreds of miles, often in a mood of deep contentment, to chapels scattered through the most marvellous countryside. The villages had names like Rime Intrinseca and Bishops Caundle, and I sometimes had to play the harmonium as well as take the service. Once in Wincanton Methodist Church I gave a recital of the poems of William Barnes. One day I might become headmaster of the primary school at Bradford Abbas, a sun-baked Dorset village (as I imagined it) close to Yeovil.

In late August 1956, about a couple of months after Daphne's departure, I went on a therapeutic walking holiday with Leslie Smith, first along the Cornish coast from Polperro to Mevagissey, and then along the Dorset coast from Weymouth to Poole. The Purbeck coastline is magnificent and as our walk came to an end we fetched up in Poole on a Sunday evening. I noticed Poole Methodist Church advertised an evening service on the very relevant theme 'Hell is other people'. As I sat down I was overtaken by an inward miracle of equipoise. The minister spoke eloquently on the theme of heaven and hell between persons, in love and in war. The climax of the service came with the choir singing George Herbert's 'King of Glory, King of Peace', and the words 'Thou didst note my working breast,/Thou didst hear me'. It was like the theophany I had experienced in Ludlow seven years before, also a time of strain.

It only occurred once more, years later in the late seventies, at another time of stress, when I was on a plane travelling by myself back from the USA. It began soon after passing the lights of Philadelphia on the left of the aircraft. Perhaps the sight of the city provided a prelude to this third theophany – what Thomas Browne in his *Religio Medici* calls an *O altitudo*. It happened as I was listening to Mozart's E flat Horn Concerto, to 'In paradisum te ducant angeli' from the Fauré *Requiem* sung by King's College Choir, and to Janet Baker singing Mahler's 'Ich bin der Welt abhanden gekommen' at the funeral of Sir John Barbirolli in Westminster Cathedral. In my mind's ear I can still hear the 'dying fall' of the phrase

> Ich bin gestorben den Weltgetümmel
> Und ruh' in einem stillen Gebiet.
> Ich leb' allein in meinem Himmel
> In meinem Lieben, in meinem Lied.

I was 'dead to the turmoil of the world', and the peace of the 'stillen Gebiet', the 'still sphere', accompanied me faithfully over the Atlantic. It was many hours before I re-entered the atmosphere of earth.

7

Reading theology and local preaching: test-bed of faith

When, in my first essay at Westminster College on my education, I ascribed as much weight to the Methodist Church as to my grammar school, that was not just hyperbole. This was the great period of church youth clubs. The post-war Labour government was in power and we 'young people' regularly talked progressive politics, and offered confident opinions on the implications of Christianity for welfare policy and issues of peace and war. I was invited to give talks as a basis for discussion, including one on psychic phenomena, like the poltergeists discussed in a book by Sacheverell Sitwell and strange doings at Borley Rectory. I gave another on Mozart's letters, which provided plenty of the juvenile humour that might intrigue adolescents.

A young female art student in the club educated me about modern art. I had no concept of modern art. I had looked at the paintings of Paul Nash at the National Gallery concerts and saw them just as paintings. When she asked for my opinion about Henry Moore I had no idea. So she gave me a book of Moore's wartime paintings of people in the London underground shelters in the Penguin Modern Art series, and literally took me home to see her etchings. I followed this up with a book on Jacob Epstein and stared wide-eyed at his rendering of a pregnant woman in *Genesis*: art as the power of fecundity.

The Wesley Guild was mainly for older people, but I was invited to give talks there on a couple of occasions, one of them on the early reception of Handel's *Messiah* in Britain and America. The minister's son, Peter Townsend, was at Cambridge and he spoke on the importance to John Wesley of Thomas à Kempis, William Law, the Caroline divines and Jeremy Taylor, which encouraged me to read about these people and about the eighteenth-century world of early Methodism.

There were also evenings where older kinds of entertainment were put on, and I was sometimes recruited as accompanist: old music-hall songs to *Chu Chin Chow*. There were readings from Dickens by itinerant performers, and occasions when people talked about books important for their personal lives. Some of these were offbeat from a Methodist point of view, but nobody seemed to notice. It just needed to sound inspirational. One was *In Tune with the Infinite*, a book of self-help spirituality by Ralph Waldo Trine, but it did not strike me or anyone else as heterodox. I was reading Khalil Gibran and had no idea he lived on another theological planet.

Various people at church were kind enough to give my education a little boost, beginning with a local preacher called George Taylor. He invited me to his fine library and gave me a history of England, Darwin's *Journal of Researches* (known in twentieth-century editions as *The Voyage of the Beagle*) and introduced me to C. S. Lewis. Mr Harding, from the ex-Primitive Methodist Church in White Hart Lane, took me on a tour of Wren's city churches and piqued me in a helpful way by saying Nicolas Berdyaev's *Freedom and the Spirit* would prove a salutary exercise in coping with something beyond me. To prove him wrong I got out the dictionary and stuck with a text that began (I quote from memory), 'We have long ago given up all confidence in the possibility and fruitfulness of an abstract meta-physic.' Now just why had *we* done that?

I don't like to think how many hundreds of times I played the banausic little jingle 'I am H.A.P.P.Y., I am H.A.P.P.Y., I know I am, I'm sure I am, I'm H.A.P.P.Y.', devising chromatic accompaniments to relieve the boredom. There was singing in the church choir and the youth club choir and playing the piano for them and for Sunday School as an accompanist; there was playing the organ for church, attending Sunday School teacher preparation classes and at one point confirmation classes. My mother commented acerbically that the children of other parents at the church were not diverted from their school work in this way. Perhaps they were merely lucky not to play the piano. Some of them came from firmly middle-class homes in the better parts of Barnes and Sheen and had parents to track their progress with understanding. I suspect my mother was in a quandary. I was doing spectacularly badly at the grammar school and she even wrote to my form teacher and had an interview with the headmaster about it. But a sense of religious obligation held her back from attempting to redirect my misspent energies, and maybe she wondered what other activities might attract me were I warned off servicing the church. Nor was the time spent at church a straightforward loss, because by trial and a great deal of error, I was learning the arts of self-presentation, public reading and exposition in a supportive environment. My presence was useful and I felt appreciated. Listening to hundreds of sermons provided me with a model of public presentation and persuasive exposition that Carlyle called 'The Speaking Man'. In spite of my shyness and gaucherie I lost the fear of public speaking. I became better at addressing an audience where I had permission to speak than at negotiating conversations.

I also intuited a mix of social and theological tensions, though I lacked a language to frame my intuitions. People like my father came from a tradition of street preaching that most Methodists believed was the great innovation of John Wesley as he went out and called on 'publicans, harlots and thieves' to repent, or moved the miners of Radstock and Kingswood, Bristol to tears. For Wesley that meant his itinerant preachers should submit themselves to programmes of tuition or self-education across a remarkable range of useful skills, but there were many like my father in the revivalist traditions of the Victorian era who felt you could rely on the inspiration of the Holy Spirit.

For my father, an approach based on the inspiration of the moment meant that academic qualifications (and the scholarly apparatus of biblical criticism) paled into insignificance compared with the deliverances of the Holy Spirit. These deliverances corresponded to my notion of genius, so maybe I was not that far removed from my father. Gradually I came to suspect that those who stood up and stood out as 'speaking men' – and to a lesser extent 'speaking women' – were likely to be very able people who had lacked educational opportunity so far. Once they learnt the arts of persuasion they rapidly acquired other arts, and easily became Protestant bibliophiles. They or their children might take up formal training for the ministry, and their grandchildren might move into business where economic comfort mattered more than the self-authenticating power of the spirit, or into the professions, where academic insignia provided recognized badges of arrival. All these jostling stages and disparate criteria were present in Barnes Methodist Church. Later I recognized the same trajectories at work among the Pentecostal street preachers of Latin America, who with their energy, intelligence, and appeal to the validation of the Holy Spirit, struck me as yet another 'buried intelligentsia'.

In spite of its apparent egalitarianism, the Methodist Church offered opportunities for individual display not available in the Church of England, at least in worship, whether through charismatic preaching or other kinds of performance, especially music. We sang anthems with coveted solo parts, and sometimes the service included a duet or a solo. To include solos left the way open for strictly musical criteria on the dangerous verge of professionalism. When a professional singer, June Wilson, joined the congregation from Australia, she greatly improved the quality of the solos but upset the pecking order. She sang such 'sacred' songs as Dunhill's 'To the Queen of Heaven' and Howells' 'Come sing and dance, come pipe and play', and 'Hear ye, Israel' from *Elijah*. Of course, *Elijah* was as central to Methodist devotion as *Messiah*, but I do not recollect anyone being bothered by 'To the Queen of Heaven' any more than anyone in the Wesley Guild was bothered by Trine's *In Tune with the Infinite*. In due course I became June's practice accompanist and understood that a decently brought up Australian might lack advancement in a singing career if all she was willing to offer was mere ability to sing.

When the Revd Professor Eric S. Waterhouse was appointed to look after Barnes Methodist Church while the minister, Eric B. Butler, was away in the forces, he appeared on the Station Road notice board with his full academic entitlement: MA, D.Litt., DD. That represented the side of Methodism most antithetic, even antipathetic, to my father: academic respectability in place of charismatic validation. So when the (Methodist) 'society steward', Ronald Humphreys, M.Sc., was appointed by the 'circuit plan' to preach at Station Road, he too appeared on the notice board with academic accreditation. An appointment to preach at Station Road and at Kew Road church, Richmond carried status. Mrs Dorothy Dalton, BA, was secretary of the English-Speaking Union and when she 'occupied' the pulpit she appeared in mortar board and gown and delivered an academically crafted sermon. Maybe Mrs Dalton pre-adapted me to women's ordination. She also did me a very good turn when I complained to her about being rejected by King's College, London. She said rather briskly that universities had 'to keep up standards'. So *that* was it! Once I realized I was just a *failure* I began to wonder whether there was something to be said for merely jumping through a standard hoop. Maybe you could succeed merely by working hard, not by some preternatural specialness beyond conventional testing. Like so many others I was in thrall to romantic ideas of creative originality springing direct from my forehead, without being able to deliver the goods. Once disburdened of inspiration all I needed was the right hoop.

We had preachers from the Richmond Hill Theological College, some of whom had been baptized in the fiery brook of German theology rather than in the inspiration of the Holy Spirit. That confirmed my father's suspicion of book learning, as distinct from the devotional reading of books of sermons. Gordon Rupp, later Dixie Professor of Church History at Cambridge, had a remarkable way of preaching the gospel *and* of drawing on learning and historical imagination. Rupp had German ancestry and preached Luther on the 'righteousness which is by faith rather than the works of the law'. He illustrated his addresses with paintings and introduced me to Milton's *Areopagitica*. He was the model I most wanted to emulate.

In spite of total immersion in Evangelical religion, or because of it, I never became what my father would call 'soundly converted'. I should have been, and my father expected it, but I never had that moment of conviction. In early adolescence in 1943, I tried hard to see if 'conviction' might be induced, and went every night to an Evangelical campaign conducted by Pastor Alan Redpath at the Royalty Kinema, Richmond. I never really wanted to abridge my solitariness by joining a happy band of believers, but I was moved by some powerful preaching and even more by the singing of Wesley's 'And can it be that I should gain'. One question I never asked: did my mother really want another 'soundly converted' male around? I knew she had no conversion experience to speak of, and speaking of it was an essential part of 'witness'. My curiosity about my mother managing to bypass conversion drove me to ask my father why. He said she 'had always been like it' (saved) – she, alone of all her sex and indeed of all Adam's fallen race. My father worshipped my mother but I still found this maternal exemption surprising. Since my mother was perfect in his eyes, conversion and conviction of sin could even have come as a shock.

At the same time as I attended the Royalty Kinema I was writing reams of bad poetry, much of it owing too much to Evelyn Underhill and *The Oxford Book of Mystical Verse* (1917). Over a period of some years in the second half of the forties and into the fifties this led me to explore the literature of religious experience, and even to read theology proper. I was deeply engaged by Hopkins, thanks to Dr Gardner, especially his intense rendering of the intrinsic grain and character of phenomena, like 'dappled things' and 'the wildness and the wet' as well as his sense of dereliction. I read T. S. Eliot carefully, and absorbed the *Four Quartets*. I responded to Eliot's invocation of East Coker in Somerset because it framed my early experiences of Dorset. I read Edwyn Bevan on symbolism and belief, Baron von Hügel, Dean Inge and Evelyn Underhill on mysticism, dipped into the poems of St John of the Cross and explored the metaphysical aesthetics of the Renaissance. I drank deep from the metaphysical poets of the seventeenth century and on one occasion heard a sermon by Lancelot Andrewes on the wireless that left a lasting impression and a latent desire to exploit semantic and rhetorical fields in the same way. I read Isaiah and Job on underground trains as though they were ecstatic poetry, and was delighted with the format of *The Bible Designed to be Read as Literature*. I remember picking up this volume with its beautiful typeface in the school library and reading John 8 on the forgiveness offered by the Lord to the 'woman taken in adultery'. I had never come across this before and was genuinely moved by it. I was also engaged by the Platonism of a novel called *The Fountain* by Charles Morgan and intrigued by Jung's *Answer to Job*. I even rummaged in monists like Haeckel, paddled in the rationalism of The Thinker's Library and books in The Home University Library like Brailsford on *Godwin, Shelley and Their Circle*. The Home University Library (with Everyman's Library) was just what I needed. I canvassed the political options it provided, first Lionel Hobhouse on Liberalism, but then, to be fair, Quintin Hogg on Conservatism and Harold Laski on Socialism.

It really is odd the eighth chapter of John came as such a surprise. After all, Methodism was supposed to be a biblical faith and we were constantly exposed to the biblical text. Yet we did not read the Bible sequentially, and faith as understood in Methodism appealed more to Paul than to the Gospels. We did not hear the Gospels for what they actually said but through some soft-focus filter: hence my mother's shocked reaction to a dramatic rendering of the denunciation of the Pharisees on one of her occasional visits to the Barnes church. This was not the 'Gentle Jesus, meek and mild' she had taught me as part of bedtime prayers or the famous picture of a benign Jesus blessing children of all colours on the walls of the Sunday School. Faith was not derived directly from the Bible but through sentiments embedded in hymns, pictures, stories, and texts like 'God so loved the world', 'Love your neighbour as yourself' and 'Suffer the little children to come unto me . . .'. The preface to the 1933 Methodist Hymn Book, which I read whenever bored by the service, claimed Methodism was 'born in song' and that was how it was transmitted. It was absorbed as a mosaic of quotation, as in 'When I survey the wondrous cross' or through evocations like 'At evening when the sun was set/The sick, O Lord, around thee lay'. Only when I went to confirmation classes somewhat late in the day did I find out that the epistles preceded the Gospels in the temporal order of writing, and at no point did I query variant readings or variant sequences of events or notice how time was fast-forwarded in the Gospels.

All the questions came to a head after adolescence. It is very difficult to remember exactly when I read what, but I do know that in 1950 I heard a local preacher speaking about Albert Schweitzer and recommending *The Quest of the Historical Jesus*. So I asked to have it for my twenty-first birthday, thinking it might evoke the Holy Land in the manner of H. V. Morton's *In the Steps of the Master* or Leslie Weatherhead's glutinous *It Happened in Palestine*. I was in for a shock. This was the first time in my whole education I encountered a sustained thesis, in this case to establish the centrality of eschatology in the Gospels. In a few traumatic hours Schweitzer introduced me to the history and scope of German biblical criticism. Once I read chapters with titles like 'The Markan Hypothesis' and 'From Reimarus to Wrede', the Gospels in their standard Sunday School picture-book format went out of the window. I think I read Freud's *Introductory Lectures in Psychoanalysis* at the same time as I read *The Quest of the Historical Jesus*, so to describe me as traumatized hardly overdoes it.

After that my reading was driven by a need to arrive at the truth of these complicated matters. I earnestly wanted to know. So I read everything that came to hand on the critical questions raised by Schweitzer, though without guidance or a map. Some of what I read was standard material like B. H. Streeter on *The Four Gospels* and Goguel on the resurrection. Some of it was radical like Loisy, or imaginative like Mauriac's *Life of Jesus*, or just wild like Robert Graves. Throughout my life I continued to read New Testament criticism, from Cadoux, Bultmann, Nineham, Farrer and Theissen to Sanders, Vermes, Ehrman, Lüdemann and Hurtado. I occasionally wondered why nobody devised a Disharmony of the Gospels to complement the ancient harmonizations, showing how widely disparate were the texts different critics dismissed as inauthentic. I did not make faith easy.

In my early twenties I also read mainstream Protestant theologians like Donald Baillie, Brunner, Otto, Reinhold Niebuhr and Tillich, as well as Bonhoeffer and John Robinson, and mainstream Catholics like Copleston, Martin D'Arcy and Gilson, as well as Lunn and Chesterton. Nicolas Berdyaev had interested me as early as 1947 because his was a mystical theology in a familiar vein, even though Russian Orthodox theosophy was not. I had read Oliver Quick in 1949, which gave me a formal foundation. Quick led on to Gore, Maurice, Lewis, Temple and Farrer. Later at LSE, when exploring the wider background for my work on pacifism, I read material that bore on the link I was developing between pacifist withdrawal and political eschatology: Mowinckel on *He That Cometh*, Brandon on Jesus and the Zealots, material on the Essenes and the Dead Sea Community,

Knox's *Enthusiasm*, Cohn on millennialism, Talmon on *Political Messianism*. I also looked out for congenial mentors on wider issues: Basil Willey on English literature, Herbert Butterfield on Christianity and science and Christianity and history, the Catholic historians Friedrich Heer and Christopher Dawson on European cultural history, Kenneth Scott Latourette on world Christianity, Arnold Toynbee and H. G. Wells on world history, the controversy between Gasquet and Coulton on the Reformation. It was a home-made course in master narratives and Western Civ.

The time frames are uncertain but I thought I should explore other traditions of Christian worship, so I went to our local Anglo-Catholic church, All Saints, East Sheen, only to be put off by the Apostolic Succession. I visited the great Anglo-Catholic shrine at All Saints, Margaret Street, only to find myself bemused by a mixture of liturgical ballet and Schubert masses. This was not Schubert at his marvellous best or I might have been seduced. One summer I was briefly called in to fill a gap as organist at a large Victorian Anglo-Catholic church in Ealing and realized how much more difficult it was to accompany a sung mass, even to fairly simple music by Martin Shaw, than to play hymns for a Methodist service. I thought it might be appropriate to introduce the eucharistic procession with the theophany in Vaughan Williams' *Job*, but the procession came in slightly late and was ushered in by the sinuous temptations of Satan. I enjoyed occasional visits to the Greek Orthodox Cathedral in Moscow Road, Bayswater. The Orthodox were marvellously uninterested in the state of my soul or my beliefs, or indeed in me. This was divine indifference and therefore inviting. I loved the mixture of intensely private devotion, anonymity and liturgical formality, and I loved overhearing an unaccompanied choir I could not see. On the wireless I was captivated by Grechaninov's Creed sung by the choir of the Russian Orthodox Church in Paris, an experience as much atmospheric as musical.

I loved most the resonance of music in the hidden spaces of churches and the plangent melancholy of mortality in Orlando Gibbons: 'Behold thou hast made my days as it were a span long and my age is as nothing in respect of thee.' I was leaving behind the sentiment embedded in Victorian hymns with tunes by Stainer or John Bacchus Dykes, though I still felt lifted up by enthusiastic singing in neat Methodist chapels with commanding pulpits. The familiar soundscape of 'Sunset and Evening Star', 'All in an April evening' and 'Brother James' Air' receded over the horizon. I was gravitating to the courtesies and gestures of liturgical worship and to words set to contemplative music as a kind of *lectio divina*.

An overlapping musical scale was forming in my head running from my father's choruses to four-square Calvinist psalm settings, Lutheran chorales, early Methodist dance rhythms, the well-made tunes of high Victorian sentiment, and hymns and choral songs influenced by folk song and the preoccupations of Parry, Vaughan Williams and Holst. Playing the piano for all kinds of musical offering, from Sunday School ditties like 'A little talk with Jesus makes it right, all right' to the Robert Bridges English version of the chorale *Lobe den Herren*, 'Praise to the Lord, the Almighty', had provided my first musical education and entry into the history of music. Now I was drawn in by the Anglican musical tradition of parish church and college chapel, in particular the seductive Trojan horse that had entered the gates of Methodism through the *Oxford Book of Carols*. This was no linear evolution. Mostly you moved sideways like a crab in muddy water. If I liked hymns taken from Bridges' Yattendon Hymnal, then I was interested to read his 'A Testament of Beauty', a Platonist philosophical poem of which I now remember just one line: 'Self expressed in not-self without which no self were'. If William Cowper had written 'God moves in a mysterious way', I might look for further instruction in Norman Nicholson's *William Cowper* (1960) and David Cecil's study of Cowper in *The Stricken Deer* (1929).

Once when I was listening to sung liturgy on the radio, my mother asked me why it sounded so sad. But the sadness touched a layer the CSSM chorus book, and the mandatory smile of Methodism, did not. One major way station on this journey was the Methodist Book of Offices, supplemented by the Book of Common Prayer (whence much of the Methodist Book came anyway), a Latin missal, and the sacramental hymns of the Wesleys as these were brought into fresh prominence by the Methodist Sacramental Fellowship, including Donald Soper. The journey took decades to complete, because I was very unwilling to cause pain to my parents or to cut myself adrift from my roots, and it was eventually made easier when my parents became themselves alienated from their Methodist church in Byfleet when it flirted with liturgical madness by introducing lads in football shorts blowing whistles and a clown with balloons in the pulpit.

My reading moved in parallel with my subconscious shift to a liturgical Christianity, and probably preceded it: Tamara and David Talbot Rice on Byzantine art, Bannister Fletcher's *History of Architecture*, large illustrated volumes on English and French cathedrals, Batsford and other books on English parish churches. Some blandishments I was utterly immune to. A couple of muscular moral rearmers tried their best to interest me but I resisted morality and

rearmament in equal measure. They seemed very anxious to assure
me they could cure homosexuality, but not knowing the disease I was
not a candidate for the cure.

It is not quite true to say that throughout this process I lacked a
map and had absolutely no guidance, because around 1952 or 1953
I decided to become a local preacher for the Richmond and Barnes
Methodist Circuit and take the prescribed examinations. After some
ten years of Sunday school teaching and assisting with the music at
church, this became a service I continued for the next 25 years. More
perhaps than any other church, Methodism relied on lay preachers.
My father was delighted I was at last responding, and said I might be
much used of the Lord once I had 'the Holy Spirit behind me'. I was
glad he was glad, but I really did not know what to say. What I did
have behind me was a perfectly serious course of study. Perhaps the
pass mark was not that exacting, but you were expected to absorb
scholarly books on the Old and New Testaments, a manual of Christian doctrine and the 44 sermons of Wesley that comprised the
Methodist doctrinal standard, as well as material on homiletics and
Sangster's *The Craft of Sermon Construction*.

My initial experiments in preaching were halting and I was told
not to share doubts or get lost in arguments along the lines of Paley
and natural theology, but to 'preach faith *until* I had it and then
preach faith *because* I had it'. And in a way something like that happened because, beginning with Blake on 'mutual forgiveness of each
vice', which I certainly needed, I rested on the Wesleyan appropriation of Luther's 'salvation by faith alone'. Morally one had no 'works'
to offer, but grace was sufficient, and that must have been important
because my life and my marriage were distinctly messy and difficult. I
also experimented with children's addresses, which were an expected
part of any morning service. I could tell stories very well, but which
stories were appropriate? Finnish folk tales just did not work and were
pagan anyway. Once I tried telling the story of the Tolpuddle Martyrs
based on a play by Miles Malleson for a Sunday School anniversary.
I gave these early Methodist martyrs of incipient trade unionism a
quasi-liturgical rendering, and it may well have been innovative, but
it plainly broke some taboo about addresses that verged on politics,
especially for children. I tried stories by Oscar Wilde like *The Selfish
Giant* and *The Happy Prince*, but there were only a limited number
of these. What then? Paul Gallico's *The Snow Goose* and *The Small
Miracle*, or the feisty Italian priest Don Camillo and his communist
sparring partner? Not really. Much of this material was not right for
Methodist purposes. Nevertheless I learnt by many mistakes of taste

and genre, and eventually turned in my sermons for adults to the kind of thinking about the Gospels and the sign language of wheat fields and vineyards, bread and wine, I had first encountered in Mauriac's *Life of Jesus*. It worked. Moreover, sources like Masefield's evocation of the conversion of Saul Kane in 'The Everlasting Mercy', and Robert Browning's 'Saul', provided a bridge between literature and the world of Methodist congregations. I was particularly moved by ''Tis the weakness in strength that I cry for! My flesh that I seek/In the Godhead!'

Maybe it is not quite true to say that I entirely lacked the kind of experience my father thought necessary to being a Christian. Between one generation and another there are mutations and transpositions rather than repetitions. Reading Gordon Davies on Blake and reading Blake himself in 'The Everlasting Gospel', I came across another version of Bunyan's *Grace Abounding to the Chief of Sinners*: 'The Christian Trumpets loud proclaim/Thro all the world in Jesus' name/mutual Forgiveness of each vice/And oped the Gates of Paradise'. I read John Donne: 'Oh my blacke soule . . . Or wash thee in Christ's blood, which hath this might/That being red, it dyes red soules to white'. This provided a ground bass for faith but it did not educate me in recipes for ordinary decent living. Once the niceness inculcated at Sunday School, and family norms of respectability, had been undermined by a combination of Blake's antinomianism and a diet of Shaw and Ibsen, together with the Swedish, Italian and French film fare available at the time, I was awash and at sea. This was the era when coffee shops took off in London and people interested in ideas discussed Colin Wilson's *The Outsider*, Sartre and existentialism. For me these advanced preoccupations were enticing noises off, though I was to meet them head on when they made a militant reappearance as part of the deadly mix of the sixties.

The foundation for a sombre and realist approach to utopianism, religion and politics was first laid down when I read Pascal's *Pensées* at the end of my teens, especially the introduction by T. S. Eliot, though it was years before I saw where that might lead when it came to my passionate pacifism. That realization only came after several years of reading Reinhold Niebuhr. It was Niebuhr who showed me how I might understand the relationship between faith and the dynamics of society and international relations, above all the problem of violence. This long engagement over more than a decade with theology, especially Niebuhr, provided a slipway to my further self-education when I decided to read sociology.

8

Exit strategy –
sociology by correspondence

———•◦•———

Lots of courses begin as marriages end. The class next to mine in Wincanton Primary School was taught by a fiery Welshman, Roy Davies, very politically committed, a product of adult education at Coleg Harlech, with experience as a union organizer in the Welsh valleys. We often walked around the little town discussing current affairs, and he told me he was doing a correspondence course in sociology. He thought it might be a way out of teaching nine-year-olds for the next 40 years, perhaps by working for the Workers' Educational Association – an ambition that also appealed to me, though probation work had also crossed my mind. He asked whether I might be interested in the course and I said I found discussions of community boring, and anyway I wanted to do a course in English literature.

In fact I had, without realizing it, read a little sociology about causes I was interested in, such as the abolition of apartheid and capital punishment. My radical uncle had put a book on South Africa my way and I had realized with a mixture of curiosity and surprise that straight questions of right and wrong giving rise to indignation had to engage with a complex web of historical causation. I had eagerly followed Ernest Gowers' arguments for the abolition of capital punishment in *A Life for a Life* and gone with a church group to the Festival Hall to hear a debate on penal practice. Bernard Shaw's Prefaces to his plays introduced me to thinking about social issues and even to questions that belonged to historical sociology, like the origins of French and English nationalism discussed in the Preface to *St Joan* and in the play itself. In common with many people unequipped with proper social scientific scepticism, I had been intrigued by Margaret Murray's dubious imaginings about a secret underground religion underlying witchcraft, and by speculations about sacrifice and

98

fertility, human incarnations of the divine and divine kingship in James Frazer's *The Golden Bough*. My reading of Niebuhr on war and peace and of Hans Morgenthau on international relations had introduced me to sociology under another name.

Roy guessed I had little idea what sociology was really about and brought in some exam papers for me to look at. I had never imagined there could be an academic discipline that dealt with the questions I asked and provided some of the answers I sought. Here was a subject corresponding to my commitments. Opinion and indignation could be fortified by arguments and evidence. I was a natural for sociology. Roy explained you had to do subsidiary economics first, so I enrolled in his Wolsey Hall correspondence course for the London University external degree, and bought Benham's famously boring text on economics. I also ordered a book called *Applied Economics* from Yeovil Public Library which they obtained on inter-library loan, provided I promised never to ask for another book. The only works that really engaged me and gave me proper understanding were Roy Harrod's biography of Keynes and Joan Robinson on wages theory. My understanding of economics came mainly through its history, because you grasp that kind of subject by following its history. I applied to read sociology at Regent Street Polytechnic, had an interview, and was accepted, but Somerset County Council refused any financial support.

Roy returned to the Welsh valleys at Pontllanfraith, north of Newport, and thereafter till finals we often met in the school holidays to chew over our course. I passed economics subsidiary and moved back home to my parents in Mortlake, teaching first in Barnes in 1957–8 and then at my old primary school in Mortlake in 1958–9. I had come full circle. At Easter 1957, I made a very special trip to visit John Chalker in Uppsala, where he was now *Lektor* in English, crossing by sea to Gothenburg. This gave me an idea of what the world of university teaching was like, though my own aspirations went no further than teaching for the Workers' Educational Association.

The correspondence course cost £18 a year and was conducted through green papers sent regularly to my home, outlining the work and reading to be done, and the key concepts to be grasped. I was assigned tutors to mark my essays in subjects such as criminology, social psychology, or ethics and social philosophy. My parents gave me £20 to buy the set books: Sorokin's 1928 work *Contemporary Sociological Theories* and MacIver's impressive analytic study, *Society*, in the revised 1949 edition written with Charles Page. Neither Sorokin nor MacIver had started as sociologists, and I suspect there is a lot to be said for coming upon sociology from elsewhere to understand what most concerns you, rather than as a professional discipline. The date of Sorokin's book should have alerted me to the implausibility of a university still using it as a teaching text, but I plunged innocently into a world of sociology long out of date, though still instructive, certainly as intellectual history, offering viable approaches temporarily in eclipse. The same was true of other books I bought, such as a volume on the history of sociology that explained the relation of the folklore movement to the origins of ethnology, Ginsberg's *Essays* written in a mode of eirenic rationalism, and Hobhouse's *Morals in Evolution*, an impressive volume, which was almost an education in itself. Reading Hobhouse, for example his *The Elements of Social Justice* (1922), schooled me in a tradition of social liberalism that provided me with the philosophical translation of Evangelical Christianity, and I found it congenial. It meant that I absorbed the philosophical tradition that had undergirded the establishment of sociology at LSE in spite of its contemporary eclipse.

I did not know that Ginsberg and Hobhouse had long been dethroned at London University, and my course tutors often appeared unaware of what had happened since. I had not heard of Talcott Parsons, then at the height of his influence, and neither, I presume, had my tutors. So in social theory I wrote essays on Social Physics, on Gumplowiscz and the social group as the core unit of analysis, and on the thesis that civilization moves steadily northward. I probably gained by lacking proper guidance about contemporary trends because that left me open to encounters I would otherwise never have had, for example, working my way through Caird on *The Social Philosophy and Religion of Comte*, published in 1885.

London University had oversight of the external system for which Wolsey Hall provided the teaching, but the university did not help much, sending me a book list that began with Aristotle and ended with Bertrand Russell. I decided to deal with that by working through C. E. M. Joad's *Guide to Philosophy* and his *Critique of Logical Positivism*, George Sabine and J. D. Mabbott on political philosophy, and a couple of books on the history of ethics, one by Henry Sidgwick. My Bible became Broad's *Five Types of Ethical Theory* and soon Kant's Categorical Imperative started to come out of my ears. It all interested me intensely and, like the villagers listening to the schoolmaster in Goldsmith's *The Deserted Village*, my friends in the pubs of Richmond were amazed at all I seemed to know. But was it sociology? I occasionally wondered. If so it was very fine and I was up for it. The Revd G. A. Utton, my ethics and philosophy tutor, a Methodist minister, always gave me the same mark, four out of ten, except just once when I made a very special effort and he rose to an enthusiastic five. But I was not dispirited. I was in the foothills of the subject, and a part-time correspondence student could expect no more.

In one or two areas the course was up to date, for example social psychology and (after a while) criminology, when it was taken over by Paul de Berker. One of my purchases with my parents' £20 had been Sprott's *Social Psychology*, which rapidly showed me that what I had learnt at Westminster Teacher Training College was so much ancient superstition based on the instinct theories of William McDougall influential in the first half of the twentieth century. My first essay on the subject was so disastrous I nearly gave up. I was asked to discuss prejudice and I wrote what I considered a nicely turned think-piece on the nature of pre-judgement. The low mark I received showed me what counts as good in one discipline is not so good in another, and sociology appeared to be several disparate disciplines under one head. In social psychology you had to cite banal experiments, usually on students, rather than engage in the free-standing thinking expected in social philosophy or deploy the comparative historical knowledge required in social institutions.

The Wolsey Hall course expected students to work through a volume on statistics that ran to several hundred pages. It was as though the course organizers had put together standard books on this subject and on that with no reference to the requirements of the university examination papers. Certainly the university did not require pages of proof of the regression equation. I tried various alternative books without great success, though some, like David Bartholomew's introduction, were obviously excellent for a general knowledge of statistics. When it came to the final examination I nearly walked out in the calculations section of the statistics paper, and only just managed to hold my nerve.

The biggest battle occurred in criminology, prior to the makeover by de Berker. My tutor was anxious to introduce himself as a retired professor of economics and informed me the mind had 15 basic faculties. That was not what Sprott was telling me in his *Social Psychology*. But my responses to questions on criminology soon developed into a critique of deterministic assumptions underlying statistical tables predicting the likelihood of a criminal career. I also wanted to discuss the nature, effects and justification of moral language in penal practice should such deterministic assumptions be taken as valid. The economics professor had no such ambitions, and matters reached an impasse reminiscent of my earlier experience with the history lecturer at Westminster College. The only solution was a change of tutor.

My problem with criminology was embedded in a wider unease that came to a head when I read Barbara Wooton's *Testament for Social Science*. The very word 'testament' is redolent of a faith in the capacity of the social sciences to solve *the* social problem rather than to provide an adjunct mode of understanding circumscribed by humility. I had not at that point read Hayek on the inherent limitations hedging the social scientific project, but Wooton's animus against religion and her triumphal declaration that few Christians survived exposure to sociology made explicit something I had so far only intuited. I began to question the philosophical assumptions underlying sociology and to wonder where I might find a coherent response. Only later did I realize there was a Christian presence in sociology in people like Tom Simey and A. H. Halsey, though the writings of William Temple and Richard Tawney were plainly Christian.

By 1957 my son Jonathan was living with me and my parents in Mortlake. At Easter 1958, nearly two years into the course, I began to slacken off, for reasons connected with the long wake of earlier marital difficulties. The most difficult period came between a holiday with my sister and her friend Pauline that Easter and a continental trip with three school colleagues, one male and two female, in the early summer. On the second night of the Easter trip we stayed in a French hostelry in Bourges called Le Coq D'Or. I do not think my parents had ever used a hotel and I was very unused to hotels myself. I found the cost of the night so unbelievably small I assumed I had no right to an actual bed. So I slept cribbed, cabined and confined in a tiny wooden cot, staring at a soft, inviting bed I believed would clean me out for the whole trip if the innkeeper realized I had used it. But Le Puy and its Romanesque cathedral on Easter Day, then Grasse, Castellane and the Route Napoléon, and finally Colmar and Strasbourg, made up for it.

Unfortunately the ambience of extraordinary physical beauty provided a slipway for an involvement with Pauline that wrecked my sister's holiday, making her understandably angry, and which over the next three months recapitulated experiences that with my first wife spread over six years. The emotional turmoil of those six years ensured that the replay would have a very short run, in spite of the charms of a young woman with a 'pash' on the Church of England, signalled by an apartment overlooking Canterbury Cathedral. Her 'involvement' with her headmaster was rekindled just in time to release me as they eloped to South Africa. She was having a house built in the Kent village of Patrixbourne, and when we looked over it I felt shades of the prison beginning to close and an encroaching gloom as I helplessly anticipated what was to follow. Had our intended marriage taken place I would once again have been diverted from pursuing my 'education'. As it was I fell behind with the work for the degree and then, when unexpectedly reprieved and released from the relationship, I started to make up for lost time with an intensity I have never succeeded in controlling even when no longer necessary. I cannot properly control it even now and it did my eventual second marriage considerable harm. Seismic tremors of all kinds are reactivated once circumstances occur that look even remotely similar.

During the summer trip with colleagues from Bruges to Trier and Koblenz, I found myself controlling my anger only with great difficulty. I conceived a hearty dislike of the other male on the trip, though I was more bemused than annoyed when we arrived at a hotel with very limited accommodation and he asked if I wouldn't mind sharing a bed with one of the women – a very tall, nice and proper person – so that he might disport himself with the other. We two virtuous persons lay there in embarrassed silence, conscious of rustlings and fragments of conversation like 'No, Brian, no!' On coming back I returned to the course with manic ferocity.

My doubts about the relevance of my course to the university examination led me to acquire past examination papers from Senate House. This had always been an obvious thing to do, but I had assumed the organizers must have based the course on them in the first place. Reading the papers with mounting apprehension, I realized some had based their teaching on the university syllabus and some had not. So I analysed the examination papers for myself for patterns of repetition and overlaps of topics, and created my own syllabus wherever the correspondence course was seriously astray. I started using the university library at Senate House, and one way of guessing what the internal students were not reading was by observing what was still there. One book left magnificently alone on the shelves was Durkheim's *Elementary Forms of the Religious Life*. I stared at it with great curiosity. I had not been introduced to this book by my course, nor indeed to anything in the sociology of religion, though I had sussed out the existence of Ernst Troeltsch and perhaps read a little of his *Social Teachings of the Christian Churches*. I had also noticed the famous Routledge Library of Sociology and Social Reconstruction contained only one volume in that category: clearly there was a gap that ought to be filled. As for the Durkheim book, it was a rare find. What, I thought, had possessed this great founder of sociology to write about convents? Turning over the pages I failed to find a single convent, and was puzzled by headings like 'Piacular Rites' that referred to the 'elementary forms' of religious life among Australian aborigines. Nevertheless I had come upon something that was to interest me deeply: the sociology of knowledge. I saw that the sociology of knowledge, meaning the distribution of ideas people took for granted, was an important part of the sociology of religion. Moreover, I was reading a classic original, not a textbook summary.

I had to make up for time lost on irrelevant byways, like civilization moving steadily northward. Fuelled by the disaster with Pauline, I worked over the rest of the summer holiday for between 50 and 60 hours a week, doing the correspondence course and my own simultaneously. Once school term started I worked from about four to nine each evening and gradually began to experience acute anxiety symptoms. First I felt as though my heart were expanding and exploding. In a panic I made my will, beginning in the name of God and other pieties, and continuing in a similar seventeenth-century manner to dispose of a minute number of worldly goods. I went to the doctor who said I was simply overstretched teaching 42 children in the day and working in the evening. He said I was psychologically all right, and treatment would only make things worse. I had better go on Diazepam to bring down the level of anxiety.

I continued to visit my friend Roy in the Welsh valleys, but now his marriage was breaking down and that too had its difficulties. We walked and talked up hill and down dale in 'the valleys' and at some time or other we watched two films, maybe on television, that shifted the way I thought. One was *Danton's Death* by Büchner, which dented my automatic progressivism, though all I remember is the last line 'Long live the king!' The other was Ibsen's *Brand*, of which I remember only the last line: 'God is love' – ironic maybe, but not to me.

On the train journeys to Newport and the Welsh valleys I made two other discoveries. I read Karl Popper and as I paused to pick up a coffee, I realized I did not *have* to believe certain things, especially about the inevitable course of history. I was free to make up my own mind rather than to replicate whatever was currently prescribed in the right-thinking world. Popper offered me the same relief offered by *Danton's Death*, not that the partisans of progress were always wrong but that they were not automatically in the right. The world was complicated and paradoxical and you could not be confident of saving the world simply by listing all the appropriate desiderata and then implementing them. I could read writers like Burke with an open if critical mind. After all, he was a Whig and favoured the American Revolution. The other discovery came from James Burnham's *The*

Machiavellians. These thinkers were Machiavelli himself, Pareto and Sorel, and I supplemented them with another 'realist', T. E. Hulme, who in his *Speculations* put forward a secular doctrine of original sin understood as a deep-seated tendency to corruption, especially the corruption of the best hopes of humankind. This kind of thinking was unexpectedly compatible with what was still my pacifist position, because pacifism is a mixture of optimism about the future if you act rightly and pessimism about the general corruption of present-day politics and international affairs. These thinkers analysed the corruption in a very convincing way, though mainly without the optimism or any expectation of a solution. I read Sorel's *Reflections on Violence* on the London tube with mounting horror, fascinated with his analysis of the interface of religion and politics.

The Diazepam half worked, but when I went with a colleague to the theatre I had rapidly to leave and found myself lying on the floor of the theatre vestibule barely able to breathe, with curious faces staring down all around me. Soon I was unable to go into banks or shops or stand in a queue. If people suddenly got in my way I felt very angry. Every evening I went for a walk along the Thames towpath at Mortlake for as long as it took to smoke a couple of cigarettes. Then, perhaps at the beginning of the January 1959 term, as I was teaching, I felt the whole of the left side of my body go numb. Later the loss of feeling switched to the right side and the explosive feelings recurred around my heart. By early May I felt unable either to teach or continue working on the course and the examination was maybe a month away.

I was sent home to rest. I remember precisely when my pen refused to write. It was a passage in Maritain where he said that by the time of Grotius' *De jure belli ac pacis* 'the natural law tradition was already in decline'. I never found out why that was so. Nevertheless in early June I got myself to the examination halls and started writing furiously for all ten papers, making up 30 hours' writing in one week. I forgot to take my pills, and the time spent writing answers within the space of two pages of A4 paid off, because it had trained me like an athlete in rapid summary, efficient organization and compression. Perhaps the sheer idiosyncrasy of my lonely intellectual journey also came through in what I wrote, for example when I compared Durkheim's 'conscience collective' with Berdyaev's theological concept of *sobornost*. At the end one finger was partly rubbed away, leaving a mark for decades, and I had lost a stone and a half. As we filed out of the Chelsea examination halls I stumbled in any direction, repeatedly taking wrong turnings until I found myself outside St James's,

Piccadilly. I saw a choir was about to perform *Judas Maccabaeus*, went in and started to calm down.

The next day I went back to teaching and settled down to the long wait to find whether I had passed. Then John Chalker rang asking me to check my examination number, which I assumed meant he wanted to be quite sure the number was correct before telling me I had failed. He told me I had been awarded a first-class degree and had aroused the interest of the examiners. I was amazed, incapable of thinking what that might imply. The next day I met a fellow examinee in sociology living opposite me in Ripley Gardens, Mortlake. He had failed seven times and had just discovered he had failed again. I was embarrassed, and he was incredulous. He said a First was impossible and I had better go up to Senate House to check the result. I did so, and there it was in the list for external students, written in unambiguous letters. Like Abou Ben Adhem in his famous dream, my 'name led all the rest'. It was the moment when I said to myself 'Look! I have come through!' On the other part of the sheet, for internal students and, as it were, parallel to mine, was the name of my future wife, though I did not actually meet her for over two years.

Luckily I had put my name down for the annual university scholarship. My instinct had been not to do so in case some superior bureaucrat should snigger at my presumption. But it was hardly enough money for someone with a child to support. I was invited to the Senate House, and a senior academic, Dr Dunsheath, told me he was able to make available assistance from a special fund for which I was eligible. The way was open. At the age of 30 I could finally go to university, as a postgraduate.

I wanted to celebrate by doing something then quite unusual, at least for me and my friends, though unremarkable now. I would take ship from Venice to Athens, travelling 'deck'. So I saw Venice for the first time. This year, 1959 was the two hundredth anniversary of Handel's death and I was able to hear *Messiah* performed somewhere below me as I stood far up at the top of the campanile. I went to mass in St Mark's, drunk with glory as the music poured from the galleries. Then I discovered what 'deck' meant. Whereas in the Coq D'Or in Bourges my expectations had been too low, now my expectations were too high. Deck meant the deck and sailors washed it down every morning at four o'clock, after which it was unusable. My body stopped functioning properly and after many days I had to appeal for medication to provide me with what I described to a monoglot Greek as a catharsis.

Nevertheless there was Korcula to look at and other exquisite replicas of Venice, and the marvellous coasts passed by as I leaned over the ship's rail. The cicadas sang in the Corinth Canal, and a peaceful numen presided over Delphi and the Castalian Spring. Walking along the greensward above the broken columns at Delphi, a fellow traveller started to hum something from Stravinsky's *Apollon Musagète*; it was immediately picked up by another of our companions, Donald Mitchell, the great Mahler scholar, who had just filed his first music review for a national newspaper. I went to the Russian Orthodox church in Athens for Sunday morning service and was introduced to icon buying by the kindly female doctor, who had not only helped with my catharsis but was willing to guide me through what she called '*bondieuserie*'. Another fellow traveller, likewise keen to talk and help, was a red-haired, freckled young woman. At one time she came into my bedroom in Athens saying it was preferable to hers and would I mind her joining me for the night. After about an hour of quiet coexistence I tapped her paternally on the behind and suggested her bedroom could not be all that bad. It was a wise as well as a moral move, because the next time I met her was at a party in Hillcroft College, Surbiton, where my future wife was teaching her.

As we returned through the isles of western Greece a Methodist minister asked me to say his morning office with him. Of course I agreed, and in any case I had plenty of spare time between the rising of the sun and the drying of the deck. We said Morning Prayer together as a solitary bell sounded from the coast of Ithaca.

Part 2

SKETCHES OF LSE AND STUDENT REVOLUTION

9

Late arrival at university and Donald Gunn MacRae

———◆•◆———

To which college of the university should I go? My first interview was at the London University Institute of Education, with Mrs Jean Floud, quick, attentive and kindly. She told me I had dented the case against retaining the external system by doing so well, and asked what I wanted to study. I mentioned I had become very interested in the sociology of knowledge, in particular the work of Karl Mannheim. I had no idea about the unhappy history of Mannheim's time at the LSE and his move to the Institute, or that Mrs Floud had been Mannheim's research assistant and had had her fill of his works. She suggested I might like to do a master's degree before moving on to a PhD on Labour education policy between 1926 and 1928. I was quietly appalled at the prospect of surviving several years on a grant of £500, and unenthused by Labour education policy just before I was born. Mrs Floud said it might not be quite as boring as it looked, because Richard Tawney had been involved. Like everyone else I admired Tawney, but even his august name was not an adequate incentive and I left the Institute to try my luck at Bedford College.

Arriving at Bedford College I had an interview with Oliver McGregor, one of my examiners and a man of craggy and politic charm. He was really a social historian and uninterested in sociology. In 1957 he had written a book on divorce in England which was excellent as history but spectacularly wrong in its prognosis of the happy future of marriage. Much the same could be said of his colleague Ronald Fletcher, another optimistic rationalist, who wrote with euphoric conviction about the future of the family, though he was also a distinguished sociologist and a fine teacher. People like Fletcher stimulated me to describe sociology as 'the documentation of original sin by those who believe in original virtue'.

McGregor told me to forget about Max Weber and all those boring Germans, and suggested I might like to collaborate in producing an English version of the Kinsey Report, a recently published inquiry into contemporary sexual habits. It struck me that I might find myself stuck with an unconvincing average of those keen to exaggerate their exploits and those keen to minimize them, like reports to doctors about personal consumption of alcohol. I did not know that 'Mac' was at the same time advising my future wife not to waste her intellectual substance on a dying subject like religion in the nineteenth century. Instead, as a product of the cotton towns, she should study the social history of the Factory Acts and the career of the factory inspector Leonard Horner.

My next interview was with Richard Titmuss, a major influence on Labour Party policy, though I also went to a pub lunch in the East End to see whether I might cooperate in the work of the people who were conducting research into working-class 'community', most famously in Bethnal Green. I crossed Waterloo Bridge as though the Thames were the Rubicon. Was this, I wondered, my future in the making? I might become one of Titmuss' young men documenting how the middle class benefited disproportionately from the NHS or something of the kind in what some unsympathetic academics called the Department of Applied Virtue. Titmuss thought sociologists had expended enough energy on working-class life in Bethnal Green, and suggested I might be interested in studying the pressure exerted by insurance companies on the legislative process.

For three days I imagined myself exposing malign influences on the body politic behind the scenes. But I followed his advice and read Professor David Ford on the subject of insurance. Time and again I fell asleep over Ford, presaging a long and notorious career as a narcoleptic, and suspected Titmuss was no more destined to be my intellectual guide than O. R. McGregor or Jean Floud. I told him insurance was not for me, and he kindly asked what I thought I would like to study. Taken aback, I reached for a thought that had occurred to me while reading the history of Methodism and William Blake. I said I would like to study the influence of Jakob Boehme on English eighteenth-century thought. He gave me a quick quizzical glance and said perhaps I might like to put that to Donald MacRae, Reader in the Department of Sociology.

Having looked up Titmuss in the library catalogue, and found a great deal, I now looked up MacRae and found next to nothing. Donald Gunn MacRae was a polymath who read everything and wrote very little. Maybe a stellar career at Balliol had permanently inhibited him from exposing his remarkable reputation to further test, or perhaps he was waiting for an assiduous Boswell to record his obiter dicta, which were often very striking. Once, when I raised a question of natural justice for a colleague in trouble for a breach of academic discipline, he commented that I could not expect the Director to do justice once when 'coercive comparisons' might be used to force him to do justice again. I realized the principle had wide-ranging explanatory power.

In university politics Donald hunted with McGregor, and they both spoke at the South Place Ethical Society. It was many years before I discovered Donald was a Presbyterian in good standing. His great merit was to be a Renaissance man with no pet subject beyond universal knowledge. On climbing the rickety stairs to his office I encountered a neat, small man with a swallowed Scots accent, a moustache and heavy-rimmed glasses. He wanted to know how I had pursued my external course and murmured approvingly when I said I had just read the classics. Enquiring about my background he foresaw a problem. I came from the 'aspiring' and 'deferential' personal service class, and this was not a good start. I needed improving, beginning with my habit of referring to myself as *Mr* Martin. He told me to call myself anything except Mister, on the grounds that 'If you were working class you could be brash, and if you were middle class you could be eccentric, but as it is you had better be correct.' When Donald eventually met my parents at my doctoral degree ceremony, my father mentioned he had been Asquith's chauffeur, and Donald drawled, 'Really? Another Balliol man – my own college, you know.'

In my first interview with MacRae I had forgotten about Boehme, but had not learnt to pause before saying whatever came into my head. I said I was interested in the social composition of audiences for different kinds of classical music, which he dismissed as impractical and not a good career choice. So I switched to the next subject that flew into my head, the sociology of art, which was nearly as eccentric as Boehme, since my knowledge of art was pretty well confined to Gombrich and Bannister Fletcher, and R. H. Wilenski on English painting, especially landscape painters like Palmer, Cox and Cotman. Art was an offshoot of my interest in architecture and landscape. Before I had time to mention alternatives, this was jumped upon, and I felt coerced and committed. For the next three or four months I was closeted with vast volumes by Hauser, Panofsky, Wölfflin and Berenson, as well as Marxist analyses, Friedrich Antal on Florentine painting and Klingender on early English industrial art. I wondered what all this was preparation *for*. Very tentatively I raised this with Donald and he said if I wished I could do something else. Had I any other ideas? This time I said outright what I had wanted to do all the time, pacifism between the wars. He agreed. Pacifism and violence lay at the heart of the problems driving my intellectual biography. It was also under-researched: just a psychoanalytic theory by Ernest Jones, an essay by Scheler, a great deal on free trade and liberal internationalism, and three thousand years of world history. It abounded in paradoxes: pacific liberal internationalists aligned with aggressive liberal imperialists, rational utilitarians who might one moment propose going 'naked into the conference chamber' and the next propose preemptively dropping the atom bomb on the Russians, revolutionary defeatists who resisted war in order violently to overturn the capitalist system, visions of the peaceable kingdom accompanied by hopeful expectation of the vials of God's wrath poured out on the evil-doers.

Donald asked me to put down my thoughts on how pacifism should be analysed along the lines of Karl Mannheim's 'sociology of knowledge' and his *Ideology and Utopia*. Once I had roughed out a scheme, he said, with a mischievous gleam of anticipation, he would find that *very* interesting. He probably guessed I was likely to deploy the sociology of knowledge against the kind of 'knowledge' favoured by sociologists. This esoteric sub-discipline could be turned against protected targets. I was told to begin by reading all the biographies of Labour and Liberal leaders from John Bright to today. Soon I was facing a large pile of these, beginning with Keir Hardie, the founders of the Independent Labour Party, Jimmy Maxton and the radical Clydesiders, Labour politicians like Philip Noel-Baker with a Quaker background, and Liberal internationalists like the Unitarian Lord Courtney, but at least I finally knew why. I was astonished when he asked whether I regarded the inhabitants of this lost world as so many dinosaurs, mischievously infiltrating the notion into my mind.

Still, not everything was clear to me even at this late stage, though I had at least settled on a subject for a PhD after several wasted months. I received written advice from the LSE administration on how to interpret 'suggestions' from a supervisor. The advice explained that if a supervisor were to say 'You might care to drop in on such and such a seminar,' this was a three-line whip and you had better turn up regularly. I received just such advice from MacRae and took it very seriously, though I could not see what the social anthropology seminar had to do with pacifism between the wars. This seminar turned out to be education in the highest sense. Like a number of things at the LSE, it was run by a combination of Scots and Jews. MacRae ran it with Maurice Freedman, Ernest Gellner and Isaac

Schapera. It was a testing ground where you either received thumbs up or thumbs down. A careless gladiator slipping in the sawdust was as good as dead. When somebody cited Macaulay's snobbish comparison between 'a squire of Kent' and the lowly head of a Scottish clan, MacRae turned this contemptuously round and round like God dangling a spider over the fire in Jonathan Edwards' sermon on hell. Some members of this august group were anthropologists from other colleges, and I sensed the anthropological tribes were socially more than a cut above the grubby sociologists. Some anthropologists were gentlemen. One or two were Catholics.

My first assignment was to discuss age sets among the Tswana, which was in the bailiwick of Schapera, and my second to analyse the role of Dutch regents in Indonesia, which was the terrain of Freedman. I survived. Then came the big test, and I think it arose in the way it did because 'Shap' referred to me as 'our Englishman'. I was asked to prepare a paper on the Bible Christians, who were a variety of Methodist, largely restricted to North Devon. Soon it became clear that this was too exiguous a subject on which to stake survival in so exigent a seminar. I would have to broaden the issue to cover Methodism as a whole and I chose the vexed question of whether it should be considered a sect or a denomination, along with other groups like the Baptists and Congregationalists. I argued that the denomination was a distinct category, not a later stage in the evolution of a sect, and for that I deployed my extensive reading in Methodist history, the marvellous (Laski) collection of Civil War pamphlets at the LSE, and my knowledge of Richard Niebuhr and Troeltsch. I argued sects displayed a dialectic between perfectionism and antinomianism, pacifism and exemplary violence, immanence and transcendence, nakedness and uniform dress. I lost my inhibitions about the kind of writing that was allowed and wrote and performed the paper with brio. I could hear people listening just as they had when I first risked all playing Beethoven.

To my surprise I was immediately made two offers of publication, one from MacRae, then editor of the *British Journal of Sociology*. He was giving me my first academic publication, and that is a boon you do not forget in a hurry. He made one stylistic emendation, pointing out that in the *BJS* one does not use phrases like 'coming to rest on the bosom of holy mother Church'. When the article eventually appeared, it so irritated an eminent Congregational scholar, Geoffrey Nuttall, that he invited me to his London club to put me right about church history. I realized that I was athwart other scholars besides the sociologists, and not for the last time either. I was soon to find myself at odds with the new breed of secular theologians, some of whom thought they were translating sociology for the benefit of the Church: it was cannon to the right and canon to the left.

To have Donald MacRae as a supervisor was gain and loss. He could be tantalizingly cryptic and he had a way of saying 'Of course, one is not allowed to say this,' before turning accepted ideas upside down. This encouraged my readiness to entertain forbidden thoughts. If I had responded to Ernest Gellner's friendly overtures and jumped ship, I might have gained an easier patron, but he would not have taken mischievous pleasure in giving me plenary permission to challenge the assumptions of the sociological establishment. Donald did just that, perhaps just for the hell of it, though maybe he thought of me as a self-steered amanuensis willing to say things he found too impolitic, especially for someone who saw himself as a university politician. I was at one and the same time opposed to the positivism that believed everything could be reduced to numbers and to the Marxism that believed everything could be reduced to material forces. There were people in the sociology department who believed both forms of reductionism. MacRae believed neither. He believed that culture matters, not only culture understood anthropologically as the sign language through which everything in society is mediated, but culture in the sense of arts and artefacts pointing beyond themselves to the transcendent. At the same time he was utterly realistic and insisted on the economic concept of opportunity cost as fundamental: whatever gain you hope for has to be calibrated against the correlative loss.

The costs MacRae exacted were very high, and he could be very cryptic. When he wrote on Max Weber in the Modern Masters series he dedicated the book to Johann Nepomuk Hummel which was mysterious unless you knew that Hummel was Carl Maria von Weber's main rival. Ergo Donald had had it up to here with Max Weber. He was inclined to mislay or forget to return your handwritten work, and he would suggest opportunities were available to you as an expression of goodwill, not because they existed. On the other hand, being sent hither and thither along byways and highways was an education, if not immediately relevant to finishing a doctorate. Reading Ernst Cassirer's *Essay on Man* was an education in neo-Kantian philosophy, if not all that closely related to George Lansbury and Ernest Bevin. One day Donald told me I ought to treat pacifism as an Ur-theme of Western culture. I was all ears. It sounded inviting, but what should I read? Donald suggested I start with the theme of *Veritas Filia Temporis*, as treated in Renaissance woodcuts by Fritz Saxl in the volume edited by Klibansky and Paton. I had to hope we had not accidentally switched back to the sociology of art. The Ur-theme idea developed further as I was directed to Ernst Curtius' *European Literature and the Latin Middle Ages*, where he discusses the history of fundamental European ideas like 'Nature'. But how might I relate Ur-themes to Vera Brittain's *Testament of Youth* or Graves' *Goodbye to All That*, Aldington's *Death of a Hero* and Remarque's *All Quiet on the Western Front*?

Then I was directed to the *locus classicus* in Mannheim's *Ideology and Utopia*, which clearly *was* relevant for the issue of chiliastic and eschatological anticipation. It was a major key to pacifist 'withdrawal' because there was a complex relation between chiliastic hope of world transformation and withdrawal from the corruptions of the quotidian world, above all its violence, alongside the dialectic between high hopes of renewal and profound fears of destruction, immanence and transcendence, an aspiration to perfection and antinomian or anarchistic rejection of all structures and rules. These ideas infiltrated my mind as I read Norman Cohn's *The Pursuit of the Millennium*, especially the sections on the English Civil War, though I rejected Cohn's psychopathological approach, but also as I read Conybeare on Russian sectarianism, A. H. Silver's *History of Messianic Speculation in Israel* and G. M. Williams' *The Radical Reformation*, which first appeared in 1962. I was later struck by the same dialectic when the student revolution precipitated a millennial movement on my own doorstep, with slogans like 'Make love not war' and threats of violence and coercive 'occupations'.

One tutorial ended with the gnomic suggestion it 'all had something to do with aestheticism' and I got together with a female student of his working on aestheticism in the 1890s. For a few months she and I enjoyed the pleasures of intellectual community, though without flushing out the role of the aesthetic movement in the genesis of pacifism. There was indeed a connection through the Bloomsbury group, but neither she nor I could make out a precise genealogy. And yet I had, after all, read Clive Bell's *Art* when I was in the Non-Combatant Corps, as though it had something to do with my hatred of violence. I plucked up courage to begin another tutorial by asking for further enlightenment about aestheticism, but Donald was a notorious back-tracker, indicated by prolonged throat-clearing, and said he must have been referring to 'asceticism'. Again, there was certainly a connection between pacifism and asceticism if one traced the Ur-theme far enough, back say to the Jains or Runciman's *The Medieval Manichee*. But I could see Donald was not to be drawn and I

David Martin, PhD, 1964

would be wise to shut up, or the tutorial would abruptly be called off. I once asked him, thinking of Marx, how wrong one needed to be to be disastrously wrong, and he said that was a good question, but he did not follow through with an answer. Perhaps there isn't one.

One of the problems of dealing with Donald was his tendency not to turn up and, if asked about it, to blame you for the mistake. You just had to learn a code of honour and shame that presumably went back to the Scottish Highlands. One excuse he repeated with outrageous frequency turned on a French onion seller who obstructed his passage between LSE and the Senate House. It did not matter that the lies were obvious, because no one cared to pay the price of challenging them. When Donald said, 'I'm sorry I could not come, I went to Poland for the night,' he knew perfectly well you could – and indeed would – meet his secretary on the stairs minutes later, and she would deny all knowledge of so implausible a journey. At times, I concluded, his mind was so fertile it generated undisposable surplus. Exactly which orchestra had he conducted when a precocious youth? When we were in Portugal together and attempting to summon up the meagre linguistic resources needed to buy ice creams, did he really 'find Trans-Lusitanian easier than metropolitan Portuguese'? When we were in Venice and he held back to allow Bernice to handle the Italian when buying a ticket, was the problem his Italian or his reluctance to fork out the cash?

Of course, there were neophytes to Donald studies who were simply baffled by him. On one occasion, a recently arrived colleague raised a rather awkward point with Donald and he immediately excused himself, saying he had an appointment with a student. He was soon back, explaining he was again available because the student had been run over by a bus. Our new colleague was stupefied by our collective sangfroid when faced by this fictitious tragedy.

Donald's style of darting enquiry, and his sudden gestures of goodwill followed by withdrawal and unavailability, renewed old feelings of anxiety in me. I found the library claustrophobic, especially as other postgraduates took out their anxieties by drumming on the floor. Moreover, librarians seemed keen to guard the books from importunate students wanting to read them. Eventually I could not bear to enter the place any longer, except much later as deputy chairman of the Library Committee.

I recognized my topic was politically and even religiously sensitive. The head of department, David Glass, was associated with a pamphlet blaming the Conservatives for appeasement rather than Labour for pacifism, and I needed to steer my way through that as well as through the antagonism between Glass and MacRae. Glass was known by some people as 'a good old Stalinist', but I never knew whether this was true, and failed to see what was good about being a Stalinist. When I gave a paper to a seminar chaired by Glass, exploring the religious roots of pacifism, one of my fellow students said it made religion sound important, which led Glass to explain there had to be a transition from religion to politics. This, of course, was the Marxist view, represented by scholars such as Hobsbawm in *Primitive Rebels*, another important text for understanding the link between pacifism and millenarianism.

Something else was happening: I was losing my faith in pacifism. I think my sense of the impossibility of strict pacifism came over me as I was reading Lewis Namier's *Europe in Decay 1936–1940*. I was beginning to think pacifist movements had made the Second World War marginally more likely. More profoundly, I no longer felt the force of the analogy between the free self-offering of Christ and a refusal to resist the evil of force and the force of evil. The action of the Redeemer in entering into and taking upon himself the accumulated weight of division, sin and death to bring peace, liberty and immortality to light for all humanity, is not a formula for deciding what we personally should do or what governments should do. In such dilemmas we are not deciding only for ourselves but have to take into account all the third parties likely to bear the brunt of our action or our failure to act. Losing one's life to gain it points in several directions. One of those directions was taken by Dietrich Bonhoeffer, when he made a personal decision that cost him his life by 'taking sin upon him' and becoming complicit in the attempted murder of Hitler. There is a clarity attending such personal decisions, even when they have political consequences, which does not obtain when governments are faced with grave and present dangers. Governments have to calculate the uncertain and long-term effects of their decisions, including pre-emptive strikes when the moral balance is dubious, rather than waiting till the moral balance is unequivocal and the encounter more likely to be very bloody and to favour the enemy.

Maybe retaining the bomb would secure peace and save suffering more effectively than banning it. I was now out of the radical Christian realm of principle and into the political realm of murky calculation. With a friend living in Poulton Square, Chelsea, I sallied out to join the Aldermaston marchers for the last couple of miles without conviction. In Trafalgar Square I listened to a hectoring address by the left-wing union boss Frank Cousins. I felt politically used and dropped out. That was it. The Niebuhrian analysis had sunk in and I had now to think about the nature of the political in a different way. I needed to explore the nature of political action and of what Niebuhr called *Moral Man and Immoral Society*. Donald advised me that pursuing the pacifist theme after my doctorate would be a mistake, and I did not return to it until I wrote *Does Christianity Cause War?* (based on my Sarum Lectures at Oxford University) in the mid-nineties.

When I did return to the issues of war, peace and religion, my perspective had changed radically. I was now interested in the way a religious repertoire – which in the Christian case strongly recommends non-violence – is adopted and adapted according to the type of society in which it has become embedded, for example the Christian inflection of feudal violence by the notion of chivalry. I concluded that, far from violence being specifically rooted in religion, it was grounded in the nature of solidarity against the other, whether that was expressed in terms of religion, political ideology or nationalism. In short, the specific identification of violence with religion was unscientific from a social scientific viewpoint, and the moralizing polemic of Richard Dawkins and others little better than the exploitation of prestige in science to pontificate on matters they made it a matter of principle not to understand.

Apart from giving me my first publication and consistently supporting me over the years, Donald did something that greatly benefited me, without intending to. He once confessed that he suffered from a poor relation between intention, or imagination, and reality. (Harold Laski also suffered from the same malady, though others had less kind words for it, like mythomania and downright lying.) When my thesis was published the reviews were very mixed, depending as much on political as on other considerations. My fellow sociologist of religion Bryan Wilson wrote a friendly review in *The Manchester Guardian* commenting on the silliness of the *New Statesman* in the thirties; Frank Allaun, a left-wing Labour MP, started his review in *Tribune* by saying he intended thereafter to ignore this objectionable book; and a Sheffield professor of politics launched an abusive attack in the *Times Literary Supplement*. Donald told me he had written a letter in my defence. When no such letter appeared in the *TLS* letter columns I wrote an indignant letter of my own to the *TLS*, complaining that I was subject to attack from the prejudiced while those who knew what they were talking about, like Donald MacRae, were denied space to reply. Soon the editor of the *TLS*, Arthur Crook, was on the phone to say he had received no such letter from MacRae, and was ringing him there and then to enquire further. My blood ran cold as I foresaw an awkward confrontation all too soon in the SCR. Next morning Donald spoke through clenched teeth and in minatory tones, saying he would very much appreciate it, should any such circumstance arise in the future, if I consulted him first before writing letters.

Happily, in the course of his phone call to me, the editor had said maybe I would like to do some reviewing for the paper myself, and more than four decades later I am still doing it. Over the whole of that time I let my reading be led serendipitously by whatever journals and papers sent me, beginning with occasional pieces in the *New States-man*, *The Listener* and *The Spectator*. I realized you become an expert by reviewing rather than the other way round.

In Donald's latter years, especially when he had retired, I felt increasingly protective.[7] He had moved to Deal and then to Sandwich with his second wife, Jean, who was a talented artist, and I went regularly to see him. I often wondered what gross anxiety or vaulting ambition had made it so dangerous to expose his work to public scrutiny or engage in easy human encounter. I thought I saw an arrogant public self adversely censuring a private humble self and pushing him to encourage others, myself included, but unable to encourage himself. Perhaps his conclusions were too contrary and pessimistic to expose in public and too remote from other people's maps of conventional connection. A 'wee dram' of whisky rather too frequently assuaged the sense of potential unfulfilled. He spoke of himself as a Calvinist but not a Puritan and I suspected this was an apprehension of bleakness without much by way of hope, though he was fond of quoting 'Betwixt the stirrup and the ground I mercy sought and mercy found'. Once he commented with mordant satisfaction that 'It is all determined from beginning to end,' which I suppose was his version of the doctrine of election. James Hogg's proto-psychological and pica-resque *Confessions of a Justified Sinner* he thought simply an ordinary account of how things were. He also said there was 'nothing but swamp between Geneva and Rome'.

A mutual friend, Roger Holmes, was another intimate, and, like me, often visited Donald in Kent. Indeed, Roger visited several of our colleagues in their difficult declining years. Donald certainly could be difficult. Once when Roger arrived at Donald's house in Deal the door remained locked, and all Roger could hear was Donald shouting inside, 'Go away, whoever you are.' As Roger was a brilliant psychologist, he was bewildered by such an opaque request. 'David,' he said, 'what do you think he could have meant by that?' One thing Roger and I discovered: Donald was, just as he said, a published poet, in a standard collection of Scottish modern verse.

In my memorial address at the LSE I said, by way of conclusion, that Donald's 'intellectual force and fascination were such (even when – as often – he was his own parodist) I could not imagine him dead'. Nor could I have remotely imagined one day saying the words of committal over him at his burial. Particularly after his stroke in 1993, Donald suffered terrible frustration which came out in fractiousness and anathema. At the same time there were moments of strange sweetness brought on by the nuzzling of a cat, or by the wholly other worlds of birds alighting on the roofs opposite. We talked of poetry, Wilhelmine Germany, early twentieth-century politics, Scotland and the architecture of Glasgow – and London. And his mind reconnoitred his remote past. Almost his last request as Jean and I sat either side of his hospital bed was for *The Times*: ending that vast appetite over seven decades for paper and print. He cared about what the public estimate of his life would be and said it would be exiguous and exigent. In my obituary for *The Times* I made sure it was not.

There was no serious loss of mental power in Donald's last years. He was often asleep in the afternoons after mixing a dram with all the pills, but he would wake up to say 'God bless you' before you left. When I said I couldn't remember a single line of Clough, he said, 'Of course you can. "Say not the struggle nought availeth".' It goes on:

> And not by eastern windows only
>   When daylight comes, comes in the light
> In front the sun climbs slow, how slowly,
>   But westward look, the land is bright.

What he made of that distinctly Victorian sentiment I never knew.

10

Getting my bearings at the LSE

———•◦•———

In the last chapter I fast-forwarded to give an account of Donald MacRae. When I was appointed at Sheffield and then LSE I had to find my bearings as an academic, having set sail in difficult waters without a compass. I stumbled by cumulative accident into an intellectual trajectory that in retrospect takes on purposeful shape and looks like a natural sequence. In these years I 'by indirections found directions out' and unconsciously created an academic profile. Several discomforts attended my arrival in what I imagined was academic paradise.

I did not at first realize that my idea of what it meant to be an academic was not universally shared. I had derived it from personal inclination reinforced by the models provided by John Chalker and Donald MacRae. My experience of academic teaching was formally non-existent, though years of local preaching had in practice instructed me in the basics: how to throw your voice to fill a given type of space; how to employ body language, gesture, pace and silence; how to emphasize what is important; how to use little props, for example simply holding up a book for inspection; and above all when to stop and how to reduce complexity to what can be grasped at different levels of sophistication. Academics often lack any sense of the basic rules for getting material across. I had honed these skills by doing extra-mural teaching and work with the WEA and the Women's Co-op movement to supplement my postgraduate grant, and had found the experience rewarding. I made friendships that lasted for many years.

Unfortunately I had such a high sense of what was required of a genuine scholar that I exhausted myself preparing careful and overlong texts. I overestimated what could be got across in a given time. It took years to overcome the fears that prevented me fully exploiting the skills of exposition I already possessed. And the effort to supplement my income cost me the third year of my scholarship because I felt obliged to fill out my schedule of activities honestly. So I needed a job as soon as possible and was taken on as a temporary lecturer at Sheffield University.

I taught at Sheffield University between October 1961 and June 1962, and remember with mild indignation an encounter with a visiting sociologist who upbraided me for drinking wine, because it was a middle-class taste acquired by 'the aspiring', whereas honest to goodness working-class people drank beer. I did not *like* beer, and in any case my humble parents were teetotal on religious grounds and indifferent to the class connotations of beer, wine or spirits. I sang with the choir in Handel's *Semele*, sank myself in Bach cantata Archiv recordings like *Herr, gehe nicht ins Gericht*, heard talks at the Philosophical Society, and became part of the lively Methodist and Student Christian Movement scene. I even imagined myself putting down roots in a region I found surprisingly attractive, particularly with the Derbyshire Dales so close by. Sometimes I went to the Dales for the weekend to spend time with Amos Cresswell, a friend from Barnes Methodist Church now teaching at Cliff College, Calver. He was editing *Joyful News*, renamed *Advance*, and enlisted me to write a regular column: my first serious journalistic venture. However, a colleague and his wife, John and Wendy Jackson, had plans for me, feeling I was lonely and in need of a mate.

The previous occupant of my room at Sheffield University had been Bernice Thompson, the internal candidate in apposition to me as an external candidate on the finals list. I met her at a Christmas conference of the British Sociological Association and found we had much in common, especially sociology and music. We listened to my little collection of records, mainly Bach cantatas like *Jauchzet Gott in allen Landen* and *Brich dem Hungrigen dein Brot*, and the B minor mass, and she took me to a concert of the Archduke Trio. She also took me to her home in Bury, one of the Lancashire cotton towns, and introduced me to the very different world of the northern working class. Bernice's mother had been widowed at 40, and she had six other siblings, all of them capable, and able to handle practical problems, like building nuclear power stations in Korea, or setting up computer systems for the Zurich Insurance Company. Bernice's academic career, as a high-flying scholarship girl to the local direct grant school, had been as starry and consistent as mine had been spotty and intermittent. Part of her education had come from a youth group at Bury parish church that paralleled my own in Barnes Methodist Youth Club. Not only was she fascinated by sociology, but she sang Anglican chant and Bach very beautifully.

125

Bernice Thompson, aged 23

Bernice was practical, like the rest of her family, as well as very clever. She was shocked by the state of my room in Sheffield, especially by my shelf of empty tins of condensed milk, and rapidly proposed improvements. Bernice was to become my lifetime's critic and interlocutor. There was just one problem. She had been the successful candidate for a post I too had applied for at Bedford College, London University, and that meant I should try to get a post at the LSE, so we might be together in London. At my LSE interview I was incoherent but the chairman, David Glass, said I could not be that bad, and I was appointed. But what was I supposed to do?

We were married and set up in a studio flat in Trumpeter's Inn, Old Palace Yard, Richmond Green, and equipped with the bare essentials of a table, a bed, a loo, a kitchen and a harpsichord, but no word came from the LSE.

As the autumn term approached I grew increasingly apprehensive, because I still could not find anyone to explain what I was expected to do. On the first day of term, I found I was to take a class in Modern Britain, which was fair enough, and to lecture in industrial sociology. I knew nothing about industrial sociology, and cared less, yet here I was expected to instruct others. Of course, you mostly learn by teaching, but my students could hardly have guessed that I was learning by teaching from scratch. The books I had to read before putting a lecture together cast me into the same boredom I had experienced reading David Ford on insurance. It is very difficult to make the fate of 'the black-coated worker' exciting or dramatize changes in apprenticeships or 'organizational theory'. No wonder I was only put to this misery for one year, for the students' sake if not for mine.

Taking classes in the social structure of modern Britain was less of a trial, since that was standard fare. Nevertheless experiences in this seminar provided my first intimation of the kind of problem I was to encounter for years to come: the ideological tilt in sociology saw class and mobility as central and my interest in religion as irrelevant. My subject was disappearing in the prescribed course of historical development, because it was unreal, just so much spray thrown up by the tides of real forces. I characterized this situation in an article for the *British Journal of Sociology* called 'The Sociology of Religion: a case of status deprivation?' The article began in a novel way for an academic journal with 'The Parable of the Righteous and the Unrighteous Students'.

The Unrighteous Student appeared to enjoy no righteous indignation about the social structure of modern Britain. He came from the Catholic working class and intended to make money as an accountant. The left-wing found him odd, especially in his attitude to the Tory working class. They assumed the Tory working class created a problem to be explained, but to him there was no difficulty. Voting conservative was evident good sense which the working class possessed in as good measure as anybody else. The more he rejected the problem as defined the more difficult it became to establish criteria for showing what should count as 'problematic' and what should count as 'natural'. The Righteous Student was a very articulate individual of public school background and agnostic development. He displayed a persuasive vocabulary no one considered susceptible to challenge. Only once was there a break in the self-validating circle of ideas when he described the Labour movement as having been 'artificially retarded' by Methodism. Somebody enquired about the criterion of 'artificiality'.

This parable had a single point bearing directly on the whole practice of sociology. Who is to say what is and is not the 'natural' direction of history, with respect to religion or indeed anything else? How far is sociology an academic subculture which socializes the mind in specialized ways and encourages certain kinds of person to undergo the process? There were two reasons I was likely to criticize the assumptions I encountered in the sociology department of the LSE, even when I agreed with them. One was that I had not been myself socialized into the expected mode of thinking. The other was that my own sub-discipline was dismissed as wasting time on a disappearing chimera. Religion was a mere footnote to the political text. I was, according to my own self-description, 'an academic deviant living by a non-existent subject'.

One colleague put it to me very directly: 'Do you think you have a *real* subject?' The question rested firmly on a dogmatic acceptance of a particular version of the theory of secularization and a unilateralist view of the direction of history. That was just the approach I believed Karl Popper had rendered untenable in *The Poverty of Historicism*. I had a strong sense of the contingent in history and how freedom within historical constraint meant that humankind is neither fated by destiny nor driven haplessly along tramlines. I had therefore to expose the illegitimate transfer of a theological *telos* or immanent direction into the domain of social science. So much sociology is over-organized history and I had read Collingwood's *The Idea of History*, and later Dray's *Laws and Explanation in History*. Clearly this would be a paradoxical exercise, but that was fine: I believed in paradox.

I would have to tangle with the dominant culture of my academic environment, and for that kind of scrap a Nonconformist background is a good preparation. The 'dissidence of dissent' would come to my aid. From time to time I was relieved to agree with my colleagues, for example, when the Marxist sociologist C. Wright Mills attacked abstract empiricism in *The Sociological Imagination*, and when sociology was denigrated by the political right. As one of my Marxist colleagues commented, I was just the right person to write 'No Apology for this Ology' in the op. ed. columns of *The Times*.

I prepared my critique of secularization by making a series of moves. One I have just described used the sceptical tools of sociology against its dogmatic assumptions. We prided ourselves on being brave nonconformists against something called 'the Establishment' when we were ourselves an establishment demanding conformity on pain of excommunication. LSE sociologists were a counter-elite and a culture with definable interests, though I did not for a moment believe my argument implied universal relativism. In Peter Berger's terms, the point was 'to relativize the relativizers' and unsettle them on their supposedly objective pedestal. The pretence of objectivity is a dishonest move in the struggle for supremacy, though it does not follow that there is no objective court of appeal. Karl Mannheim's 'unattached intelligentsia' was itself chimerical.

Another move was to unsettle the sociology of religion itself, in particular by investigating everyday religious practice in the past as well as now, and not taking some arbitrary point in the past as normative, whether Victorian piety or the faith of the High Middle Ages. The years 1250, 1860 and 1960 provided 'a handy historical tripod' for laying down the tracks of secular destiny. The existence of two points, six centuries apart, at two periods of intense urbanization and 'progress', was itself suspicious. Once you defined a given period as normative for what 'religion' *essentially* meant, it followed all too easily that change counted as secularization. I was not arguing secularization was impossible, but interrogating what counted as *real* religion and a *truly* religious period. That interrogation included the sociological tendency to treat a strong version of Christian orthodoxy, held by clergy, or even a fundamentalist like Ian Paisley, as the appropriate criterion. We 'needed to look at our religious beliefs not as if we were testing them for congruence with the Athanasian Creed but from the point of view of the religious and superstitious frameworks by which men live'. That was my aim in a paper I gave in September 1965 for a meeting of the British Association entitled 'The Unknown Gods of the English'.

My British Association paper was later included in a group of 'Studies in Secularization' I published in 1968 as *The Religious and the Secular* in which I canvassed the internal contradictions of the concept of secularization, and criticized 'the over-secularized concept of man' as a case of Prometheus Unbound. I also characterized the varying understandings and trajectories of secularization among sociologists, theologians and historians of the arts. I was interested in what looked like a major difference between secularization in music and secularization in the other arts, like painting and architecture. If you walked through the Accademia in Venice it seemed to tell a straightforward story, from Siena to the glorification of the secular city. But as you moved in music from the *Vorklassik* composers to Beethoven and then to the worship of nature and the nation in Romanticism, as well as the recovery of the Middle Ages and the mythic, whether in Friedrich or the Romantic composers from Mendelssohn to Mahler or from late Beethoven to Wagner's *Parsifal*, matters appeared much more complicated. I became suspicious of 'from–to' stories in principle. The sacred returned in the twentieth century, even in the special musical variant of modernism. The engagement of some important modern composers with liturgical Christianity made me wonder whether that was connected to the recovery of the Byzantine and the Baroque in art history and sensibility. I thought it raised questions about the assumptions underlying art history and intellectual history, including the history of science. So I read works like Burtt's *The Metaphysical Foundations of Modern Physical Science* to find out.

Before I dealt with sociologists and secularization I had to deal with theologians and secularization. The chapter on the theologians, 'Sociologist Fallen Among Secular Theologians', started life as a BBC Third Programme talk in which I satirized the proceedings of three conferences:, one at Swanwick in 1962 dealing with 'The Death of the Church', one organized by the Methodist Renewal Group, and one at the Catholic University of Nijmegen on 'The Death of God and the Advent of Modern Man'. The Methodist Renewal Group debated with some passion whether they should continue to pursue their aim of supplanting mere 'maintenance' with real life by organizing yet another conference and appointing a secretary and officials. At the Dutch Catholic conference I wanted to know just how many modern men actually existed, and was greeted with the scandalized riposte: 'Do you mean in a *percentage*?' It was one of those rare occasions when I appealed to numbers. I recommended some attention to where 'modern man' hung out, and to how many modern men and women actually existed.

The theologians at these conferences were too excited about their liberation from the confinement of settled forms, roles and duties to waste time on complicated facts. There were those who wanted continuously to mint new symbols lest old ones dull real experience with familiarity, and to translate Holy Communion into a once-for-all happening. As I put it: 'Reject any historic image of God and you are that much freer to construct him in your own.' The Christ of the Gospels could be remade even by New Testament scholars, first as a political zealot and then as a first-century hippy or a homosexual. John Wren-Lewis, a scientist working for ICI, promoted Jesus as a prototype of a scientist working for ICI and the Church as an anticipation of the international community of scientific research. One genuinely brilliant Dominican, Herbert McCabe, demythologized the Assumption of the Blessed Virgin to show it had something to do with the war in Vietnam.

The demand for reality ate up the necessity of institutional maintenance: it was more entertaining to rip off your clerical collar with its constricting conferral of an identity and celebrate the secular city as a real person. In Bishop Robinson's terms, one should strip down for action. The Methodist minister of Carver Street Chapel, Sheffield, told me he was doing his best to disband his old, dull congregation without explaining just where his new, young, exciting congregation was coming from. Another well-known Sheffield clergyman argued personal sin was irrelevant in view of the structural sin of capitalism, which led me to wonder whether *mea culpa* would come into its own after the Revolution or the eschaton, whichever came first. *Existenz* ruled, 'religionless Christianity' became a slogan, and the word 'structure' was anathema. I doubt whether anybody, apart from Hugh McLeod,[8] has canvassed the role of a sixties vanguard within the Church in undermining the very idea of institutions and institutional continuity in favour of the untrammelled self-made man, born free but everywhere in institutional chains. This is the approved variant of what is in other contexts greatly disapproved of: the self-made businessman. The theological votaries of liberated selfhood never for one moment paused to ask what lay behind one of the graffiti scrawled in 2011 on the walls of Benghazi, after 40 years of the arbitrary dictatorship of one self-made man: 'We want institutions'.

The paper for the British Association was a five-finger exercise, but it pointed me towards a further exploration of English religion in *A Sociology of English Religion*. Perhaps its flaws were understandable, but I am embarrassed to have missed the decline in the second half of the sixties. I insouciantly ignored what the statistical experts in the Church of England were telling me, for example, about declines in rates of confirmation. I was dubious about using church statistics, even when, as in the case of Methodism, they were very good. If I had looked at the statistics of Methodist decline as a proportion of total population, as Robert Currie did somewhat later, I would have seen them marching steadily downward year by year. Yet the book had good ideas: it identified what I called the 'subterranean theology' of everyday believing and anticipated how the practice of women might alter as they became more integrated into the mainstream economy.

My critique of the secularization thesis lay always latent but its crystallization was adventitious. I have to step back to 1963–5 for more background about the Department of Sociology at the LSE. Soon after my arrival I was greeted with the comment 'We are divided twenty to two; which side are you on?' Donald MacRae belonged to the minority of two, which could prove awkward. I listened to heated debates over *The End of Ideology* (1964) by Daniel Bell, and was disinclined to accept the majority view that Bell's thesis about the decline of ideological thinking could be dismissed. The debate was a precursor to the issue of secularization, except that most colleagues were seriously engaged by the end of ideology because that was about politics, whereas they took the end of religion for granted. Some time later I became friends with Bell, and he confirmed the link between the end of ideology and the end of religion by coming out on my side in the secularization debate in his LSE lecture 'The Return of the Sacred'.

Secularization made its first appearance in departmental debate when a colleague, Alan Little, asked how we should treat religion in the Modern Britain course. He suggested it should come under the head of secularization. Donald MacRae asked 'Why?' in a challenging way, and said that by 1963 we should have got beyond such simplistic approaches. I knew better than to ask what he meant, but when Julius

David Martin, lecturer at LSE, 1964

Gould, the other member of the minority of two, asked me to contribute a chapter to *The Penguin Survey of the Social Sciences* I worked it out for myself and engaged in a provocative work of demolition.

In 'Towards Eliminating the Concept of Secularization', I suggested the concept of secularization fused several incompatible elements and that whenever one ran into contradictory empirical evidence, one changed the criteria of what was to count as secularization. I set out three ways in which secularization worked simultaneously as description and as prescription: liberal rationalist, Marxist and existentialist. I argued that the ideological underpinnings of the concept expropriated Christian imagery such as ages and stages and the metaphor of light. The Enlightenment expropriated the Christian metaphor of light to proclaim man's release from an age of superstitious darkness to an age of scientific truth. On Julius' advice I added a final sentence: secularization should be 'erased from the sociological dictionary'.

Knowing Ernest Gellner was a famous iconoclast, I dropped the piece in his room, imagining he might appreciate my own exercise in iconoclasm. I had stupidly forgotten he was a liberal rationalist who believed in the Great Transition I was tilting against. Far from appreciating my iconoclasm, he cast himself as the icon, and lampooned my argument: 'David Martin believes secularization is internally incoherent, therefore God exists.' Others reacted differently. Peter Berger, the most creative intellectual force in the sociology of religion, wrote me a charming note to say that I might well have a point, but *something* had happened with the advent of modernity, and we needed to elucidate what it was.

Yet Ernest Gellner was responsible for my next adventitious move, though in retrospect it looks inevitable. We were taking a seminar together and when the reader of the paper failed to turn up Ernest instructed me to make one up. I had nothing to lose, and invented the kind of relatively modest and contingent secularization theory I believed would not fall foul of my critique of the Great Transition. I sketched out a historically *contingent* theory of secularization, apart from certain broad empirical tendencies with regard to size of urban concentration, presence of an industrial working class, gender and so on. There was also the key process of social differentiation whereby the Church ceased to exercise power and ideological control over such sectors of social life as administration, education and welfare.

Broad empirical tendencies apart, the pattern of secularization varied with the concatenation of various historical components today renamed 'path dependency'. These components included 'crucial events' such as the English, American, French, Dutch and Russian revolutions, and the failure of revolution in Lutheran countries. They also included whether or not the relation of religion to the local Enlightenment and the local nationalism was positive or negative. Religion was positively related to both the Enlightenment and nationalism in the USA, and negatively in France, and in Russia nationalism had first fused with Marxist Enlightenment and then reverted to an older model of the church–nation. The spectrum of possibilities ran from the USA to France and Russia with varying degrees of religious diversity and unity, individualism and collectivism, church–state establishment and separation. It yielded fundamental patterns: the American, the British, the Latin (Southern Europe), the extended Latin (South America), the Russian (Eastern Europe), the Calvinist (Scottish–Dutch–Swiss), the Lutheran (Northern Europe), and the Polish–Irish.

Gellner sponsored a publication of my ideas in the *European Journal of Sociology*, which duly came out in December 1969. Almost without noticing I had devised the initial critique of secularization theory, and now the first general theory of secularization. It was amazing no one had combined these various elements before, and much later Charles Taylor marvelled something so patently true had so long evaded notice. Paradigms are powerful, as Thomas Kuhn noted in *The Structure of Scientific Revolutions*: another truism that evaded notice until someone said it.

From then on I elaborated my fundamental patterns and put the drafts in a drawer as unfinished business. In 1976 my secretary, Judy Strang, found them, and asked if she might type them up. I told her this was no part of her duties, but she went ahead and I realized this was a book-length theory of secularization. It was published unrevised in 1978.

In the most recent summary articles on secularization, all this is forgotten prehistory. As new generations add new storeys the foundations become invisible, and if you live long enough you may observe your own oblivion. The problem lies in the occlusion of sociology as a humane discipline dependent on history, including its own history, in the dominance of the technician with the research grant, as well as an accelerating expansion of the universe of production that separates research communities into worlds hermetically sealed off one from another.

My critical trajectory took off from my work on the alternation of aggression and quietist withdrawal in *Pacifism*, and my analysis of those I called 'anarchs of reason' like Bertrand Russell. That was hinted at even in my *A Sociology of English Religion*, more particularly in its 'Concluding Unscientific Postscript', where I set out some ideas that in retrospect were to engage me for decades, but especially after the anarchic and histrionic episodes of the student revolution of 1968–9. I was interested both in the issue of freedom and determinism raised by the way sociology analyses patterns of behaviour and by the dependence of freedom on hierarchies of predictable habit. My favourite analogy was drawn from my experience of musical performance: freedom of interpretation was totally dependent on wide-ranging, cumulative and automatic hierarchies of habit. That entails a defence of hierarchy and habit as necessary for a viable social existence and providing the preconditions of freedom. No doubt I was also influenced by my knowledge of the costs of freedom without boundaries and of the absence of firm pre-emptive decisions illustrated in my first marriage. I was against the sixties notion that life should consist of meeting constantly in solemn conclave to decide what is to be done next, and invoking the inherent virtue of the workers while castigating them for being so readily duped by the wiles of consumer capitalism.

I was on a direct collision course with the student revolutionaries, who believed liberation followed from the disruption of habit and the destruction of hierarchy (or 'imperative co-ordination', as sociological jargon had it). Having been responsible for postgraduates in the sociology department, I had much experience of liberated people, so I entitled my 1972 inaugural lecture 'Order and Rule', in order to expound the role of good habits in sustaining order and rule, and not just in monasteries. I edited a book called *Anarchy and Culture* where I analysed the crisis in the university as yet another 'dissolution of the monasteries'. These themes had germinated in my head ever since I started reading sociology and realized it could provide a defence of rule-following rather than spontaneity.

My inaugural lecture came a day after a lecture I gave to the whole first-year intake to the school, 'Parts and Wholes, Objectives and Objectivity', contrasting ritual, following the prescriptions of a pre-ordained order, with the vacuum of pure self-expression. I argued that 'to act "as if" and to see and play a part is the precondition of seeing the whole'. Both lectures were critiques of spontaneity, and the LSE printed them together. Initially I planned to give my inaugural as a series of disruptive meditations like Pascal's *Pensées*, but I decided eventually on a through-composed meditation based on the semantic fields generated by the etymology of key words like 'mark', 'habit' and 'rule'. My model was the sermon as practised by Lancelot Andrewes, pondered, poetic and intricate, and just as Andrewes uncovered a theology by the excavation of webs of meaning embedded in key words (or the Word as logos and as text), I intended to uncover a sociology. Moreover I would compound the offence by suggesting how the two webs of meaning might intersect. I was defending markers and habits against those who lauded spontaneity as the source of authentic creativity. Creativity depended on the habitual and the automatic, just as freedom and choice depended on the pre-existence of settled hierarchies. I was also defending the university against the market model that has since then exercised so destructive an influence on the disciplines of scholarship, especially the imposition of criteria based on size of grants and 'impact'.

I began with a meditation on the family as a prelude to meditations on schools, churches and universities. I argued:

> The dependency relation of childhood is very inimical to the logic of the spontaneous self. The requirements of survival require pre-emptive decisions, and the requirements of economy in decision-making suggest using ready-made cultural modes rather than the confusing invention of new ones. Thus, the universal openness of the child is pre-empted willy-nilly by a name, a nation, a role-definition and a set of normal cultural recipes. Where there are siblings, equality and justice according to aptitude, interest, and age depend on the firm exercise of authority. Both the

psychological health provided by stability and definition and the needs of justice are rooted in authority and hierarchy. If participatory democracy were instituted in the family it would have the usual consequence: uni-dimensional determination by peers.

I said the university

is less conformable to market and media models than to the model of the family. Like the family it transmits a good by a prior act of qualitative judg-ment; like a church it takes a novice, tests his calling and socializes him into a way of life. As in the family there is a clear hierarchy of knowledge and experience which does not respond to demand but *makes* demands on those who desire to attain the good which is offered. It sets out the mini-mal conditions which must precede the achievement of certain ends. The custom is not that of the customer but a custom of disciplined criticism.

I concluded by saying that 'To obey the rule of one's order is to dis-cover the possibility of a new order.'

A sympathetic colleague in another discipline commented that I was trying to combine Wittgenstein and the Prologue to St John's Gospel. An unsympathetic colleague in sociology regretted having to misspend a whole hour. Ernest Gellner wanted to know who had made *me* professor of metaphysics in the University of London. I replied there was nothing metaphysical in what I had said: it was experiential without being empiricist. I saw the address as no more than obvious sociology. It was my good luck to live when 'the obvious' could seem a baleful metaphysical revelation. I had been looking back to my own experience and my own mistakes, for example when I was a primary school teacher and discovered by harsh experience that only meticulous forethought, firmness in making decisions and the creation of settled sequences and rituals could generate the creative murmur of satisfying activity. The anarcho-syndicalist mob at LSE had conferred originality on common sense and only a Nonconform-ist born and bred dared defend it. But then Ernest went on to make a very perceptive remark: 'Having gone back to Catholicism your next step should be back to Judaism.' After all, Christianity both abolished *and* fulfilled the law, and Jewish survival and creativity had depended on devotion to statute and the most minute disciplines of exegesis.

After the publication of the fully worked out version of my general theory of secularization, I turned to something very different: *The Breaking of the Image: A Sociology of Christian Theory and Practice.*

It reflected my engagement with faith understood as the solid poetry of a transforming vision encountering the stubborn resistance of human nature *and* social nature. I wanted to release the potentials locked in religious imagery, to explore how images mutate under social pressures, and to show how the radical repertoire of Christianity is inflected by the dynamic of power and violence, in particular the varied kinds of power and violence associated with (say) the Roman Empire, feudalism, enlightened autocracy and early capitalism.

It also took off from my analysis in *Pacifism* of the strictly limited spectrum of fundamental religious attitudes to 'the world' as they generated what I called tables of symbolic affinity or alternatively the symbolic logic of the main world religions. Here my sociology of religion was as indebted to Max Weber's seminal essay on religious rejections of the world as my sociology of politics was indebted to his essay on politics as a vocation. I held not only that different relations between acceptance of and rejection of the world bred different tendencies to pacifist withdrawal and eschatological expectations of an imminent overthrow of the world order – with pacifism likely in Christianity and Buddhism, and less likely in Islam and Confucianism – but that there was a persistent movement back and forth between pacific withdrawal and overturning the reign of evil to establish the kingdom of God. This dialectic in the religious sphere was mirrored by a dialectic within secular utopianism between liberal pacifism and liberal imperialism and between an anarchist rejection of force and exemplary murder. Once you understood these varied symbolic logics, you could analyse how they were inflected in particular societies.

Once you analyse how religious images of renewal, alteration, restoration and revolution are inflected and partly expropriated by structures of power, righteous abuse of religion *as such* has to give way to social scientific understanding. Once you have understood how radical images are taken on board by an empire or a nation state for its own purposes, and yet work inside their welcoming hosts to undermine as well as underpin them, moralistic spleen is exposed as intellectual self-indulgence. A potent idea, like Luther's affirmation of conscience against both emperor and pope, can only take off when mixed with other motivations and forces, like the greed of nobles, or the ambition of absolutist monarchs anxious to secure supremacy in their own realms, or the rivalries of nation states. Once you unmask the rhetoric that identifies religion as *the* cause of the so-called 'wars of religion' you cannot, in the style of 'the New Atheists', conduct hit-and-run raids on history. You cannot, for example, gesture in the direction of the entanglement of religion with British imperialism and Irish nationalism in Ulster, in order to load the onus onto religion and goad others to easy indignation. The rejection of analysis and understanding in favour of abuse has become an intellectual scandal. Internecine wars long preceded the emergence of the God of Abraham, Isaac, Jacob, Joshua and Jesus, and the abolition of God was attended by yet another reign of violence and intolerance. Indeed, the abolition of God is another of its malign manifestations. This was the position that underpinned my book *Does Christianity Cause War?*, published in 1997, but was already implicit in everything from *Pacifism* to *The Breaking of the Image* (1980).

The Breaking of the Image reflected on the refraction of the sign by the social medium of its reception but it started life as a five-minute paper about how people in different historical times overhear 'the double entendre' of Christianity, as it sustains and subverts the family of procreation, maintains and undermines institutional hierarchies and their mediations, reinforces tribal solidarities in promised lands and converts them into visions of universal fraternity. This paper was supplemented by sermons I gave as Select Preacher to the University of Cambridge and by a series of addresses given in Durham University and Westminster Abbey. I pursued the symbolic logic of Christianity through the categories of sociological analysis, above all the revolutionary dynamic unleashed when 'the world' is accepted as potentially good and rejected because contrary to God's once and future kingdom.

The Breaking of the Image was written under great stress. It wrote itself as though in a dream, and was the closest I came to writing poetry under the constraints of social science. Proliferating metaphors did my sociological work without conscious intellectual government. The 'double entendre' was exposed and revealed itself in the closely linked images of the Servant King and the potent Child, the Virgin Queen and the humble Mother, the earthly city and country juxtaposed to the heavenly Jerusalem and the kingdom of heaven. You overhear the 'double entendre' in the poisonous serpent in the garden who becomes the healing serpent on the cross; the broken stone that becomes the corner stone. In contemplating the broken body of Christ stretched out on the cross you absorb the marring of the image of God in man on account of sin, and in contemplating the glorious body of the resurrection you participate in that image restored through the travail of redemption. Images are always being broken and restored. When I fall I rise, when I am abased I am exalted, when I offer myself without stint I receive back a hundredfold. 'The One who descended is the One who ascended': the shape of the creed and the groundwork of the sermon.

11

Bryan Wilson, the Jews, secularization and its discontents

———◆•◆———

It was during my early period at LSE that I became aware of the work in the sociology of religion of Bryan Wilson at Oxford. This was material I needed to come to terms with. I might be on my own at the LSE, but the sociology of religion in Britain was being resurrected as a serious theoretical discipline by Wilson after a long period of neglect that extended back to Herbert Spencer. Of course, there had been serious empirical work of a very illuminating kind such as I deployed in my *Sociology of English Religion*, for example the inquiries carried out by Rowntree and Laver, and the writings of William Pickering. About the same time as I wrote my book on English religion, arguing religion was more extensive and resilient than you might think, Bryan Wilson had published his *Religion in Secular Society* in which he first articulated a standard model of secularization that later developments in Britain, if not in America and elsewhere, might well be thought to support. I was dubious about his claim that American religion was internally secularized, because I thought the criteria for internal secularization could nullify evidence for lively religiosity anywhere and could well imply religious societies in the past were really secular: religion in Victorian Britain might be seen as internally secularized in its conformity to the secular imperatives of power and profit.

Bryan had developed Troeltsch's understanding of the Christian 'sect-type' into a set of sub-types, one of which was 'the conversionist sect'. This was a major advance, incorporating suggestive empirical connections that would be exploited by Bryan's students for years. Unfortunately, the 'conversionist sect' was precisely what I had meant by the denomination in my very first academic publication, where I had argued Methodism had not gravitated from sect to denomination but emerged from the church as a denominational movement. That was a serious difference. The denomination emerged from what Joachim Wach called *ecclesiola in ecclesia* (that is, a ginger group like Wesley's Holy Club) rather than being a stage of sect development when the early fervour had cooled off. I had suggested that there was a dialectic within the sect, more narrowly defined than in Bryan Wilson's formulation, between perfection and moral anarchy, total transcendence and absolute immanence, subordination to a uniform and egalitarian style of dress and the (dubious) egalitarianism of streaking naked with no markers of social distinction.

Bryan disliked this approach, and I suspect he was irked by the way I imported hints of dialectic, irony and paradox into my presentation, my use of non-sociological materials, like Monsignor Knox's *Enthusiasm*, and what he took to be my condescending attitude to sects. He disliked Anglicanism and detested Catholicism, and something of his attitude to Catholicism came out in his later dismissal of the multi-volume sociology of religion by the Catholic scholar Werner Stark. I received a letter from one of his students upbraiding me for not referring to – and deferring to – his analysis of sects in the *American Sociological Review* for 1959. I could only confess I did not know the article existed: the *ASR* was not a journal I had canvassed for my particular purposes. When I read a review by Bryan of my *The Religious and the Secular* I realized we were at odds across a whole range of sensitive issues, including my interest in theology, for him proof positive of an unscientific approach.

I feared the sociology of religion might become as fractious as other sub-disciplines. I decided to see whether he would respond to a friendly approach. He did respond, and in due course I gave regular papers at his Oxford seminar, and examined his meticulously prepared doctoral students. Bryan attended to his friendships with Ciceronian care and you were admitted to his circle through induction into civilized behaviour. That meant being introduced into a set of personal protocols, for example about the appropriate treatment of 'college servants', and the rubrics of eating, and drinking good wine. Bryan explained to me that the bouquet of a good wine was more exquisite than Mozart and that he 'only came to London to visit his wine merchant'. Friends on probation, especially foreigners, were informed that 'We don't shake hands', and on one occasion when we were together in Toronto Bryan declined to take off his jacket on a very hot day on the ground that one never knew where divestment might lead. Bryan hated middle-class disorder and the cult of the tactile and the tactless. He thought English 'respectability' meant 'worthy of respect' and he respected people like the office clerk who attended to 'my station and its duties'. In opposition to Sartrean existentialism, he thought of roles as the means whereby people found themselves, not as constrictions of their individuality. He was dubious about excess, and responded to the quiet world of the English watercolourists. He believed in times and seasons, and when he took me to breakfast at All Souls made sure to go early in case our quiet reveries were interrupted by people anxious to address us with important questions, like Rodney Needham.

We became friends and I enjoyed his company, his courtesy, kindness and hospitality. He had made an extraordinary journey to Oxford by unconventional routes like evening classes, from beginnings even humbler than my own, and we could agree on many matters, in particular the absurdist gestures of radical student demonstrations and the proper role of the university teacher, though his fulfilment of the role was far more exemplary and meticulous than mine. For Bryan there were affective, diffuse and humane obligations embedded in the role of teacher, threatened by functional specificity, the notions of training and career development and a corrosive 'in-group scepticism'. The sociologists of religion in Britain were not like that, and long remained a friendly and cooperative group outside the mainstreams of contention, even though some felt that only showed the sub-discipline was irrelevant. There was an unspoken compact between me and Bryan never openly to criticize the other, and that meant we rarely referred to each other's published work, a virtual silence that colleagues noticed and commented on with some amusement. We were regularly paired in textbook summaries as holding opposed views, yet our disagreements remained implicit and our friendship intact.

Bryan was safe in All Souls, Oxford, and I could assume my job at LSE was safe enough, but advancement could easily be jeopardized by stepping outside the accepted consensus. Luckily my peculiar route into the academic world made me indifferent to prospects of promotion because I did not expect it, and was content to be part of the academic world. More than that, my independence and willingness to say exactly what I thought did not in the event amount to professional suicide, though when my name was proposed for a prestigious academic society it met with 'ferocious opposition', and the damning suggestion 'Isn't he really a theologian?' Maybe my insouciance even worked to my advantage, in spite of a degree of stress that was nearly fatal.

Bryan also broke with the accepted consensus by an analysis of demoralization. He built demoralization into binary oppositions, contrasting the religious past with the 'demoralized' secular present. I was critical of linked binary oppositions and felt Bryan worked with too simple a contrast between dense and close-knit communities held together by religiously sanctioned mores, and rational bureaucracy where moral behaviour became utilitarian calculation. But whatever the historical truth behind this contrast, Bryan was sufficiently committed to the theme of demoralization to risk professional excommunication. He knew demoralization was on the index of prohibited words, yet refused to bow before the weight of established opinion. It exposed him to sneers and denigration and I admired him for it. At the same time I thought such schemata as community and association, or traditional and rational-bureaucratic, or theological and positive, worked in combination to imply that we were living on an inclined historical plane. They made us unwilling to ask by what criteria we defined a past period as *really* religious. In just what sense was the world (say) of Hogarth more religious than our own?

Bryan and I shared a Protestant background, but in Bryan's case that came out in an intense dislike of religious ritual and of the idea it was replete with content. He was singularly unhappy when in a seminar in California I challenged Frits Stahl over his contention that ritual was meaningless by analysing the meaning of the mass. He was also scandalized when I compared the crepuscular rites of commensality in the All Souls dining hall with the courtesies of Holy Communion in All Souls chapel. For him what was precious and sustaining in the fraternity of scholars became pretentious flummery in the congregation of Christians. Moreover, the rites of the fraternity were easily profaned by alien presences, including women, and ritual infringements shook his social universe, because that was how a precious membership was defined and made secure. There was an Unseen Monitor at every meal and excommunication followed infringement. Once when I was at high table in All Souls, an irate Fellow threw a glass of water at a colleague who had displeased him. Bryan felt that only condign reproof could wipe away the stain and restore the shattered order. Yet Bryan was the kindest master of novices. A neophyte willing to learn was always granted prevenient grace.

When Bernice and I took him out for a meal to recompense his kindness, he subverted our intentions by insisting on a particular restaurant and picking up the bill rather than take a chance on our untutored taste. In the end I fear my name was erased from the inner circle of his friends, which saddened me. I had always been under suspicion for mixing the sacred protocols of social scientific truth with theology and expressing scepticism about any trust we might put in the multitudinous deliverances of reason. I was the more glad when the Warden of All Souls, John Davies, asked me to speak alongside the historian Simon Green at Bryan's memorial.[9] This was my chance to celebrate his gifts and virtues, above all his gift for friendship. As we sat at lunch before the event, there was a moment of unexpected revelation when Bryan's sister said he had once been seriously interested in Christian Science. None of us knew of this episode because Bryan drew a protecting veil over early indiscretions to wrap himself in the mantle of disinterested scholarship. Now the truth was out and I allowed it a suitably inconspicuous place in my eulogy.

Living in a Jewish environment

In a recorded account of his early experiences in Leeds, Bryan Wilson described how he became the star of his school once the Jews left. There were hardly any Jews in my grammar school but my arrival at LSE introduced me to a brilliant subculture that was part Jewish, part Scottish. Bryan illustrated how Protestantism could mutate into secularity and my Jewish colleagues illustrated how Judaism might mutate into secularity.

My Englishness and my Christianity marked me out and I was distinctly bemused when Asher Tropp responded to a modest kindness by calling me 'a real Jewish gentleman'. I began to realize where I was when Ernest Gellner objected so strongly to my critique of secularization. When Ernest tried to mend matters by expressing his respect for Puritanism as expounded by Max Weber, I had to confess my roots lay in revivalist enthusiasm not Puritan intellectuality and constraint.

My Jewish colleagues took Freudianism far more seriously than it deserved, even when they dissected its principled indifference to contrary evidence, and recognized how threadbare it was as a modern myth of the soul. It was *their* religion, and they went through its rituals whether or not they believed. When a young woman from Rochdale was recruited to the sociology department and showed signs of distress, she was told to 'get yourself psycho-analysed and join the middle class'. That was *not* how North Country women understood social mobility.

I understood the hostility to religion of some of my Jewish colleagues: they saw Judaism and Christianity as the sources of their exclusion and persecution, and believed secularization might relieve their historic burden. They found Protestant philo-Semitism ambiguous, if they even knew of its existence, which is why I wanted it included in Hans Hillerbrand's *Encyclopedia of Protestantism*. Only recently have scholars cared or dared to recognize the role of secular Jews in the promotion of secularization, especially in the United States but also in Europe, for example Vienna. However, there were other currents pushing Jews into the secular camp, like the demand of the secular Enlightenment and its Marxist extension that they assimilate as the price of inclusion. It was all very complicated and terribly easy to get wrong.

The traditional anti-Semitism of Russia had been revived under secular communism, and as the left turned against Israel as 'racist and colonialist', many Jewish intellectuals reassessed their commitment to Marxism. Eventually I discovered that some of my Jewish colleagues, like Julius Gould, retained their loyalty to the faith that had sustained their existence over nearly three millennia and recognized what Jonathan Sacks has called 'the dignity of difference', as well as sharing my concern about the way new educational nostrums worked against outsiders anxious to learn and succeed, whether Jews or Christian Nonconformists. Some Jews knew the communist left from the inside. They no longer cherished illusions about the USSR and had no truck with student neo-Marxism.

I responded to the writing of Talmon and Aron without much ideological self-consciousness and I was merely glad to be welcomed and befriended by Jews like Freedman, Lipset, Bell and Shils. Some acquaintances were acquired accidentally at conferences. I remember the conference in July 1969 arranged by Konstanty Jelenski where I first encountered Edward Shils, George Steiner and Melvin Lasky, and found them well disposed to what I said and how I said it. Steiner in particular interested me with his writing on words, music and silence (and later on 'real presence'), and Shils with his work on tradition.

Over time I became an honorary associate of the Jewish intelligentsia in North London and New York, and (later) in the suburb of Brookline in Boston when I worked with Peter Berger and others at the Institute for the Study of Economic Culture. In London I chaired a meeting between the Chief Rabbi and Liberal Jews, and in Jerusalem I spoke at the centenary meeting of Reformed Jews at the Hebrew Union College with the renowned Yeshayahu Leibowitz. Leibowitz spoke movingly of the obligation to obey Halacha without hope of reward, emotional or otherwise, and at one point he said, 'Our Christian guests will now leave us to perform *their* religious duties.' It was Easter Eve and we arrived at the Church of the Pavement just as the priest was intoning, 'O certainly necessary sin of Adam . . .' Bernice and I shared a Portuguese seder with Zvi Werblowsky and his family on this visit. Later we became friends with Allon Gal, historian of Zionism, who took us to Zionist shrines in Tel Aviv, and made the acquaintance of Shmuel Eisenstadt with whom we shared an interest in 'multiple modernities' and the modern character of fundamentalism.

My philo-Semitic background helped. I shared Anthony Smith's views about the overlapping sources of nationalism and religion in God's covenant relation with Israel, and while in Prague with Adam Seligman I shared his critique of the modern cult of sincerity as a criterion of true religion. In Prague I visited all the synagogues as a matter of obligation, and when in Bratislava with Neal Kozodoy, a friend and the editor of *Commentary*, we went together on a fruitless search for the site of the old synagogue.

Not all my Jewish contacts were so easy to negotiate. With Shirley Letwin I felt I was being tested for ideological soundness as a possible ally but could not divine her criteria for inclusion and failed the test. On one occasion I was consulted by Keith Joseph, at that time talked of as future leader of the Conservative Party, about 'the logic and empirical base' of an important speech he proposed to make. I warned him a Conservative politician could not possibly regret the reproductive habits of 'classes four and five' without disaster. He persisted 'as a matter of personal integrity', claiming 'My record will protect me', and when overwhelmed by the negative reaction sent me a charming note to say I had been right. Joseph also introduced me to Margaret Thatcher to brief her on the student revolution. With Midge Dexter and Norman Podhoretz I spent a weekend with Lady Thatcher and gave a lecture on the family to which she was the respondent. Thatcher was another migrant from Protestant Nonconformity who appreciated the ethos of English Jews, and I wanted to stimulate her to recall her Methodist family origins. She did so enthusiastically, adding that her early memories included 'Handel and all those lovely oratorios'.

I had my most unpleasant experience at a conference on artificial intelligence at Yale, when Alfred Ayer described my contribution as the 'worst he had ever heard'. What seemed most to incense him was my characterization of Beethoven's last quartets as marking a summit of the distinctively and creatively human, and my evident belief this was no emotive opinion but apodictic truth. I think Ayer picked up a religious sensibility antithetical to everything he stood for, and recognized how alien I found his rationalist cleverness. The brain scientist and Nobel Prize winner Sir John Eccles came to my defence, and Ayer apologized for having introduced 'a note of fanaticism' into the debate.

12

More on LSE and student revolution

In 1968–9 ordinary academic existence was disrupted by the student revolution, partly imported from California, and more disruptive at the LSE because so many postgraduate students were American. Robin Blackburn, the immediate cause of the upset at the LSE, was a student in my classes, and I gave him his reference for the LSE post from which he was sacked, mentioning that if the LSE wanted to 'live in interesting times' he might provide them. Those interesting times are no longer interesting and I do not want to add to the mountain of ink spent since, or to my own comments on disruption that lasted no more than three years. When a small group of us, Robert Mackenzie, Edward Shils and Martin Lipset, met in Norwich in 1970 to defend the university, another student generation had arrived, anxious to be lawyers and accountants.

As someone amazed at my good fortune in being at a university, I disliked the way radical students regarded their presence there as an automatic right they could treat with contempt rather than embrace as a privilege. They took for granted what I had acquired at great personal cost and still experienced as precarious. Some of them saw themselves as 'the workers' in the knowledge factory, which stirred me to coin the phrase 'prolier than thou'. They were chronically suspicious of the knowledge produced in the bourgeois university and despised liberal freedoms as covert repression. They had to expropriate the expropriators and either turn the university over to 'workers' control' or establish their own counter-cultural institutions with a 'critical' curriculum. They thought sociology ought to unmask a bogus social reality, whereas I thought it an analysis of limits and a warning against utopianism. Yet when they went 'on strike' they asked me to take classes for them in a nearby pub.

All this came to a head in a lecture by Peter Berger I chaired in the Old Theatre of the LSE on 'Sociology: Radical and Conservative'.

Berger had been misconstrued as a radical because he had written on the social construction of reality and the students assumed he was in favour of deconstruction. In fact he cherished a mild nostalgia for the Habsburg monarchy *k. und k.* Once he reached the conservative (small 'c') section the temperature dropped below zero. The prophet had failed to prophesy, and reactions were so hostile Berger threatened he would not continue unless they displayed proper European manners. He added that it was some relief to him to know they would one day have children and spend part of their politically hyperactive lives sleeping. The moment a fiery Hungarian emigré, Imre Lakatos, stood up to contribute, I realized it was time to close the session. Lakatos believed we should station a machine gun by the cornice of Connaught House covering Houghton Street. Berger and I were the same age and in the twinkling of an eye we aged a generation.

There were LSE academics who thought the student ideology infantile, yet criticized the administration as maladroit and counterproductive whatever it did. The very word 'administration' and the surname of our director, Sir Walter Adams, were spat out as expletives. I found this as annoying as the pronouncements and the rudeness of the students themselves. These critics from the sidelines were always right because never responsible for decisions. Moreover, when criticism of the administration was combined with contempt for British institutions in general on the part of people who had left countries with less benevolent institutions, I felt outraged. One day I vented my feelings in a speech to the Academic Board. I forget exactly what I said, except that it included a three-fold 'I am tired . . .' – for example, 'I am tired of picking up my copy of *The Guardian* only to read in the letter columns yet more captious criticism by colleagues of whatever action the administration has felt obliged to take' – and 'We are exposed to a daily service of commination from those who renounce all responsibility for our collective life.' Commination was not a word regularly pronounced in the Academic Board (and to judge from the red underlining on my computer not regularly pronounced anywhere).

This statement was naïvely courageous, because it was bound to annoy senior people in my own department on whom my future depended, and the silence was furious and palpable. The administration might have a moment of secret satisfaction but could not save me from the consequences of my open declaration of dissent. I was taken on one side by Lord Robbins to receive kindly advice to the effect that though forthright comment was noted and not entirely unacceptable, nevertheless, pointing out in public how ridiculous goings on were at 'the School' gave a handle to its enemies.

LSE academics had the full range of views on the student revolution, and the lawyers in particular were divided into conservatives, vocal left-liberals and Marxists. Some of the Marxists in my own department thought the revolutionary students the 'spoilt children of the bourgeoisie' and one muttered darkly, 'We shall deal with these Bakuninites one day.' They were understandably concerned with the facts of inequality and mobility and complained about the indifference of student revolutionaries to facts. Most colleagues did not at all conform to a stereotype of the LSE academic modelled on the far left politics of Harold Laski. I had friends, like the anthropologist Maurice Freedman, who imagined the brutal suppression of the Prague Spring would educate the students in some realism about the revolutionary alternatives they espoused. For a brief while I thought they might be right. But when I taxed a student with observations about the rather more important revolts in Eastern Europe against Marxist regimes, he replied that the capacity of these regimes to arouse passionate dissent rather than pallid protest showed how superior they were. Robin Blackburn once told me revolutionary governments put their opponents away because they at least had the grace to take intellectual criticism seriously.

Other colleagues were taken aback by the reappearance of an earlier Marx still under Hegelian influence. As a philosopher, Ernest Gellner thought this backward-looking, as Hegel had been rightly expunged from the history of philosophy. Ernest added, 'We are not the London School of Phenomenology.' I never knew quite what to expect from Ernest. When Maurice Freedman gave his inaugural lecture in anthropology on Chinese marriage ceremonies, Ernest was afraid the subject might lead hard-nosed economists to believe the softer social sciences were *feminine*. And who but Ernest could complain that the canons of Chichester Cathedral all looked like Wittgensteinians?

Ernest was a classic liberal and he and I agreed we were facing an outbreak of chiliastic fervour. He wrote an excellent piece on the 'Troubles' for my edited book *Anarchy and Culture*, called 'The Panther and the Dove', where he utilized my approach to the alternation and intermingling of pacific and aggressive motifs in revolutionary movements. Later, during the miners' strike, when students were busy leaving all the lights on to defeat Edward Heath's attempt to conserve fuel, Ernest thought it essential for Mrs Thatcher to defeat the miners. Academics with a background in the political convulsions of the Continent held much sharper views of student revolution than the native born, who often retained a rather British fuzziness. Robert MacKenzie, our media star, commented on politics for radio and television, and greatly admired Harold Macmillan. Early on he warned us trouble was travelling our way from California, not least because we had so many American students, many seeking exile as dissidents. MacKenzie was very upset when a picture of Lenin was installed in the departmental office, but such was the atmosphere he dared not take it down.

I am surprised in retrospect just how extensive my comments on the student revolution were, particularly when I look over a collection of critiques I published in 1973 called *Tracts Against the Times*. Some were on Radio 3 (and in *The Listener*), others in *Encounter, Dissent, The Times Literary Supplement, The Times Higher Educational Supplement* and *The Christian Century*. For a while I did quite a lot of work for radio, sometimes talks on Radio 3 but also talks on the World Service in Bush House, and even some work for television, though opportunities for extended argument on television are very

Family photo in 1974 in the garden of Cripplegate Cottage, Woking, with David, Bernice, Jonathan (aged 18), Jessica (aged 12), Izaak (aged 10) and Magnus (aged 3); used in an article on social mobility by Time–Life *for a popular sociology volume edited by Paul Murphy, 1977*

rare and your comments are often taken out of context and woven into a producer's essay to give weight to his views not your own. Over the years I grew increasingly resistant to being misused in this way, or even to being asked to save broadcasters intellectual work by explaining issues for hours at a time on the phone.

Encounter threw interesting assignments my way, for example, opportunities to review Adorno's *Minima Moralia*, and to engage the New Left academic Perry Anderson's bold and contentious thesis about a 'white migration' that had made up for the absence in Britain of an intelligentsia with a coherent social scientific worldview. I thought British performance not all that lacking, and coherent worldviews dangerous, given one could never engross their unintended consequences. That was precisely the argument of Hayek and of Popper (dismissed by Anderson as 'a fluent ideologue'), and I had been happy to find it convincing, even though it sharply circumscribed the scope of social science. I was not a Hayekian but I thought he was right about that. Some cautious modesty in prediction was entirely in order, given the previous history of failed predictions, and events that had defied prediction. Who for example predicted the student revolution or (later) the fall of communism and the Soviet Union, or the rise of Pentecostalism?

One of my targets was the psychiatric guru R. D. Laing, about whom I wrote a piece entitled 'Psychiatry and Apocalypse' for a book on *The New Left* edited by my colleague Maurice Cranston. Laing sought to replace the experience of politics by the politics of experience, and I suggested debating with him was like an exchange between a Pentecostal in the pulpit and a Unitarian in the congregation. After that it was surprising he should suggest me as chairman of a radio debate between him and Thomas Szasz, the alternative guru at the time.

Ironically I had to reverse my critical tack and trim in another direction when the Conservative government of the 1980s attacked sociology. Everything had happened as Bernice had anticipated in an article she wrote for the Black Papers, 'The Mining of the Ivory Tower', reproduced in *The Times Higher Educational Supplement*. The Black Papers had been violently attacked by the Labour education minister Edward Short for their critique of contemporary educational trends, but Bernice's argument was that the net result of student revolution would be more of the bureaucracy and the rationalization the revolutionaries so abominated.

Since then the academic role has been increasingly undermined by the imposition of criteria based on output, impact, and the cash nexus of research grants. Academic integrity is now threatened by absurd arrangements allowing students to monitor the academic services provided, not just with regard to their efficiency, which is fair enough, but in terms of how far teachers pander to student preconceptions and their preference for good grades. I joined with Conrad Russell in co-chairing an association to defend the autonomy of the university and with a group of American academics led by Charles Frankel to produce a *Report on German Universities* focusing on disturbances at the Free University of Berlin. Once I saw what the Free University looked like under occupation, I caught a whiff of the antinomian chaos that descended on Münster in the 1530s, but with no disbenefit of religion whatever, unless you ducked the whole problem of moral disintegration by defining all such outbreaks as religious. Compared with the Germans, the English outbreaks were fairly mild, though I have never forgotten one child of privilege from Cambridge demanding the university be burned down in a final purification from all the false beauty that hid the *damnosa hereditas* of the past. At the Cambridge Union I seconded the motion that 'Marx is dead', and lost, but not by a humiliating margin. Perhaps it was a minor victory given the atmosphere. Leo Labetz, a Polish émigré, was the main proposer, and we were opposed by a communist member of the House of Lords.

I was also involved in a group called The International Council on the Future of the University with Richard Löwenthal, Alan Bloom, Martin Lipset and Edward Shils, and we produced volumes like *Universities in the Western World* (1975), edited by Paul Seabury, and *The Western University on Trial* (1983), edited by John Chapman. This was a revolt by Jewish intelligentsia, in alliance with 'the scholarship boys' – and girls – against the destruction of institutions that had in their independence lent a unique character to Western civilization. In the Seabury volume I contributed a chapter entitled 'Mutations: Religio-Political Crisis and the Collapse of Humanism and Puritanism'. This piece originally appeared in *The Times Higher Education Supplement*, and it earned me my only reference in the 'Pseuds Corner' of *Private Eye*. It was an accurate summary of what I said. There was much more critical writing of this sort by academics responding to the university crisis which has not been canvassed by people looking back later on the eruptions of the late sixties and seventies. My engagement with R. D. Laing, Jeff Nuttall and Timothy Leary was only a minute and unimportant part of this response. This material is not now part of the accepted story line, but then it was ubiquitous.

In the university during the sixties and seventies it was not always easy to trim in the right direction at the right moment, defending reason but not embracing rationalism, attentive to the facts but not adopting the restrictive protocols of positivism, acknowledging the role of perspective and interest without toppling over into relativism, aware of how intellectual work is shaped by lived life but conscious of an independent logic working in tandem with the experiential thread. I have already said my chief advantage over some colleagues lay in not being a disembodied intelligence. I was just lucky to have major problems donated by my background that I was motivated to work out.

One problem was the nature of the political, and the sources and role of violence in human affairs. Here, as a person who had worked through the logic of non-violence and the role of reconciliation in politics, I heard what the radical generation of students were saying about making love not war, and disagreed profoundly. I remembered my own self-indulgent righteousness and was embarrassed to see it writ large in a whole student generation. My sources had been the 1930s and the 1890s, and before that the pacifist and antinomian strains in the radical Reformation, and in the sixties I watched it all in action replay in an institution dedicated to understanding it. When it came to understanding violence and the nature of the political, I was influenced by the realist school and by sources that I found shocking as well as convincing, like Sorel's *Reflections on Violence*. International relations provided a model of political action which I thought inadequately integrated into sociological accounts. In particular I believed that the 'ethical dimension' in politics and foreign affairs was differently available depending on the role you occupied.

All this I set down in my piece on R. D. Laing, 'Psychiatry and Apocalypse', envisaging it as an appendix to Max Weber's 'Politics as a Vocation' and his defence of an 'ethic of responsibility' against 'the irresponsible romanticism of new ideas'. I delineated the character and role of a politician faced by impossible choices, unable even to boast of public martyrdom for some good cause, and subject to the superior scorn of bystanders as ignorant and naïve. I later added that such a person would face questions from inquisitors in the media who hide behind the requirement of 'balance'. They refuse to acknowledge the opportunity costs of alternative policies, snipe from behind hidden positions, and feel no conscientious pressure to pay even the minimum costs of consistency. The contemporary media inquisitor is a moral parasite needed to maintain the healthy ecology of democracy. As a man of high principle, Raymond Williams used a review to take exception to my portrait of the politician, and there were hints he would have dismissed it as Fascist, except that it lay too clearly in another part of the political landscape. My manifesto was written with burning indignation. These were very exhausting years for me, since the LSE was the epicentre of trouble. The graduate section of the sociology department was a centre of trouble in the LSE, and I was in charge of it.

Some of the debate turned, very unfairly, on the record of Walter Adams in Rhodesia. As one student put it to me, 'There are three great contemporary causes, Rhodesia, Vietnam and the LSE.' Another student commented, 'They dare not do anything to us. We are the future.' Yet another demanded I be 'more existential'. I explained that I only had about ten minutes' *Existenz* available per day and rapidly used it up. This kind of infantilism led me to write a piece for *The Spectator* entitled 'The Day Nursery of Revolution'. I also asked on Radio 3 whether they were expecting to have a quiet punt under Waterloo Bridge or to meet Karl Popper over a pint in the Three Tuns. Once the streaking started, I took an obvious opportunity on Radio 3 to compare their symbolic nakedness with streaking radicals in the English Revolution.

A little later, Talcott Parsons from Harvard was to give three lectures at 'the School', and when I got wind of a plan to streak at his final lecture I realized as department convenor that there was a lot to be said for not interfering. Notoriously Parsons produced rapidly diminishing audiences. So a crowd at the final lecture expecting an incident was entirely desirable. Halfway through the third lecture, Parsons was describing a typical Parsonian convergence between the USA and Russia, when three naked students appeared behind him. But they had not noticed the exit from the stage on the other side was blocked, which caused them serious embarrassment. There was a gale of laughter, but Parsons, physically and psychologically deaf, merely supposed he had made an inadvertent joke and proceeded imperturbably.

Some of the manifestations at LSE made me think Donald MacRae was right when he commented that a nation going through a utopian and antinomian revolution of this kind was bound to be badly shaken. For example, a writer in the student newspaper asserted that a particular chair was funded in an inappropriate way. I was one of the four academic governors and we invited him to offer us the evidence. He said that the truth of the assertion was irrelevant because it 'served its purpose by symbolizing our implication in the capitalist system'. On one occasion I was in charge of the School as Evening Dean and was tried by a mob for the offence of being on their premises. Somebody called the police, maybe one of the students or someone among a

David Martin, Professor, at home in his study

largish group of London anarchists, and I was then roundly abused for my stupidity in calling them. Next morning the School had quite a number of broken windows.

One very bright student wanted to undertake a study of Zen Buddhism. At his second tutorial he presented me with a blank piece of paper on the ground that any positive statement about Zen was false to the spirit of Zen. I suggested that he might look at the actual people who believed this ineffable doctrine. At the next tutorial he turned up with another piece of blank paper, saying that people thinking they truly represented Zen were by definition not true followers. After that I could only think he deserved a blank piece of paper in lieu of a PhD. *Ex nihilo nihil fit*. Another student insisted on writing without the conventional constraints of punctuation, and yet another carried on his discussion of sociology and phenomenology by writing in bilious red ink and continuing all round the page once he had reached the bottom. A radical young scholar was anxious for me to comment on his study of the Hungarian Marxist, Meszaros. I read his virtually impenetrable prose with increasing lassitude and could only point him to a construction worker on a crane just outside my sixth-floor window. I suggested he keep this member of the proletariat steadily in mind as the potential recipient of a message when expounding the logic of revolution.

The revolutionary students were a bright and fractious minority, and some, like David Maxim Triesman, emerged later as Labour government ministers. Other bright students described themselves as 'militant moderates' and later became colleagues. Eileen Barker became my immediate colleague in the sociology of religion, expanding the work of Bryan Wilson on sects into the analysis of the new religious movements that emerged in parallel with the cultural upheaval of the sixties and providing information to mediate between them and anti-cult groups and the often distressed parents of their converts. Colin Crouch was the 'moderate' President of the LSE students' union: as a colleague he worked with me on an article about religion in Britain, moved to Oxford and became chairman of the Fabian Society and Curator of the Bodleian. Another future colleague, Christopher Badcock, adroitly evaded political identification by wearing a badge with a gnomic 'NO' on it. He carried forward understanding of religion by work on Levi-Straussian structuralism, psychoanalysis and (recently) cognitive psychology, working on the autism of atheism.

Like Durkheim, Badcock cooperated with an anthropologist working on Australian aborigines, and it was the anthropologists, including Maurice Bloch at LSE and Mary Douglas at University College, who most of all gave the study of religion a secure institutional footing. The sociologists of religion at LSE kept up a relationship with them and also with historians. David Starkey, for example, had written his doctoral thesis on what was in effect the anthropology of the Tudor court at the time of the Reformation. At a crucial moment in his LSE career I defended his work against hostile critics, and I persuaded him to talk to the religion seminar I ran with Eileen Barker on the role of Anne Boleyn in the English Reformation and on other platforms about religion and kingship. I also reviewed the work of Keith Thomas for *Encounter*, and realized he was another pioneer of the use of anthropology in excavating the role of religion in early modern society.

Religion also had a place in the study of nationalism at LSE, and Gellner, Elie Kedourie and Anthony Smith, all Jews, had transformed its study, Gellner by arguing nationalism was an essentially modern phenomenon that replaced religion and Smith by an ethno-symbolic approach that placed the origins of national consciousness much earlier and allowed constant interaction between nationalism and religion. Clearly the debates within nationalism paralleled the debates in the sociology of religion over secularization. Changes in other subjects also allowed more space for religion than the kind of positivist Marxism focused on class and social mobility popular in the previous generation. Criminology had benefited hugely from the anthropological and ecological approach of my Catholic colleague Terence Morris, and it was Paul Rock, one of his students among the sixties generation, who espoused 'symbolic interactionism' at LSE. An approach that emphasized the interpretation of signs and symbols as well as the analysis of 'facts' helped bring the study of religion back to the central place it had occupied for the founding fathers, Weber and Durkheim. Whatever else the sixties did, they helped open sociology up to themes central in other disciplines like utopianism and its relation to millenarianism. One of my colleagues sent me a student essay on the Troubles that compared the multicultural assemblages of revolutionary students with the three thousand assembled in Jerusalem from Crete, Libya and the furthermost parts of Asia on the first day of Pentecost.

It fell to me, as the person in charge of sociology graduates, to take over several young scholars with unusual and creative ideas not fitting the conventional categories. I made it my business to nurture younger scholars, not only because I recollected my own unhappy experiences but because conversation with the next generation is one way to keep abreast. Two of these have stayed with me as maybe geniuses. Will Keenan had been a porter at Paddington Station, and his exam papers as an external student had shown such understanding of my arguments that I asked to meet him and we became lifelong friends. He wrote a multi-volume thesis on changes in the Marist dress code that anticipated the shift to an emphasis on 'materializing religion' in sociology and anthropology; in its brilliance it overwhelmed the requirements of a PhD.

Another extraordinary student asked me to read the extensive correspondence he was holding with a friend who lived with him in a balsawood simulation of his new theory. At some point I made a frivolous comment, opaque in a rather British way, and now impermissible, suggesting he find a nice girl and spend some time in Vienna. I do not know about the girl, but he went off and returned some considerable time later, saying he had something for me. First he deposited two volumes on my floor, then another two, and another two, and finally he placed a seventh volume on top of the other six. I began to regret the Vienna idea. This was a much more onerous task than absorbing the balsawood correspondence.

I rang up the great, good and learned Professor Rickman, one of the few people I knew steeped in German social thought, asking whether he would mind looking at this unusual work. I did not emphasize its precise length, and to my amazed relief mixed with some rather faint qualms of conscience, he agreed. About two months later Rickman rang up to say he was now into the third volume, and that this kind of thing might have been all right in Heidelberg a century ago, but was seriously overblown for current English purposes. It needed to be reduced to two volumes, including the diagrams. I passed on the news to the student, he complied, and after great difficulty we found an appropriate and willing examiner. Soon after this, concerned relatives rang me enquiring after his welfare, and I had to tell them that when we had last met he had become a Sufi.

My final contact with him came many years later through the internet, by which time he was a designer for Boeing. I was not entirely surprised when he sent me some more of his work to read and comment on, or by the fact that I did not entirely understand it.

Part 3

ANOTHER CULTURE WAR?

———◆•◆•◆———

13

The Book of Common Prayer and the KJV

Everything about my education came to a focus in my attempt to save the Book of Common Prayer and the King James Bible. These texts, with hymnody, were what I most obviously shared with my father, and now the generations were being separated from each other just where they might expect continuity. To maintain something of that continuity I found myself in correspondence with the intelligence and imagination of England. The Prayer Book, the KJV and classic hymnody for me brought together poetry, music, poetry set to music, the poetics of place, the Church in a place, and articulate speech. I thought the revisers had misdiagnosed the role of traditional language in the problems of the Church and suspected it was easier to take away and divide than to add and multiply. Our sense of the divine is not straightforwardly separate from the 'earthen vessels' in which it is embodied. What you say is not that easily divorced from how you say it, just as the message of music is not easily divorced from a sequence of notes. A liturgy is a pondered score. That is why I wrote an article about God-forsaken liturgies, even though I was as much engaged by the project of liturgical renewal as the revisers.

I did not want to write this chapter, because it was painful at the time and painful to recall. No one wants to argue about prayer, and those most concerned for the Prayer Book and the KJV were less inclined than most to argue about prayer. They were not a flash-mob in the making. It was their sense of being taken for granted to appeal to less automatically loyal constituencies that made them angry, and now I have found irenic distance I want to keep anger out of it. Prayer Book people did not want to be told what the Greek of the Lord's Prayer really meant, or asked to say 'Do not bring us to the time of trial' where their mothers had taught them 'Lead us not into temptation'. They did not greatly care what Dom Gregory Dix had to say about the four-fold shape of the Eucharist or what liturgical archaeology had unearthed from Hyppolytus Romanus. They were above all indifferent to the ecclesiastical politics of high-level ecumenical commissions that produced prayers supposedly held in common but in revised versions familiar to nobody. Quite a number wanted to be 'left in peace' rather than to 'share a sign of peace' in effusive hand-shaking, though the 'kiss of peace' had more appeal than most innovations.

Of course, for many clergy, sacred traditions 'from the time man remembereth not' were only the innovations of the generation before the last. Innovations rapidly morph into 'invented traditions'. I cared passionately about Anglican chant, but it is hardly ancient. It was all very complicated because some of what was proposed, for example about participation and the position of the altar, made good sense, and yet one could enter churches rearranged according to the best contemporary practice that contradicted the meanings and dispositions of the architecture. Once, in the great Byzantine cathedral of Périgueux, Bernice and I felt unable to last out a celebration that mocked its architectural setting and was little more than a disorganized singalong.

This memoir is not about painful emotional episodes, but about close links between personal life and intellectual engagement. It is not a history of the Prayer Book controversy with all the main players on stage, but my response to the planned ruination of my inner imagined landscape. If it retains any edginess, I am sorry, but not at liberty to pretend otherwise. There were, of course, very close links between my personal motivations for attempting to prevent the demise of the English Prayer Book, and my engagement with sociological issues. Ritual is central to both anthropology and sociology. I was attempting in sociology what Mary Douglas achieved in anthropology, above all in *Purity and Danger* and *Natural Symbols*. She understood the symbolic enactments that underpin our solidarity one with another and had a female and domestic sense of dirt as 'matter out of place'. From time to time I cooperated with Mary, and Bernice developed Mary's analysis of dirt in a piece entitled 'You Should Have Seen the Mess', which was in part a critique of the middle-class cult of disorder.

So much of the addiction to 'anti-structure' has dripped down from a sector of the upper middle class. Bernice knew what working-class respectability meant because she had been brought up in it, and her aunts had been pillars of Bury parish church, terrorizing its upper-class curates, and incumbents like the Wingfield-Digbys. Bernice also set the ecclesiastical scene in a wider context in her *A Sociology of Contemporary Cultural Change* (1981). Of course the

Church picks up and even anticipates social change. If the universities were affected by antinomian and anti-structural cults and later succumbed to bureaucracy and utilitarian criteria of impact, the Church was unlikely to stay immune.

Victor Turner was another Catholic anthropologist and friend who had a delicate sense of the relation between what he called 'liminality and communitas', and he too was an ally in the debate over ritual and the linguistic register of worship. The Catholic historian Eamon Duffy later exposed the psychological disruption of the Reformation in *The Stripping of the Altars*, and when I eventually met him we were natural allies against the cult of functional oversimplification. Of course, there is a paradox here: what I defended was a liturgy that destroyed the inner imagined landscape before the 1540s. The medieval Catholic stripping of the altars is one of the most profound enactments of the liturgical year and the Protestant service of the Royal Maundy no more than a relic of the sacrament of feet-washing. I applauded any recovery of the richness of symbolic action but deplored the functionalist doctrine of language.

The most recent defence of ritual and habit against the corrosions of spontaneity and sincerity has been launched from a Jewish perspective by another ally, Adam Seligman. If any group owes its survival to the repetitions of the rite and everything involved in Halacha, it is the Jews. One or two Jewish scholars, Gerald Hammond for example, argued that the KJV reflected the rhythms of the Hebrew Scriptures better than the modern versions, and the great scholar-rabbi Louis Jacobs read a psalm to me in Hebrew to test this, maintaining that anyone who knew the KJV ought to be able to identify it. I failed the test.

Jews and Catholics were historically better able than Protestants to understand how commitments are sustained by diurnal rhythms. In many ways the reforms actually reinforced the sense of liturgical time and space, in particular the lectionary with its subtle typological references and sequences, but most lay people do not engage with the lectionary and anyway some Evangelicals have their own freelance arrangements of topics. There is a strain in Protestant thinking which values individual spontaneity to the point where each day begins anew rather than following settled routines. The urge to make *everything* sacred easily renders everything secular by destroying boundaries and markers, and in a profound sense we no longer know where we are. The fear of times and seasons, habits and memorization by heart, is so widely diffused in contemporary culture that its Protestant roots are no longer visible. Good habits are dismissed as automatic ruts and we realize too late what has been erased by the purifying fire of iconoclasm. Perhaps new generations, many of them the highly educated women on whom the future of the Church is likely to fall, will have a more balanced retrospect of 'the darkling plain' where once 'ignorant armies' fought by night. All we can claim for our mountains of effort is that the texts are still there to be appropriated by those who care, whereas without us they would be gone for good. In 'quires and places where they sing', young people can still overhear the music of Coverdale's translation of the Psalms, and come, with time and age, to care.

Many tiny rivulets came together in the mainstream of my concern with liturgy. I had read the celebratory material published by the Church on the four hundredth anniversary of the 1549 Prayer Book while in the Army. My Methodist minister had given me Bernard Manning's *The Hymns of Wesley and Watts*, which not only confirmed my love for classic hymnody but celebrated the common inheritance of the Prayer Book and the Latin of the mass. I had also been influenced by wartime invocations of Englishness and of a historic church in a particular place you find in the paintings of John Piper, by early encounters with matins and evensong in Dorset churches, by BBC broadcasts from cathedrals, as well as by the close association of liturgical words with plangent music, like Orlando Gibbons' setting of Psalm 39. One source far upstream was playing the Passion chorale on the organ during Holy Communion in Barnes Methodist Church. The Methodists used a version of the Prayer Book, and after a dousing in soteriological cliché in a thousand sermons I found its sober cadences consoling.

At the same time I held the conventional view that the language of the sixteenth century was a barrier. My Methodist minister asked me to go away and when I had found a passage I did not understand, to ask him what it meant. To my surprise I could only locate one: 'By his one oblation of himself once offered'. He then explained to me the desire of the Reformers to avoid any suggestion of a repetition of the once-for-all sacrifice on Calvary. Occasional obscurities stimulate enquiry.

I soon realized that there was little appetite for compromise when I ran into one of the London suffragan bishops, Bill Westwood, in St George's, Bloomsbury, and he told me with some vehemence that 'In a clerically led church *we* decide.' When I mentioned the supposed role of the *laos* under the new dispensation he added, 'That's all eyewash – and anyway the Prayer Book has had its chance and we now have to try something else.' He complained that many of those

I had mobilized to defend the Prayer Book were not Anglicans: an odd retreat from the idea that the Anglican Church is the Church of *England*. If I did not want to be told how to pray by Bill Westwood, he did not want to be told how to run a Church by Beryl Bainbridge. The signature of Glenda Jackson on the petition I devised about the Book of Common Prayer aroused his particular ire.

People like Bishop Westwood genuinely believed the mission of the churches could be revived by rewriting the classic texts. This justified them in introducing the new services as 'experiments' when they had no intention of subjecting them to the judgement of effectiveness or democratic accountability. It was a respectable point of view, and I would have respected it more if enough room had been found for those whose affections lay elsewhere, and if the case for change had not been hidden behind smokescreens and false justifications. I agreed about the dubiety of doctrines of substitutionary atonement. But that was where the reformers were least open about their intentions, in part because there were articulate Evangelicals who felt their theology of the atonement best protected by the traditional text.

I had not spent many years on the causes of secularization for nothing. I was sure the decline in churchgoing had little to do with linguistic registers, and equally sure linguistic changes would not increase the appeal of the Church to young people. The whole debate felt like a struggle between the in-house movers and shakers in the Church and a wider intellectual constituency, and that impression was reinforced whenever the issue was raised in the letter columns of major newspapers. Of course, some churchmen were far more open than Bishop Westwood to that constituency, for example Victor de Waal, Dean of Canterbury, and David Stancliffe, who later chaired the liturgical commission. It was Stancliffe's father who as Dean of Winchester deepened my understanding of the Eucharist through his exposition of the poetry of David Jones.

I became confirmed as an Anglican in 1979 after years of 'occasional conformity', and tried to find a Prayer Book church, only to discover they were locally non-existent. This felt like internal exile and I wondered whether anything could be done to secure some mainstream availability of the BCP and the KJV. The cue came in a conversation with the poet and critic, Donald Davie. As a Baptist who had become an Anglican, he wondered in a musing way why there had not been more critical opposition to the deposition of the classic texts. He admired the KJV as an example of 'the plain style' he himself practised, not the 'majestic' text some of its defenders liked to talk about.

We had not joined the Church of England to find the Prayer Book no longer available. It struck me Dame Helen Gardner might be the right kind of Anglican scholar to raise the issue nationally. I wrote to the editor of the *Daily Telegraph* suggesting he approach her for a contribution, and was invited by phone to walk down to the *Telegraph* offices and meet the editor, William Deedes. Once in his office I was plied with whisky until he was free. When he came in I had a confused impression of someone who might well have consumed much more whisky than I had. He asked me what I wanted and I referred vaguely to my letter 'about the Church'.

'Ah yes, of course,' he said, 'Marxism in the Church. But we have Edward Norman for that.'

I ventured to mention the Prayer Book and he assured me this was an absolutely super idea and he would expect an op-ed piece from me in a week's time. I felt I should not further confuse him by reverting to Helen Gardner. So off I went to write 'This Great Act of Forgetting'.

When it appeared, William Deedes told me gleefully it had stimulated the largest number of letters since the issue of dogs fouling the pavement. I answered all of these letters, some of them from sad elderly spinsters, one of whom became a regular correspondent and indeed a friend whom I sometimes visited in Salisbury. I wrote another piece for the *Telegraph*, commenting on this reaction and quoting a speech of the Bishop of Southwark to the General Synod in which he said the dear old Prayer Book people barely knew whether they were praying for Elizabeth I or Elizabeth II. The editor rang me to say the Bishop was very upset, because he 'liked visiting the palace and had found the Queen not amused'. I was to be summoned before the Press Council and he would come and support me. The Bishop turned up flashing his episcopal ring and the *Daily Telegraph* editor agreed to some emollient form of words, though I am not convinced the Press Council took the matter all that seriously.

I had acquired a public profile as a controversialist I did not want and one which obscured my interest in liturgical changes that would work. I wanted conversation not contestation. Certainly I had no ambition to mobilize so-called traditionalists against progressives. I wanted to talk not to organize, and for a while I kept my distance from the Prayer Book Society. I felt I would be more effective as a lone ranger, though the Society and its leaders did most of the legwork needed to keep the issue alive. Once I acquired the incubus of a public profile, I found myself constantly rung up to engage in debate or offer comment and ruefully realized 'leadership' was a constraint not an opportunity. My comments were monitored and I had to listen to my own echo-box. Leaders are the prisoners of followings, though to say I had a following is quite an exaggeration.

I was in a dilemma, because I had no firm standing outside my expertise as a sociologist of religion and that meant calling in celebrities just to secure a hearing, even though the clout they added could boomerang rather than convince, or be confiscated by political causes in which I had no interest. Well-known figures might have their own agendas able to drive my own modest agenda off course, as I found out during an otherwise genial lunch in Fleet Street with a friendly journalist on a popular newspaper.

My new-found 'constituency' included parts of English society and of the Church where I lacked a detailed map. I discovered ins and outs of the Church which I might have preferred not to know. Some 'traditionalists' thought the Prayer Book bound up with loyalty to Queen and country, some Evangelicals thought it a bastion of Reformed doctrine, and some 'Prayer Book' Catholics thought it a repository of doctrines sustaining a 'Catholic' interpretation. Cranmer had clearly been a master of politic ambiguity.

Some of the people I met were impressive, others unusual. Earl Waldegrave was one of the most impressive and decent. He turned up one afternoon at the LSE Porter's Lodge and asked to see me. He said he was much encouraged to think that someone of the 'New Thought' had expressed what others felt in their bones but had so far been unable to express. He added that he understood me to be canvassing names for a petition and would I care to have the signatures of 'all the Knights of the Garter minus foreign royalty like the Shah of Iran'. I paused before saying that such a galaxy might well cause an imbalance or arouse negative comment, so perhaps just half a dozen Knights of the Garter would do. He looked surprised and asked if I meant that some signatories were more equal than others. That was indeed what I meant. Maybe I should have accepted the signatures of the whole Order. It would certainly have caused a stir. Earl Waldegrave left saying that it was all so simple in the old days: 'Matins at eleven o'clock, feed the horses, and into dinner.'

The Labour MP Frank Field was another impressive and decent person, who wrote to me castigating a Gang of Four as responsible for liturgical disaster, but I cannot now identify them, and in any case finding the prime movers always proved elusive. Enoch Powell proved surprisingly pleasant apart from assuming I knew Greek. He wrote saying his comments on liturgical change were so like my own I might conclude we had drawn on a common source, 'Q' (*Quelle*, source) just as the writers of the Synoptic Gospels were supposed to

167

have done. But then, as I no doubt knew, he did not believe in 'Q'. He thought difficult passages in translations of the KJV added a layer of fascinating mystery: not at all the 'simple style' that appealed to Donald Davie. He outlined a brilliant political strategy we should follow to save the Prayer Book, but so complicated I could not remember it. But I did retain the impression it would have wrecked Church–state relations as successfully as Powell had wrecked his own career by ill-judged remarks about the consequences of too many migrants in Britain.

Lord Sudeley was unusual. He 'cultivated his sensibility and ancestor worship' and traced his genealogy back to Frankish counts. He held conferences on his family history to which he was kind enough to invite me. His most famous ancestor was Katherine Parr, the last and surviving wife of Henry VIII. Merlin Charles Sainthill Hanbury-Tracy Sudeley was Vice-Chancellor of the Monarchist League and happy to remember another ancestor, one of the knights who murdered Archbishop Becket near the high altar of Canterbury Cathedral. Perhaps the old aristocratic dislike of the clergy still lodged in his mind. His family had mislaid Sudeley Castle when some financial scoundrel had relieved them of their money in the nineteenth century. When he invited me to lunch at Boodles he wanted to know whether I minded eating in close proximity to parvenu City people.

Some members of the Prayer Book Society were unhappy that the new prayers were more concerned with the spiritual and physical health of bishops and clergy than of the monarch, whereas I was put off by petitions that conducted tours of world trouble spots whenever these grabbed media attention. Those concerned for the monarch wondered what the Queen thought of it all. They felt particular pleasure when Prince Charles came to the annual occasion where young winners of the Cranmer Prize spoke the sacred texts by heart, and gave a witty speech on education, articulacy, the KJV and the Prayer Book. It was not that difficult to guess the sympathies of the Queen if you took the trouble to attend the royal chapels at Hampton Court and the Savoy.

Part of the Church of England wanted to slough off establishment associations in the public mind while not wanting the more disobliging aspects of disestablishment. At an evensong in Westminster Abbey for the Prayer Book Society, one of the canons offered prayers for a renewal of the spirit of Cranmer, implying that the actual substance of Cranmer was less desirable. Perhaps this illustrated clerical ambivalence about awkward inheritances. Following the service, the Dean asked me to look after Princess Margaret, and though I was tongue-tied, she was less inhibited and made it clear that at least one member of the royal family felt no ambivalence about awkward inheritances. The princess was for the Prayer Book.

My closest literary allies were Donald Davie and Charles Sisson, both poets and critics associated with *Poetry Nation Review*, and I came to know them well. Sisson was a man of curmudgeonly kindness with great learning in the classics and French and Italian literature. He had a surprising history which included a time in the civil service and a longish period when he was interested in Charles Maurras and French monarchist radicalism. This gave his writing an acerbic edge and one might describe him as a radical Tory like Jonathan Swift. He did not believe in the existence of a personal self, which came out in his novel *Christopher Homm*, and I wasn't sure he believed in a personal God either. He did not pray, and was clearly surprised by the idea he might. But he said the creed, and thought about it seriously, and he was passionately attached to the Church of England because it was the Church of England, not the Church of anywhere else, in particular not the Church of Rome.

I wrote an appreciation of Sisson in a special issue of *Poetry Nation Review* for his seventieth birthday which he called his 'mortuary volume':[10]

> There is no generalized nostalgia for a mythic historical past in Sisson. It is simply that for him certain things are deleterious, such as the media, the Bien Pensant style, the myths and misleading defences of 'the religion of democracy', the superstition of individuality. These are not disliked because they are modern, but because, in his view, they can distract our attention from how things are . . . The problem for anyone who reads Charles Sisson's poetry and prose is that the distinction between religion and politics is very unclear. You cannot look for the markings of religion in an inward sphere: rather they only emerge clearly in the public realm . . . Read him on William Barnes or Henry Vaughan and you find a piety which links itself to buildings, places, rites and successions . . . the church comprises a location, a building and a 'congregation of meaning': he sees it as a continuation of the historical polity in its religious aspects. Only this institution is a continuous plantation over 1800 years on this particular earth . . . So we have pietas, but do we have piety?

Mary Hesse, Basil Mitchell, Rachel Trickett, Brian Morris, Derek Brewer, Ian Robinson and Stephen Prickett were close academic allies in England, and Cleanth Brooks and Margaret Doody in the USA.[11] I naïvely took it for granted there were major issues of language and the religious 'register' (such as had been raised by Ian Robinson), and supposed the Church would be interested in the thoughts of people who understood writing. Philip Larkin wrote to me of his frustration at the way his contributions were ignored. When Rachel Trickett talked to a group of Anglican liturgists about the nature of religious language, she was shaken by the sheer hostility she encountered. Brian Morris, a poet, academic, later principal of Lampeter University College, as well as deputy Labour leader in the Lords, was particularly helpful and felt we should present the issue as one of national patrimony. We edited a book called *Ritual Murder* and the press suggested we should be sequestered together for a weekend to see if we could come up with something better than the liturgical commission.

I am glad we did not agree to this, because writing modern liturgy is difficult and takes time. What seems immediately appealing to the sentiment of the moment rapidly looks dated. You have to avoid the didacticism, typological overload and sentimentality favoured by in-house liturgical experts. The experts were scholars not writers and simply could not let a symbol do its work without telling you it was a sign. They had little sense of the close union between the signifier and the signified. Some of the services lacked any consistent vision because they represented the net consequence of a partisan tug-of-war. For example, the baptismal service halted unhappily between adult professions of faith and a potent sacramental gesture marking children with the sign of the cross to affirm their rightful presence in the kingdom of God.

Later I devised a baptismal service in contemporary English. There were problems with the Prayer Book service, and the contemporary service was verbose and required parents to make distinctly Evangelical commitments. My service began with a short homily on the meanings of water, because 'Life began in water' just as new life begins in what Philip Larkin called 'a devout drench', after which I left the 'signs' to do their work. I kept the typological references down to three: water, light and oil. I also built in the typological references about passages through water in one of the traditional prayers in the Prayer Book and modelled them on the plainchant responses in Elgar's *The Dream of Gerontius*:

> Through devout washing we are purified and cleansed and made part of new creation;
>
> By safe passage through water we enter into the promises of God; Noah in the Ark receiving a dove of peace and reconciliation; Moses in the bulrushes waiting discovery by care and love; the People of God passing through the Red Sea from slavery to liberty . . .

and so on.[12] I knew there were many people who wanted to mark the birth of their children and to have them accepted and blessed but not ready for the language of Evangelical commitment. In 2005 my chance came when I was asked to baptize the children of a lapsed Catholic woman married to an agnostic man with two charismatic Evangelical sisters. I carried out the baptism in a marquee in their garden, and the Catholic grandparents spoke of their relief at now having 'Christian' grandchildren. I had another chance to graft the contemporary onto the traditional when an ex-student asked me to officiate at a church blessing after his secular wedding. I revised the promises somewhat and set the service in the context of the dialogue in the Song of Songs between the lover and the beloved, with the congregation speaking the part of the Daughters of Jerusalem. I was asked where I had 'found' that beautiful service.

The petition mentioned by Earl Waldegrave when he called on me at the LSE came about because people had been very frustrated by indifference to their concerns conveyed quietly and privately. Tradition had to borrow modern clothes to survive and I had the idea of a petition followed up by a Gallup poll and maybe by very reluctant recourse to Parliament. I wrote hundreds of letters long-hand, each letter mentioning the interests, achievements and background of the recipient, and soliciting a signature. When I wrote to the former Prime Minister Edward Heath, I referred to his time as organist at Balliol and as correspondent for the *Church Times*. Writing to Sir Bernard Lovell, I began with his love of playing the organ, and for Laurence Olivier I recalled his years as a choir boy. The reply from Olivier first of all conveyed a polite refusal from a secretary, but Olivier had scrawled across the top in his own handwriting 'I'll sign'. My letter to Michael Foot recollected a sermon given by his father, a Methodist lay preacher and a member of the radical Liberal government of 1906–14. Foot had written a commentary on the William Tyndale translation that lay behind the KJV and knew very well the tradition of sermon writing going back to Latimer's 'Sermon of the Plough' in 1548. Occasionally I encountered profound grief, for example when A. S. Byatt told me of the tragic death of her son and how difficult it had been to persuade a clergyman to use the Prayer Book burial service. Her letter was a poignant reminder to me of the recent occasion when our youngest son, Magnus, had been close to drowning in the treacherous currents of the Dordogne before being pulled out by a French fisherman.

I started with figures on the left like Michael Foot and Edward Short and left the people one might expect to be favourable to the end, including politicians, like Lord Butler, who genuinely cared about the Church. Most of these signatures were collected by Sir John Colville, who had been private secretary to Winston Churchill.

The petition was included in a special issue of *Poetry Nation Review*, edited by myself through the kindness of Michael Schmidt its founder, and delivered to all the members of Synod just before one of its sessions. They were furious. They had done their best to update the Church and were now being criticized for it. *The Guardian* ran a headline, 'Half the people you have ever heard of'. That included many people in the creative arts, especially drama and music, because I saw liturgy as poetry and drama accompanied by music. The great names of the theatre signed the petition, often fervently: Peggy Ashcroft, John Gielgud, Anna Neagle, Flora Robson, Ralph Richardson, Peter Hall, Joyce Grenfell, Paul Scofield. Joyce Grenfell was a Christian Scientist and Paul Scofield a Catholic, so their signatures underlined the national character of affection for the Prayer Book. Journalists, being daily practitioners of the word, proved very supportive.

I also devised 'The Saint Cecilia Petition' to draw in the great names of the English musical renaissance. In my mind there were underground passageways linking the Sound of England with English poetry, including the KJV and the Prayer Book. You had only to look at the texts that inspired Benjamin Britten to have some sense of that. Britten was dead but Peter Pears signed, and so did Ursula Vaughan Williams, in company with Lennox Berkeley, Edmund Rubbra (both Catholics), William Walton, Malcolm Williamson, Peter Maxwell Davies, John Tavener and Andrew Lloyd Webber.

I particularly wanted the support of church musicians, and so I initially approached well-disposed people like Herbert Howells, Herbert Sumsion and Francis Jackson, before approaching others explaining who had already signed. Herbert Howells was a major church composer and a devout agnostic who told me he felt as though each church that abandoned the Prayer Book had a black mark against it. He was not the only devout agnostic to care deeply about the Church of England. I was particularly interested to receive a positive response from Janet Baker, because she represented the total commitment to the union of voice and verse I believed at the heart of the kind of English sensibility now under threat.

Some surprising people contacted me to express their concern and to encourage me to continue trying to secure a place for the BCP and the KJV in Anglican worship. Sir Adrian Boult, for example, rang me at home during Sunday lunch specially to alert me to other support-ers in the musical establishment. An even more surprising phone call expressing support came from the woman editing the gay and lesbian journal *Stonewall*. A distinguished journalist who had been a prime mover in the Campaign for Real Ale was just as anxious to support a campaign for Real Prayer. On the other hand some surprising people and institutions were unsympathetic, like the BBC, especially its department of religious broadcasting. I recollect a bruising radio interview about our Gallup poll with Rosemary Harthill. The BBC that had been so important for my education was fast disappearing.

The Gallup poll made just as large a splash as the petition, and *The Times* ran an editorial entitled 'Gallup to the Rescue'. But it elicited no response from the Church because it was nobody's business to deal with an informal pressure group, and we concluded, against all my instincts, that nothing remained except recourse to Parliament. I met Viscount Cranborne at his home in Chelsea. Cranborne suggested a draft bill to be voted on in the course of 1981, but only taken to its second reading. It was, he said, rather like the Eastbourne Pier Preservation Bill. It duly went before Parliament and received a favourable vote.

That *did* elicit a response and I was asked to go to Lambeth Palace to speak with Robert Runcie, the Archbishop of Canterbury. I thought I should ask the chairman of the Prayer Book Society, Tony Kilmis-ter, someone I regularly consulted, to come with me. Robert Runcie said he could 'not negotiate'. But we were not the kind of people to expect him to negotiate: we merely wanted to be heard. Gradually we reassured him and realized he was genuinely afraid of a serious rift between Church and state. There were, he said, people at the sharp end of liturgical change already threatening to campaign for dises-tablishment. At this point he invited a 'loyalist', Richard Chartres, to join the conversation, and I worked with Chartres on the outlines of an article for the *Daily Telegraph*, which included an invitation from the Archbishop suggesting that provision for the Prayer Book should be available wherever a sizeable group of parishioners wanted it. That had been precisely what the bill before Parliament had asked for.

On 11 April 1984 a revised version of the Prayer Book (Protection) Bill came before the Lords for a second reading. Almost all I recol-lect of this occasion was Lord Hailsham holding forth with forensic brilliance in favour of ecclesiastical autonomy, which on almost any other issue I would have applauded. The freedom of the Church to order its own affairs had always been a major concern of the Arch-bishop. But when I look at the account of the debate provided by my friend and collaborator Roger Homan in an issue we edited of *Faith and Worship*, I realize that the tenor of comment, beginning with a speech by the Archbishop of Canterbury, was sympathetic to the concerns underlying the bill. Some other bishops made sympathetic noises and acknowledged mistakes had been made. Earl Waldegrave spoke, along with Edward Short, Lord Glenamara. The bill was formally withdrawn by Lord Sudeley. We had achieved all we might realistically hope for. The Prayer Book was not to be consigned to the museum, and its services would remain available to worshippers.

Visiting the USA and Australia I encountered a much stronger Anglo-Catholic presence among Prayer Book 'loyalists' than in England, and felt embarrassed whenever the liturgical question became mixed up with the question of women priests. Eventually the partial conflation of these issues led to a painful 'parting of friends' who had worked together for years to save the Prayer Book in England. In the *Church Times* I argued that pressure groups were most effective when they stuck to the logic of a single issue, and that adding other issues alienated constituencies that might otherwise be favourable, as well as landing us in a generalized conservatism. A few people who embraced a generalized conservatism, including politicians like John Gummer and Anne Widdecombe, left the Anglican Church to become Catholics, and others became Orthodox. P. D. James and I agreed about keeping the Prayer Book issue separate from the debate over women priests, and we met to think over how we might work together. We approved strongly of women priests, and I felt we might have maximum effect if I resigned from the Prayer Book Society while she stayed. I do not know whether my resignation had any impact, but I expect P. D. James, in company with other influential people, like Douglas Hurd, helped keep the Society to its original purpose.

At the height of the controversy over the Prayer Book my friend John Nurser, Chancellor of Lincoln Cathedral, put it to me that, since I was exercised by liturgical change in the Church, I might consider offering myself for ordination, though I felt a distinctly grubby Christian to be publicly identified with the sacred ministry. I had twice been approached about chairs in theology and in 1983 Arthur Peacocke, Dean of Clare, Cambridge, asked me to let my name go forward as the next Dean, hoping I might continue the work he had done on theology and the biological sciences but in the area of theology and social science. However, Rowan Williams emerged as the alternative candidate, and I probably owe him a great deal for preventing what might easily have been a disastrous move. As for my ordination, the Bishop of Guildford, David Brown, proved far from encouraging, and told me I had set myself up 'against the mind of the Church and the Holy Spirit'. But the Dean of Guildford, Anthony Cyprian Bridge, was a doughty supporter, smoke poured out of the Deanery and the Bishop calmed down. I was accepted and went to Westcott House, Cambridge, for just one term.

I wanted to be assigned to a parish but I was seriously exhausted. Only a little earlier I had spent three weeks in the Westminster Hospital in the Fulham Road recovering from chronically high blood pressure. On leaving hospital I was too tired even to grasp the instructions about dosage and took pills in amounts that caused walls to cave in on me and gave me a lightness of being that tempted me to step out of a fast-moving train. There were many reasons for all this, but one was the difficulty of combining my various roles at the LSE with public campaigns, not just about the Prayer Book but about the state of education generally: so-called 'progressive education' by osmosis as well as the outbreak of anarchy in the universities. Trying to do something about the situation in the comprehensive schools, to which as people who had relied on scholarships to make up for lack of money we sent our children as a matter of principle, was as exhausting as defending the classic texts of the Church and the nation. The tension caused by so many calls on my time, as well as other emotional pressures, meant I was assigned to light liturgical duties at Guildford Cathedral.

I now had the chance to combine priesthood and poetry through the discipline of sermon making. Charles Sisson had edited three volumes of the sermon and I wanted to practise the ancient craft in a modern way. It is not easy to write sociology decently, because it deals in passives and abstractions. The sermon is very different because it deals with generic human experience of divine epiphany and the waste of sin, with acceptance of 'the world' as good yet flawed and in need of restoration, and with the paradox of a descent into the earthly to ascend to the heavenly. I could draw on the solid poetry of the liturgy as well as on English poetry from 'The Dream of the Rood' to Hopkins, Eliot and Auden, and English hymnody. The sermon is an art form that juxtaposes quotations and releases the charged-up energies stored in minute atoms of text and the multiple meanings of single words.

Two books stimulated my invention when faced by emptiness of spirit and blank paper: Northrop Frye's *The Great Code: The Bible and Literature*, and *The Bible References of John Ruskin* by Mary and Ellen Gibbs. Like poetry, a sermon is designed to be spoken, and you

David Martin with the Very Revd Anthony Cyprian Bridge,
Dean of Guildford, at the author's ordination as deacon in 1983

Practising the Eucharist in the kitchen of Cripplegate Cottage,
with granddaughter imitating, spring 1985

find out what is wrong and what will work by reading it out loud beforehand. It is a performance art, but one where you need to subordinate yourself to the text message in every sense of the word. Illumination depends on discipline as much in preaching as in musical performance. These two kinds of performance have been the most satisfying privileges of my education.

Part 4

EXPLORATIONS IN SECULARIZATION AND PENTECOSTALISM

14

The ecology of secularization:
the Balkans, Scandinavia – and Rome

———◆·◆·◆———

Throughout my academic life I embarked on research journeys as part of the project handed me by my early experience in a revivalist home. There was first the issue of secularization. Then there was the reappearance of Christian revivalism recognizably like the world of my father, but in places he had never even heard of in 'the Global South'. These were the two nodes of my work and I had to canvass them *in situ*. When I compared different kinds of religion and trajectories of secularization I evoked visual images of *place*: landscapes and cityscapes. I worked with visualizations of the shrines of Bavaria, the juxtaposition of mosques and churches in Sarajevo, the French and German architectural styles representing the *paté de foi* in Strasbourg. The religion of a place could never be separated from its politics. There is an isomorphic relation between religious and political patterns and this was brought into play years later in May 2003, when Romano Prodi, then President of the European Commission, invited me to speak to a reflection group about the issue of an *Invocatio Dei* in the Preamble to the EU Constitution.

These patterns were embedded in much larger cultural areas: the Alpine region, the Mediterranean littoral or the North European plain or the eastern borderlands of Galicia and Transylvania. Between 1964 and 1969 I had opportunity to look at the astonishingly uniform pattern of secularization in Lutheran Scandinavia, and the more variable pattern in south-east Europe. The contrast between north-west and south-east Europe provided two patterns of secularization. I not only needed to contrast Dover and Calais but Bergen in Norway and Plovdiv in Bulgaria.

I went first to Bulgaria and then to Bergen. Bulgaria offered me the kind of material that can yield pleasing paradoxes if you stay around long enough. A Marxist sociologist not only told me that Bulgaria represented the true Marxist dénouement of secularization whereas Poland was artificially held back, but added that England would in due course catch up and become as secular as Bulgaria. Early in the twenty-first century his prediction came true, because decline in England matched recoveries in Bulgaria.

The Balkans first arrived at my door with the advent of an admirably resourceful would-be migrant. Some time in 1954 I received a letter out of the blue from a student at Ljubljana University in Slovenia, called Smilja, in which she described herself as of medium height, with green eyes and brown hair. She was studying 'the English literature' and had a problem with a late Middle English text, a *fabliau* of five or six hundred lines, which maybe I would translate for her. I was astounded but also intrigued by the idea of translating this esoteric and erotic text. She appeared gratified by my efforts and wrote to say she was now coming to London and hoped I would meet her 'at the station'. I missed her at Victoria and on arriving home found her already there, chatting with my wife, Daphne. I arranged for her to stay with my mother while we worked out what to do, including what to do with her large pile of £50 notes. I took Smilja to the Bank of England, only to find the notes were part of Hitler's plan to drop currency on England and destabilize the economy. The Bank expropriated them, leaving us looking after a young woman in total penury.

I took Smilja for a chat about her future along the towpath by Chiswick Bridge. She astounded me by asking me to marry her. My reply was equally astounding because I said marrying her would be problematic since she was a Catholic.

She rapidly dispatched this: 'I become Protestant.'

I resorted to the clincher. 'Smilja, I am married already. It is really difficult.'

It seemed best to introduce her to a London Yugoslav club. There she met a very nice young man and they left England to live happily in the United States. Soon after I wrote to the BBC World Service, saying the class war in Shepherds Bush for the next 40 years was not what I really wanted, and I would do anything, even learn Romanian or Bulgarian, to get out. They wanted evidence of my ability in languages, and I heard no more.

The next encounter with the 'gorgeous East' came with a British Council visit to Bulgaria. I went because a radical student, Robin Blackburn, told me of an article in the *Revue française de sociologie* by Professor Ochavkov, claiming the census of 1962 showed Bulgaria had become the first country to approach complete secularization. Women, the old, rural people and those separated from advanced means of production, as well as those who had lost power and wealth by the revolution might lag behind, but the march of statistics and history was inexorable. As backward elements passed away, religion would pass away with them. The Bulgarian Committee for Cultural Relations was happy to cooperate with the British Council to subject this achievement to sociological scrutiny.

Unfortunately, the Bulgarians could not imagine anyone arriving by rail rather than air, so there was no one to meet me at the main station in Sofia. This took a lot of contorted French and German to sort out. My guide, and future friend, was Kyril Delev, a philosopher working on bourgeois philosophy and a member of the ideological powerhouse in Sofia University. He was interested in what use Marxists might make of my colleague Ernest Gellner's critique of Wittgenstein in *Words and Things*. He enjoyed this critique: it had a 'witt' on every page. He also introduced me to Bulgarian philosophers, one of whom informed me 'We may now praise Jean-Paul Sartre.' Kyril said this was not ironic because Sartre's recent move towards Marxism had made him acceptable. I asked whether Bulgarian intellectuals had any dialogue with Christians and Kyril said truth could not debate with superstition. Religion might once have been a positive force but now it was ineluctably negative, like bourgeois nationalism. I also met Professor Ochavkov to discuss the 1962 census. He said if the figures had shown Marx was wrong about religion, he would trust the figures. Happily Marx was right. Belief of all kinds stood at 78 per cent among those over 69 and at 12 per cent among those between 18 and 23. One day 'Anglia' would catch up with Bulgaria: a touch of 'negative' bourgeois nationalism, perhaps.

Kyril warned me the women who infested the hotel were likely to be informers anxious to trap foreigners. I was never propositioned, but while I observed the portraits of leaders of the revolution in a special museum a young woman sidled up and rubbed my arm with her breast. Kyril asked if the forwardness of young Bulgarian women surprised me and explained this was a regular hazard for Western visitors, because they wanted a passport to the West. Later, when I invited him to Britain I took him to Tolpuddle in Dorset, where six Methodist labourers started a trade union. He asked whether I had registered with the local police. When I said it was not something I needed to do, he commented this made adultery very easy in Britain. 'In my country,' he said, 'registration either makes you liable to blackmail or the police want to be included.' He also commented on the very different origins of British Labour and Bulgarian communism. Kyril constantly oscillated between his Marxist persona and acute observation of historic difference. Walking around Woking with me, he wanted to know where the guards were protecting the homes of the bourgeoisie. After reading the dissident historian Roy Medvedev, he made some incautiously critical remarks about Russia and had a nightmare in which Lenin appeared as his accuser.

Whenever Kyril and I talked about politics in Bulgaria he insisted we do so in the open air. He suspected my hotel was bugged, and at home he was afraid his son might overhear our conversation and accidentally drop something incriminating at school. Maybe I was indeed under some kind of observation, because when I did some writing and dropped rejected text in the toilet, men rapidly appeared and drained it. I mentioned this when a discussion got very hot after I gave a talk to Kyril's department. The discussion turned on Krushchev's secret speech of 1957 about the nature of Stalin's tyranny. The atmosphere was already acrid before I mentioned the bugging,. It did not improve, and Kyril was quite defensive on my behalf. He said bugging was routine.

I visited the cultic sites of Bulgarian religion, beginning with the cultic sites of state atheism, in particular the museum of 'scientific atheism' in Plovdiv. The museum was liberally spattered with quotations from Dickens on the Catholic Church, Pavlov on religion as the consolation of the weak, and the usual material from Lenin, Marx and Engels. The scientific section began with a comparison of religious and scientific cosmologies. The comparative religion section assumed what is derived or paralleled between religions cannot be true. The rest was mostly social critique: Paul on women and slaves, Protestant pastors as American spies, religious leaders promoting violence, the Inquisition, and nuns with rifles in the Spanish Civil War. The main site of state ideology was the mausoleum of George Dimitrov, hero of the Reichstag trial, which is close by party headquarters in Sofia and guarded by two motionless soldiers. There I saw a quiet and respectful queue waiting to enter the chamber. As for the party HQ, a Bulgarian academician asked me to observe carefully the symbolism of its architecture, resting weightily on the foundation of the people.

My most sobering visits were to a small Catholic minority near Plovdiv and to Protestants under suspicion as foreign subversives by Orthodox and communists alike. The Catholics were mostly descendants of Bogomil heretics (Paulicians) converted by Italian Franciscans in the sixteenth century, just as some Bogomils in Bosnia and some other Paulicians in Bulgaria were converted to Islam. The area was dominated by Italianate churches, but I found the priests living in chicken runs. Some priests had been executed in the early fifties, but an account I gave for the Third Programme on my return omitted the dire conditions of these people to protect my informants. The Catholic bishop was very wary, and met my enquiry about the social sources of recruits to the priesthood with the dead-pan answer 'Pious people.' The survival of Catholicism he attributed to the grace of God: no sociological quibbling about the solidarity associated with small and distinctive territorial minorities.

The Protestants were even more wary, since a number of pastors were still in prison, even though it was nearly 20 years since they were convicted of spying in show trials. Before that Protestantism had been making progress, as it was to do again, later, in response to Pentecostalism. When I asked the pastor of the Methodist church in Sofia about his imprisoned colleagues, he gave me a quick, anxious look and said, 'Don't you imprison traitors in your country?' I met the wives of the imprisoned pastors at morning service, and soon after visited them in a run-down part of town. To get to their apartment I had to step gingerly through human excrement deposited in the stairwell. They made me a cup of tea and spoke longingly of a visit to England many years before, and pointed to a picture of a water-mill, which I recognized as Pyrford Mill, five miles from my home. At least one of the pastors died soon after release. In the Congregational church in Plovdiv the pastor told me his congregation had once been large and lively, but was now much reduced. When I asked why, he said some were dead and some had jobs in the public administration. Cutting further discussion short, he suggested I play the organ, and put in front of me a hymn from the Bulgarian Congregational Hymnal. The tune was 'God Save the King'.

My time with the Orthodox was less a matter of interviews than soaking up the way Orthodoxy was intertwined with ways of acting, with the history of the nation and the language, and with sacred buildings in a sacred landscape. Rila monastery lies in an idyllic mountain bower, though I am not sure if its monks had yet returned. I looked at the premonitions of a renaissance parallel to the West in the murals of the Boiana church, cut short by Ottoman occupation, and I listened to the plangent singing of the choir in the Alexander Nevsky cathedral in Sofia. The name of the cathedral reminded me of the deep if ambivalent connection between Russians and Bulgarians.

Of all the religious groups in Bulgaria the Jews were the saddest remnant, though they had been protected from deportation in the war by a tradition of tolerance in Bulgaria and by the Orthodox patriarch. Nevertheless they came under economic pressure under communism, even though many were politically on the left. Most left for Israel in the late forties. The beautiful main synagogue in Sofia was in 'Old Mauretanian' style and some Jews still spoke Ladino, a form of Spanish, in the home.

The Jewish situation contrasted with that of the Muslims, whether Turks or Pomaks. (According to one contested version of history, the Turks had given the Pomaks the choice of massacre or conversion.) The Muslims were concentrated in particular parts of the country, notably the south-east near the Turkish border. I went to the mosque in Kardjali with Kyril, and encountered male socks uncomfortably close to my nose when my head touched the ground. As we left the mosque I was confronted by a line of mendicants, many of them disabled. When I went on to Istanbul, my Turkish hosts said the Bulgarian communists had recently forced many Turkish Muslims to adopt Christian names (*sic*) or to emigrate to Turkey. Once in Istanbul I had arrived at a city long imagined, and entered the Blue Mosque and the Church of the Divine Wisdom with awe. I walked by the walls of Byzantium and looked at 'the gong-tormented sea'.

Turkey was a Muslim country attempting a modest modernization under the Ottomans, and imposing a secular regime after defeat. It was not easy to fit Turkey into an account of secularization based on Europe, which suggests profound differences of civilization and development. But the (seeming) homogeneity of Turkey did alert me to the logic of modern nationalism in enforcing ethnic, religious and ethno-religious unity. Apart from intermittent massacres by the Ottomans to secure obedience, Christians, Jews and Muslims had lived in close proximity, in Beirut, Alexandria, Mostar, Sarajevo, Smyrna, Heraklion, Salonika, Jerusalem, Amman and Baghdad. With the rise of nationalism, maybe first in 1492 in Spain, there began a constant exchange of populations to secure homogeneity, above all in times of war and civil conflict, for example, Turkish attacks on its large Muslim minorities, and the murder or expulsion of its Christian minorities. These were paralleled by the expulsion of Muslims from the Crimea, Greece, Crete, and Bulgaria, and by the expulsion or anticipatory withdrawal of Jews from almost everywhere.

This was something I was very much aware of in 1986 when I visited Lebanon, where ethnic and religious mobilization destroyed the fragile balances of power for which it had once been celebrated. Latent tensions, particularly where civilizations overlap, as in the Balkans and the Caucasus, are fuelled by memories of forced conversions, and by victories won, and crucial battles lost. In Lebanon a Catholic at the University of St John told me, 'The Muslims are trying to avenge Poitiers' which occurred 13 centuries earlier, while in Jordan I was told, 'We are in mourning for Granada.' Carefully tended memories of traumatic defeats like Kosovo and Mohacs, or recollections of victories like the defence of Vienna in 1683 and of Malta, as well as of the (temporary) triumph of Lepanto, never lie down and die, they are so potent in maintaining national unity.

That is as true in Scandinavia, where I made my second research journey in the late sixties, as it is in the Balkans, except that Scandinavia is unusually homogeneous and the crucial battles mostly long ago. Anyone who has joined the vast crowds for re-enactments of the semi-mythic founding history of Olaf in Norway has some sense of the unifying power of myth, including myth reconstructed by nationalist intelligentsias. Scandinavian countries are unified both religiously and politically, in spite of times when either Denmark or Sweden has been hegemonic. Any sociologist interested in the paradoxes of secularization, in the interaction of political and religious patterns, and in similar effects arising from similar causes, finds Scandinavia a rich source of evidence. How has it come about that these five Lutheran nations have all engendered a social democratic political culture, and a uniform pattern of secularization where between 2 and 4 per cent of the population attend church on any Sunday, but a very much larger percentage are confirmed? Are we all following in the wake of the Scandinavians? Why are they so religiously active in the USA, so ardent in missionary work abroad and so religiously inactive at home?

I first took ship to Bergen and then train to Oslo and Copenhagen to find out. Bergen is a major example of a periphery in relation to the centre, now in Oslo. It fits the dialectic of centre and periphery, just as the 'periphery' of religious Wales once did in relation to London. Bergen has a distinctive dialect and has been the home of the Haugean movement, parallel to Calvinist Methodism in Wales, as well as a stronghold of the 'old Left'. Those who have travelled along the indented coast of western Norway, as far north as Trondheim and beyond, will sense the role of geography in shaping insular and peninsular pieties resistant to metropolitan influences. Just as there have been insular pieties in the western isles of Scotland or in north Wales, such pieties have flourished in the protected enclaves and islands of Norway. Whether a pious periphery can resist a secular centre partly depends on its size and modern communications. If Bavaria, with its great shrines, is a periphery, it is a very large one, and so is the American South.

In Denmark I was visiting one of the most secular countries in Europe. Church and nation are so closely integrated citizenship is as much a criterion of membership in the Church as baptism. My host had carried out a study of baptism, and the Danes, like the English, had remarkably inchoate and inarticulate reasons for having a child baptized. As one later study reported: why should one go to church on Sunday when one could live in Denmark all seven days in the week? During my stay in Copenhagen I spent time with students, one of whom came from the pietist periphery of rural Jutland. It occurred to me that a number of radical students opposed to certain kinds of capitalist modernity came from pious peripheries. An old friend, Pal Repstad, has considerable sympathy for the small, often independent, pious communities in parts of Norway and has taken me through mountain, dale and fjord in a spirit of loving enumeration. My Danish student successfully drew me into his world, and when I was interviewed on Danish television my interlocutor commented I displayed 'a typical Jutland attitude'.

I saw Denmark through the lens of Kierkegaard when in fact his great antagonist, Grundvig, was far more influential. Our family had once stayed in the rectory of the biographer of Grundvig in Asperup-Roerslev, near the Little Belt, and there I had gained some idea of his influence on the creation of a Danish national spirit, especially through the folk high school movement. Denmark is homogeneous in a way our disunited kingdom is not, and I think the combination of an overall homogeneity in Scandinavia with any number of resistant peripheries mirrors a splintered geography which nevertheless does not favour the kinds of difference created by the geography of Scotland and Ireland, and even of Wales, Cornwall and East Anglia. Jutland and the Bergen hinterland provided me with a model of difference and dissent transferable much later to places as far away as the Yucatan peninsula.

My road led me to the resistant centre: Rome. In 1969 an invitation came from the *Secretariatus Pro Non Credentibus* to join other sociologists to discuss 'The Culture of Unbelief'. They included Peter Berger, Bryan Wilson, Talcott Parsons, Robert Bellah and Harvey Cox. The presence of Harvey Cox was intriguing because he was a major influence in the currently fashionable movement of secular theology, including the 'Death of God' theologians. This movement embraced secularization, both as a social process and as a working out of Christianity. A cautiously sceptical sociologist like myself, who questioned the immanent *telos* secularization theory had taken over from theology, had to argue against theologians who believed that was a thoroughly good thing. They were not interested in my analysis of variable patterns, but in recommending a theology of history, culminating with Harvey Cox's brilliantly written book *The Secular City*. Secularization was all the rage in theological circles, especially in Holland, where I had attended an excitable conference in Nijmegen. 'The Death of the Church' was a favourite theme in the sixties: it mirrored a zeitgeist opposed to institutions in every sphere and anticipated the advent of 'spirituality'.

Rome had been through the metamorphosis of the Second Vatican Council, but had not embraced the Secular City, being aware it would rapidly put the Eternal City out of business. Peter Berger made me convenor of a discussion group, but seeing it was a marvellous day we agreed a walk in the park by the Villa Borghese would be better than talking about the culture of unbelief. However, when we returned, refreshed but guilty, Italian television had turned up, and wanted an account of the afternoon's deliberations. Being naïvely honest I confessed to Peter we had strolled in the sun instead. 'Make it up,' he said, as the whole conference assembled for the TV interview. I gave a version of the paper I had written, 'Towards Eliminating the Concept of Secularization', while my companions on the stroll in the park gazed in astonishment. Afterwards I apologized profusely, but they understood the call of necessity.

The climax came with our private audience with the Pope. I went on the coach with Bryan Wilson, who was exercised by two problems. A priest had given us each a medallion and had requested we either keep it or give it to a Catholic relative or friend. As a man of honour, Bryan was desperately trying to think whether he knew anyone in either category. Though determined to be his usual courteous self, he was equally determined to make no obeisance to the head of an organization he cordially detested. Obeisance to our queen well befitted a true-born Englishman, but this Italian foreigner was a very different matter. As we made our way through the Vatican, Bryan noticed a reference to Paul VI and queried which of the many popes he might be.

In the audience hall Pope Paul VI took time to arrive and elegant ladies gathered expectantly behind us. When the Patriarch of the West eventually entered in dazzling white, he omitted to give his usual benediction, perhaps out of sensitivity towards sociologists he could not assume were devout believers. The elegant ladies immediately moved their arms rhythmically so that the numerous objects of devotion they carried made a pleasant jingle, apprising the Pope he had omitted something. He raised his hands in benediction, and said, with admirable inclusiveness, 'All is blessed.'

Each of us met the Pope in turn, and he was kind enough to assure Talcott Parsons he was acquainted with his work. Harvey Cox had promised to break with protocol by talking to the Pope 'man to man'. 'After all,' he said, 'here we are meeting one of the loneliest men on the planet and surely he would appreciate a truly personal word.' As Harvey met the Pope he was thrown off balance by the Pope saying he had been very stimulated by *The Secular City*, though Harvey would understand he had certain reservations. This seemed to be Harvey's moment for the personal word, but instead he held out his hippy rosary and murmured, 'Bless this rosary, Holy Father.' Afterwards I asked him what had happened to the personal touch, and he confessed the Eternal City had blotted out the Secular City just at the crucial moment. But afterwards at a reception Harvey 'got the girl', and she was Audrey Hepburn. That is all I remember about the occasion, apart from a black-coated priest gliding past me to ask yet another elegant lady, 'And how is the beatification cause of your dear uncle?'

Meeting Pope Paul VI at a conference on 'The Culture of Unbelief'
at the invitation of the Secretariatus Pro Non Credentibus, *Rome, 1969*

15

Buddhist revival in Japan, Islamic revival in Lebanon

———◆◆◆———

Pentecostalism crept up on me by unexpected routes. I knew it was making inroads in Latin America, but I supposed the future lay with Marxism and liberation theology, or even maybe with secular liberal democracy. But experience began to change my mind. In 1978–9 I went to Japan and realized there was more than one way to modernize and these ways might include a role for religion. Buddhist revival movements were making a mass appeal to millions of Japanese in what was otherwise a very secular society. In 1986 I went to Lebanon, and the representatives of the large Christian (Maronite) minority asked me whether there was any Christian equivalent of Islamic revival. It took me a while to realize that Pentecostalism in Latin America, and soon all over the Global South, was not only analogous to Buddhist revivalism in Japan and elsewhere but was the global equivalent of Islamic revivalism.

It began when Eimi Watanabe became my student at the LSE. She was a Finnish Lutheran and a member of a famous Japanese musical family. She could recite the fractured Latin retained by Japanese Catholics throughout an underground existence after the terrible persecutions of the seventeenth century. Eimi expressed contempt for the Western obsession with Zen, but she did want to study the Japanese new religions. She needed a framework and I dared for her what I would not have dared for myself. She should compare the 'new religions' of Japan in the north-east Pacific with the 'new religion' of Pentecostalism in Chile in the south-west Pacific. Japan and Chile were similar in their socio-economic development. The intensification of faith among expanding religious minorities in two rapidly modernizing countries, one Buddhist, the other Catholic, could parallel the historical intensification of faith through Evangelical revivals in Britain. In Britain it had been Methodism. Nowadays it was an offshoot of Methodism: Pentecostalism. My father's Evangelical faith was burgeoning in places he had never even heard of.

In 1978 I became a Japan Society Fellow and was invited in my role as president of the Société Internationale de Sociologie des Religions (SISR) to visit Japan for a conference and an extended visit in the company of SISR colleagues. The trip was initiated by an invitation to meet a Japanese representative in a London club with another prospective visitor, Lord Long. Lord Long was to meet the crown prince, whereas I, being under 50 and interested in religion, was to meet the Shinto high priest. In due course Bernice and I, with our children Jessica, Izaak and Magnus, were on our way to Japan via Pakistan International Airways (PIA, aka Please Inform Allah) and Islamabad. The outward journey proved uneventful, but on the way back Allah was gracious and compassionate. A door fell off and stranded us in Istanbul.

Once in Japan our learning curve was steep, especially when adjusting our bows for differences of status. Other adjustments took longer, for example when our liberated female guides asked questions of priests on our behalf considered impertinent coming from a woman. A young woman was assigned to accompany us to the Ise peninsula to a traditional Japanese inn. I thought she might help us decipher train times at crowded termini, but it seemed her role was to sleep with us. We indicated we could handle sleeping on our own, but she took some persuading.

Honour mattered seriously in the conference, because senior Japanese scholars did not want to be shamed by criticism and had their papers read for them by juniors. Later we were addressed by a former Japanese minister of education who explained in how many ways Japan had overtaken the West, Britain in particular. I replied his unfavourable comparisons were no doubt correct, but part of the answer might lie in the unfortunate fact we in Britain had never been conquered by the Americans. The silence following was long and furious. Rules had been broken on both sides. Happily, when I later inquired into the meaning of my hosts' names, like 'little cherry tree trailing in the water', and wrote haikus on them, all was delight. On one occasion I was confused because the chairman of a lecture I was to give at the Oriental Institute was still introducing me after half an hour. The point was not to hear what I had to say but to prove I was worth hearing.

Almost the first 'new religion' we visited fulfilled my best expectations of a 'functional equivalent' of English Nonconformity. We were taken around a large hall, like the Methodist Central Hall, Westminster, and with similar galleries, except that each corner was occupied by people acquiring useful skills. Then we met the leader of the religion, which numbered three million or so believers. He was a 'living god' and we should prepare questions appropriate to our privileged access. This task was initially mine, but I fell short by asking a question about burial rites, which our translator, Father Jan Swingedouw, hinted showed mere curiosity. Big occasions demand big questions.

This was brought home when the living god told me he had recently met another living god in the Vatican. So I asked what were the three most pressing problems facing the world. Half an hour later it appeared this was the right question and it was the turn of my colleague, Hans Mol, who mistook the occasion for a sociology seminar. Since the living god was plainly concerned about world peace, Mol wanted his solution to the way solidarity at a subordinate system level exacerbated conflict at the super-ordinate system level. Father Jan stared, promised a properly idiomatic translation, and suggested Mol refrain from elaboration. Later he whispered to me that our host really had 'wrapped that one up', so he must have done a virtuoso job.

The visit to the Perfect Liberty Church was charming. It began with its art gallery, replete with modern erotic masterpieces for the better edification, or pleasure, of the members. Pleasure and edification were not sharply distinguished. Then we looked in on the hospital, where appropriately insured church members received diagnoses in modern medical language surrounded by personalized horoscopes. As it was Sunday, Jessica, Izaak and Magnus were offered morning worship on the equipment in a magnificent pleasure park. Finally we ascended a 500-foot 'peace tower', built with a wobble in the middle because that was how it had appeared to the leader in a wet dream. At the top of the tower the names of the dead on all sides in the Second World War were recorded.

The next 'new religion' was extremely popular because the leader had a hot-line to God. He sat surrounded by devotees with a telephone to his ear while he phoned God with their problems and relayed the answers.

The largest new religion in Japan was the Soka Gakkai, which had disputed relations with Komeito, the third largest party in the Japanese parliament. The leader explained the relationship was less close than critics suggested. Religion should steer clear of too much political involvement. I sat opposite him for our talk, while a beautiful young Japanese woman sat demurely and supportively at his side. Meanwhile a Japanese professor played music to attend the happy occasion, which was supplemented by drinks all round. The appalling frankness allowable after the slightest sip of alcohol had to be treated as though it had never happened. Later the leader phoned me to suggest we meet but I admitted I had a prior engagement, not realizing priority did not trump status. The invitation was not renewed, much to my relief because the leader was in the habit of having very long conversations with foreign visitors, later to be published.

We did the usual things, like visiting the shrines of Kyoto and the imperial shrines, as well as attending the vast popular ceremonies at the New Year, and having the scheduled meeting with the Shinto high priest. I had a particular interest in the curious status of Christianity in Japan, especially as compared with its variable penetration and status in Korea, China and Taiwan. There was little doubt about why Christianity took off in Korea and not in Japan. In Korea it was allied with nationalism over against China and Japan, while in Japan it was associated with foreign intrusion, hence the rise of Buddhist rather than Christian new religions.

Yet at Christmas, overhearing carols in the university, you might have supposed Japan seriously engaged by Christianity, at least in the educated urban middle classes. We soon discovered the millions celebrating in Tokyo on Christmas Eve were the non-Christians, whereas the Christians were in church. We found many universities and colleges were linked to religious groups, including the Soka Gakkai, and a remarkably large number had Christian foundations, some of the most impressive being for women. When Bernice gave a lecture in one famous Christian college for women the different attitude to women was palpable. Elsewhere she had been introduced as 'the wife of David Martin'. One academic we visited in the Quaker-like quiet of his home belonged to the Japanese 'no-church' movement, a Christian group that eschewed organization.

While staying at a beautiful Quaker guest house in the country, we attended Sunday morning service in a Pentecostal church on a poor housing estate. Once the pastor knew we were present, I had to give a greeting, and the pastor then translated his address into English as he went along. Afterwards we gathered for what I took to be a shared agape, receiving rice into our hands rather than bread: that kind of inclusion in the body of Christ you do not forget. During the war many mainstream Christians felt an obligation to conform to the imperial cult, but some Pentecostal pastors (and some leaders of Buddhist new religions) did not, and were executed.

Our visit to Japan altered our view of modernity and its relation to religion. Back in the sixties I had argued that the future of humanity was not necessarily prefigured by the contrasting forms of secularity in France and Sweden. There were many possible roads to modernity, including the alliance of religion, enlightenment and science found in the USA. But Japan seemed to be an example of a genuinely 'alternative modernity', in the sense later used by S. N. Eisenstadt. Up in the mountains we watched a violent exorcism performed by a traditional practitioner on a woman while the Japanese watched television. The fastest train in the world took us to the marbled temple of Daisekerji, a 'stately pleasure dome' raised by Soka Gakkai under the sacred shadow of Mount Fuji. The television tower in Tokyo was dedicated to the tutelary gods of Japan. In Islam and in Pentecostalism, or even in the earth mysticism of the ecological movement, the most modern technology coexists with religious forms that thrive on its use. Sociology has been constructed on the opposition of ancient and modern, but it ain't necessarily so.

Islamic (and Christian) revival in Lebanon

Just before taking up the study of Pentecostalism in 1986, I looked back to the gorgeous south-east and agreed to speak at a conference in Beirut on Christian and Islamic revivalism, though my task was to compare the conflict in Northern Ireland to the conflict in Lebanon. The relevance of Islamic revival was obvious but the issue of Christian revivalism struck me as opaque, unless I concentrated on the Evangelical traditions that linked the north of Ireland with the American South, and the Welsh revival with the emergence of Pentecostalism. Yet the answer to the question of Christian alongside Islamic revivalism lay precisely here. Christian revival had taken the form of Pentecostalism, just as the Buddhist revival had taken the form of the Japanese and Taiwanese new religions.

The invitation to Lebanon appealed to an old interest in the borderland of civilizations, and in religious and cultural enclaves and peripheries: Swedish-speaking and Orthodox Finland, Alsace, Ulster, the Waldensians of Piedmont. I weighed the dangers against what might be a uniquely instructive experience and decided to go, with my wife. Lebanon, after all, was a broken-off fragment of the Greek vision of a reconstituted Hellenic and Byzantine eastern Mediterranean, and a fragment of the Turkish and French empires, as well as a Catholic foothold in the eastern Mediterranean littoral, like the Latin Kingdom of Jerusalem. It was also a Maronite enclave in an Islamic sea, like the Egyptian Copts, and Beirut was a religious entrepôt like Strasbourg, Sarajevo, Salonika, Odessa and L'viv.

The visit was initiated by a mysterious letter from the *Mouvement Antélias*, asking me to meet two Maronite priests at the Worplesdon Hotel, near Woking. They were anxious to re-establish Beirut as a cultural meeting point in spite of the kidnaps and violent conflicts. The Foreign Office suggested we might travel by sea from Cyprus to avoid passing through Muslim Beirut. The priests waved that aside, promising we would be escorted through Muslim Beirut to Christian Beirut by the Lebanese army. I did not realize the Lebanese army only controlled a couple of villages, and at Beirut airport there was no sign of it. Instead a Christian taxi driver said he would take us through Muslim Beirut and across the notorious 'green line'. We would be followed in another car by a trusted Muslim guard armed with a machine gun, though the guard would peel off just before we reached the green line. We travelled safely through Muslim Beirut, a mainly Shia area full of Khomeini slogans, and, after some scrutiny, we were allowed to pass over the green line. Our taxi-man crossed himself devoutly and the sight of a Christian church told us the danger was over.

Our destination was a nunnery overlooking the city, a serene place, surrounded by cedars, except for the regular sound of firing from other hills overlooking the city. Some of the Christians we met had been expelled from their ancestral villages in the Chouf Mountains and had taken refuge in the city. One of our meetings took place in a sand-bagged monastery underground where I met a Shia scholar who had become a Christian monk and now devoted himself to the translation of Persian literature. Another monk took us by car into the mountains above the Bekaa Valley, a journey made perilous more by other drivers than rival militias, and entertained us with ancient Syrian folk melodies, of which he was an assiduous collector.

The main venue for the conference was the largest church in the Middle East, a new concrete building with modern facilities. Sunday morning mass in Arabic was a lively charismatic affair, with a packed congregation and a youth band. So, here it was – the Christian revivalism my hosts wanted me to talk about, and it so shook a French participant sitting with us on the platform that he murmured 'La renaissance de l'église.' Evening services in a nearby older church were also jammed tight, mainly with young people, some of them sitting in the recessed windows, and it was clear the priests were trying to lead the community towards peaceful resolution of the conflict, in spite of the interests of the numerous rival militias. People we spent time with down in the city phoned around every evening to find out where the firing was coming from, and the word was it only stopped when *Dallas* was on TV.

The conference was mainly conducted in French, and the Shia did not turn up, so the contributors were mostly Maronites, Sunni and Druzes. They dismissed Northern Ireland as child's play compared with Lebanon: there were only a handful of religions and ethnic groups to reconcile in Ulster, while they had dozens. The French priests were too sophisticated and the Muslim contributors too dogmatic, but the spirit was good. A sometime Syrian minister of culture was a typical French-speaking sceptic. He took us to the mountain shrine of Our Lady of Lebanon and to ancient Byblos to observe what he called 'the chute of the gods', though we also observed churches and mosques side by side, witness to an older and more amicable proximity, before the rise of modern nationalism and political ideology. The American University invited me to give a lecture on the British stereotype of the Arab, but as the university was in Muslim Beirut I thought this a needless hazard. As we left to cross the green line again a woman embraced us, offering us in a moment of profound emotion 'l'union de la prière'.

Arriving back in Britain we were shocked by the contrast between the vitality of life and faith in war-torn Beirut, where every thing and every moment was precious, and the banality of British concerns, where peace and prosperity could be taken for granted.

16
Southern Methodist University

———•◆•———

Pentecostalism became my main intellectual contribution after secularization, the one following naturally from the other. But I only had the chance to study it by near-accidents leading me to Pentecostalism in Latin America by way of Southern Methodist University in Dallas, Texas. I went to a lecture by Peter Berger in London on a Saturday, something I was normally quite unlikely to do. Appropriately enough the venue was on the site of Aldersgate Street where John Wesley in May 1738 had the experience of a 'heart strangely warmed' which gave major impetus to the English and American Awakenings preceding Pentecostalism. Peter asked if I had noticed the spread of Pentecostalism in Latin America and parts of the southern states of the USA. Would I be interested in studying it?

I had seen Spanish-speaking Pentecostal churches in California, Arizona and New Mexico, but the presuppositions of sociology led me to suppose Pentecostalism in Latin America would remain a back-street affair. I expected mass movements to be political not religious, in spite of my critical approach to secularization theory.

Peter Berger's suggestion was attractive, backed up as it was by the offer of research money from his Institute for the Study of Economic Culture at Boston University. The Institute had an interest in the economic implications of any extension of Max Weber's Protestant ethic in Latin America. My brief would be to follow the trail blazed by Weber and trace the consequences of the latest wave of Protestantism in fostering an economic ethos and a disciplined lifestyle. I would also ask how far it promoted democratic participation, education and literacy, pluralism, the increase in political actors, the growth of civil society and non-violent movements for cultural change rather than violent insurrections. In the event I cautiously concluded that, other things being equal, Pentecostalism did contribute to these changes, though perhaps not to the same extent as earlier waves of Protestantism. Religion was once again playing a serious role in modernization, more so than the emphasis on the Enlightenment preferred in the academy. Many scholars were dubious about the modernizing potential of Pentecostalism, but I was willing to ask how far it could be a major modernizing agent. I would be challenging the elite ideology of the Enlightenment in the field of modernization as I had earlier challenged it in the field of secularization.

Then I received another offer which I did not immediately see was complementary to Berger's suggestion I work with him at Boston University. I was telephoned at home by the Provost of Southern Methodist University (SMU), Hans Hillerbrand. His suggestion took me aback, because I had never contemplated moving to the USA. I had not taken into account the possibilities now open to us, given both my parents had died and Magnus, our youngest, was now in his mid-teens. Hans Hillerbrand said he was ringing from the 'distinguished' state of Texas and that, though he could not offer me the Scurlock Chair of Human Values at SMU on the phone, perhaps I would like to hear the conditions. He made clear I would be twice as well off at SMU for half the teaching, and I put up the first roadblock by pointing out that my wife also taught in the University of London. He inferred I wanted two jobs, and I responded in a cautious subjunctive. I added there was the further problem of our children, which only inspired him to ask what he could do for them. By now I was desperate and indicated I was happy where I was. But he had been happy in Munich, and now he was even happier in Dallas. Surely I would not turn down the offer on the phone without looking the joint over. When I feebly mentioned the autumn term was nearly upon us, he explained tickets would be available at the airport in three days' time and we would be picked up by SMU university police at Dallas-Fort Worth airport.

We arrived at Dallas-Fort Worth in a temperature of 105 degrees, and saw the vast greensward of SMU, surrounded by 'eighteenth-century' buildings, complete with a white church, New England style, and crowned with a reproduction of Jefferson's Monticello. In the dome were the rooms of the Professor of Human Values. When I met the university president he urged us to come right away, but I said I had a prior obligation to Boston University. He assumed, first, that I wanted more money, then that I wanted less teaching, and finally that I was a tough negotiator and wanted more money *and* less teaching. When I mentioned the mysterious word 'obligation' again, he offered me immediate opportunity to 'talk to BU'. To my surprise Boston University thought it would be a very good idea to teach in Dallas and use it as a springboard for research in Latin America. I could always take the plane from time to time to Boston. That was what I did, though my students were puzzled by these occasional visits to the east coast. One even asked why I would spend time in Boston when Bostonians were 'no better than Europeans'.

Soon after settling in at SMU I met the donors of the chair and two members of the governing board. The donors, the Blantons, were a charming couple, 'in oil', from Houston. They arrived at the dinner party in Rosewood Mansion, Dallas, congratulating them-selves their separate helicopters had arrived at exactly the same time. Hans Hillerbrand warned me against British modesty in case anyone should think me less than a bargain. Later I met a member of the governing board, Edwin Cox, who was a cattleman, and lived in a heavily protected mansion in the wealthy district of Turtle Creek. On being admitted to the vestibule I noticed a couple of pictures by Degas, followed by a couple by Cézanne (and so on) and when I had identified half a dozen pictures correctly, my host complimented me on 'having quite an eye'. In the drawing room I noticed four pictures by Van Gogh, and Cox explained that normally he collected pictures in twos but his agent thought these so delightful it made sense to buy four. In the library there was only one Renoir, but it did take up a whole wall. Ed Cox said it was good to have me around, with all the moral mayhem going on in the fraternity houses. That forced me to explain I had not been hired to patrol the morals of what some people called 'a party school'.

The next member of the governing board I met was more doctri-nal than moral in his concerns. He had a mission to make SMU more godly than it had been of late. I decided this was not the moment to drink a gin and tonic before eating. He asked what I thought of humanism, and I foolishly treated the question as academic. No sooner had I mentioned four possible meanings of humanism than I caught the eye of Hans Hillerbrand, and paused nervously, hoping for more enlightenment. My interlocutor said, with a faint suggestion of menace, 'What I'm asking you, Dr Martin, is *this* – what do you think of the Ten Commandments?'

I replied that I was very much in favour of them, which went down very well. 'See here, Dr Martin,' he said, 'I am a tolerant man, and I don't care whether you are a pre-millennialist or a post-millennialist.'

In Texas we became friendly with people we would never encoun-ter in the British academic world, like the donors of my chair, who lived in the River Oaks enclave of the super-rich in Houston, with its famous country club. They attended St Luke's Methodist Church, which for Mr Blanton was a social and charitable duty incumbent on any responsible citizen. Laura Blanton (neé Scurlock) had endowed my Scurlock Chair, and the Blantons had together endowed a wing of the local hospital. They also supported the new art gallery in the same spirit that had animated Unitarians like the Courtaulds and Tates, and represented a philanthropic social and religious tradition all too modestly represented in Britain. Blanton commented that if the newly rich of Houston did not cooperate in philanthropic endeavour, 'We run them out of town.'

Not all the people we met in Houston were as amiable as the Blantons. At a concert given by Joan Sutherland and Luciano Pavarotti, the super-rich gathered afterwards in the Four Seasons Hotel to meet and to be seen to meet the celebrities. In the mêlée I encountered a corporate lawyer who responded dismissively to my appreciative remarks about New Zealand, saying 'I hate the place. No rich, no poor, just people in between.'

Ron was a Dallas multimillionaire with a different charitable style. He was interested in social relief in Guatemala, which he visited frequently, and now proposed spreading 'the Christian thing' to assist economic and social progress in China. Progress and religion go together in the USA, just as conservative attitudes to the Bible go along with technical sophistication. The compartments of the American mind are as capacious as they are practical. When we went for a spin around Ron's vast ranch he wanted to know which Christian radio I preferred. He explained the rocks on his ranch were three hundred million years old, and asked what the Bible had to say about women riding valuable Arab horses. His elegant second or third wife was with us and she liked careering around the ranch on these aristocratic beasts. Ron wanted to know whether the Bible cast a critical eye on female horse-riding. No text came to mind to support either of them, and I had the feeling she did not much care. Ron was an engineer and a highly intelligent man playing the stock market. 'But I have to tell you, David, some of the Jews on the market have IQs so high that if it wasn't for Jesus I would be finished.' I kept quiet about the ethnicity of the Son of God.

I liked these people, including one lady who told us it was 'real sweet' of her husband to bring her back a Gainsborough for Christmas, and a philanthropic man who 'redeemed' prisoners in state penitentiaries using Renaissance techniques of memorization to 'teach them all the facts of world history from the Resurrection to George Washington'. Yet another friend took us to see the Cow Girls for Christ parade near Billy Bob's in Fort Worth, which included 'native'

Americans performing the Lord's Prayer in smoke signals before a large and devout assemblage.

All this was part of coming to terms with Texas. Peter Berger argued every nation ought to have a Texas, combining religion and economic dynamism, and this was why he liked Evangelicals (while actually worshipping in the Orthodox or the Episcopal Church), and approved of Pentecostal expansion in Latin America. SMU, however, was only physically in Texas, and I suspect rather few of its out-of-state faculty met the kind of people we did.

We met another area of Texas life through Bernice's secretary, whose social existence turned around the roles available to her in the Lions, an American organization like the Elks in Britain. This is where I heard the heartbeat of America, unsophisticated and profoundly hospitable. Faculty people were mostly liberals trying to educate conservatives and they turned classrooms into arenas for prosecuting culture wars. Even when I sympathized, I disliked their misuse of charisma and authority. Like Bernice, Magnus also met unusual people. One of them, a very attractive student whose father had connections with the Italian mafia, told me over dinner she 'had been able to help' my son. I realized what kind of education she had offered when they went off to Acapulco together.

In some ways SMU was a 'party' school, divided between those who believed it was a university that happened to have a football team engaged in dubious practices of recruitment among blacks, and those who believed it was a football team with a liberal arts annexe. A different dichotomy operated in the prestigious Perkins School of Theology, between those who saw it as a major school of Methodist theological and historical scholarship and those who treated it as a religiously toned version of liberal ideology. Some faculty made up in political righteousness what they lacked in religious conviction.

SMU had a distinguished faculty in several areas, and there was a splendid theatre school enabling us to watch classical Greek and Spanish drama and a music school that introduced us to Couperin's *Leçons de ténèbres*, and performed Byrd's four-part Mass (on Reformation Sunday!) for Sung Eucharist in the university Methodist church. I found it difficult to stomach a university culture proclaiming the virtue of equality while exploiting the devotion of helots, often female, who did the bulk of the teaching, while stars performed on the public stage. I also disliked the grade inflation following the corrupt practice of teachers marking the scripts of their own students. I did not understand how an education system inducing comprehensive ignorance of everything except food hygiene, cosmetics and pop music could also sustain world-class graduate schools and magnificent bookstores and record shops. Some of the teachers at SMU showed me how it was done because they gathered little groups of enthusiasts around them, whom they taught intensively, while doing what was required for those who were there just to be processed.

Processing had its problems when you had to teach sports stars. One bronzed tennis hulk in my class had become so educationally retarded in the course of his exertions on the court I was appealed to by colleagues to pass him. They said it was my responsibility to rid the university of an encumbrance. Yet I must have stirred up a faint sense of something beyond tennis, because he requested an interview to ask if I could recommend 'a good religion'. I asked what had been provided by way of 'a good religion' in his background. One parent was a Jew and the other a Polish Catholic. Another bronzed hulk regularly sat at the back drinking iced water, providing a persistent soundtrack of clunking ice. One day my patience broke and I shouted at him, 'Please stop making that barbarous noise.' A sudden silence followed. They had not so far encountered words like that nor the contrast between civility and barbarity: all that mattered could be calibrated by the dollar sign.

My arrival at SMU coincided with the deposition of Hans Hillerbrand as provost, so nobody knew why I was there. I found myself with a class of students in the first year all of whom had been rejected by the courses they really wanted. When I mentioned Hillerbrand's initial idea, natural enough in a scholar of German background, that I might give lectures open to anybody, or of interest to a theology faculty concerned with social science perspectives, I risked incomprehension. Nothing could attract support unless it offered credits. University education was the accumulation of credits without cumulative educational impact or coherent links between topics. A credit gained was a credit forgotten. I got used to students telling me they 'needed' an A, sometimes to maintain a sequence of As, and I began courses explaining I knew about this ubiquitous need, and would indicate the steps required to meet it. My requirements included historical sequence and geographical location. I asked them to imagine a criminal investigation where there was no time line and no spatial evidence. Time and space are of the essence in social as in any other form of science, and I would not listen to anything until they were both specified. Their sense of geography was non-existent and I told them that once they took off from Dallas-Fort Worth airport they had no idea where they were going except that it was called Cancun or Hawaii. Once, in desperation, I said, 'If you are going to rule the world, find out where it is.'

As I entered my first class I began by asking what motivated the students to be interested in religion and politics, and they candidly replied that they were not interested at all. At the end of the initial session I asked if anybody had a problem. One student said, 'Yes, the *words*.' She explained she had never heard of 'Cathol- something' or 'a-thism', and added plaintively she had never imagined there were so many religions in the whole world, having hitherto supposed there were 'only Methodists and Baptists'. That was an extreme instance, and at least my American students had none of the withdrawn in-group scepticism of some British students. The problem was their lack of an organizing structure, leaving them prey to random impressions derived from the media and films. They really thought you could understand the world through popular media and the execrable CNN news programmes. As I tried to explain the conflict in Northern Ireland, one bright and interested student commented, 'You said these Ulsters had been mostly Scots, so why doesn't the king of Scotland intervene?' I wondered if she had Macbeth in mind.

One incident revealed the depth of the educational disaster, because it suggested that in the so-called information age too many of my American students were incapable of absorbing information. They had attended lectures on the Russian Revolution by a major Russian scholar, Daniel Orlovsky, and were tested on what they had understood. It seemed that Stalin had led the Germans in some kind of war, perhaps between 1917 and 1945, and had killed thirty million peasants in the course of it. After that, the notion that Kruschchev was a ballet dancer who defected to the West was merely amusing.

Next day I walked into the class dressed in black, and was asked what was the matter. I explained it was a private grief. They pressed me and finally I said that they were intelligent, that I loved them and loved teaching them, but they were the victims of an unprecedented educational disaster: vast sums of money spent for nugatory results. There was total silence until a hand went up: 'Sir, what can we do about it?' Here was my chance, and I suggested we look at how they had been taught, and we identified testing by multiple choice questions rather than through the pursuit of coherent understanding. Some grasped what I wanted, but feared to take the risk. In a world of ticking boxes and formulae, thinking had become dangerous.

When I taught the SMU summer school in Oxford I took my American students to Purbeck in Dorset, partly to show them where in 1944 their grandfathers had gathered for the largest sea invasion in history. One of them commented, 'You don't mean to say there's water between here and Europe?'

Back in England in the 1990s, I lectured on the history of English religion in Lancaster University and a bright young woman said, 'I didn't know we had a Civil War.' When I asked what she had done in English history, she said: 'We didn't study English history. We studied women in Brazil.'

I said, 'Well, at least I don't use jargon,' to which she replied, 'I wish you would. I understand that.'

My grandson, classified as gifted, is in his pre-GCSE year and is answering a question on the Catholic attitude to contraception. I make suggestions. He explains taking my approach would lose him marks. 'We have formulae for giving points in the right order.'

17

Victorian England in Latin America

———•◦•———

I had always regretted my father never visited the USA. Of course, he liked Americans, because they tipped well, and because he admired American evangelists like Torrey and Alexander, and Billy Graham. But a visit to the States would have assured him he had a religious homeland where his lay enthusiastic faith was quite normal and acceptable. What I did not anticipate was finding people like him in Chile.

My first journey was not to Chile but to the Yucatan, a periphery of Mexico as Wales was a periphery of England. I phoned my local contacts, one of whom asked me whose side I was on. Academic curiosity seemed not to be an option in a highly charged atmosphere. When Bernice and I arrived, a Mexican anthropologist took us to a Protestant village not far from the ancient Mayan ruins of Chichen Itza, and a few miles from the provincial capital of Merida. The village was neatly laid out, with a school, small park and medical centre, and had received some money for development from Switzerland. The Catholic church was ruined and locked and there was a new Presbyterian chapel, in pastel shades, looking as if it had been flown in from the Welsh valleys. I took a photograph, making sure to include the palm trees, in case anyone should doubt its Mexican provenance.

We visited an Evangelical training centre for young people, many of whom tumbled out of their bunks to form a girls' choir with guitars, and offered us a musical taste of what they sang in the Maya language as they went around neighbouring villages. The minister gave us a copy of his Maya translation of the Psalms. Finally we spent time in the new La Esperanza hospital, set up by Protestant missionaries with some interestingly Scottish names. Perhaps I was finding traces of British peripheries, no doubt via the USA, here in a periphery of Mexico. Periphery calls to periphery: Scotland to the American South and the American South to the Yucatan. I found a cache of information about the growth of Protestantism in the University of Merida, much of it written by a young Mexican scholar living just five miles from my Woking home.

Our other Mexican visits were equally amazing. On one occasion we climbed the vast Toltec/Aztec Pyramid of the Sun outside Mexico City at Teotihuacan, and found an ancient and colourful pre-Hispanic ceremony being enacted. This revival of ancient customs and culture heroes is something some anthropologists approve of, certainly by comparison with Pentecostalism. Folk revivals appeal to nationalist intelligentsias all over the world, from Guatemala and Ghana to Uzbekistan.

Another encounter was accidental, because we had taken my mother-in-law for a few days in Mexico City, and found ourselves invited to his parents' house by our taxi driver. He started off by talking about Baudelaire's *Les Fleurs du mal* and 'L'Albatros', before giving us the history of his family's conversion to Protestantism and his role as 'the black sheep' of the family, no longer Protestant. This was our introduction to the 'revolving door', people converted in one generation, ascending the social scale, and leaving a generation or two later. But we also saw an illuminated Bible in the niche where one might expect the Virgin and numerous diplomas on the walls testifying to educational aspirations and achievements. The patriarch of the family had begun by reading the Bible and ended by extending his reading in every direction, including Ouspensky. What began with an enthusiastic embrace of salvation among the brothers and the sisters had veered towards to the literature of spirituality, self-help and psychological insight. It was a pattern I easily recognized. My mother-in-law was the matriarch of a large family in a Lancashire cotton town and was delighted to find that Mexicans had families just like her own, and she felt very much at home. Perhaps she felt rather less at home when a meal was serenaded by a musician singing songs of the war of Mexican independence, while I was force fed donkey meat to assist my virility.

We visited Guadalajara and attended worship in a vast temple built by La Luz del Mundo, complete with hospital and school. La Luz ran its sector of the city, and each neighbourhood was named after biblical places around Jerusalem, like Bethesda. The group claimed, in the words of the Song of Songs, that there were 'many concubines, but only one that is my dove', that one being La Luz. At morning worship the women anticipated the arrival of the leader by keening more and more loudly, and when he made his triumphal entry, torch bearers went before him in what felt like a re-enactment of Palm Sunday. His seat was placed at the exact spot where the sun would strike at the solstice.

Guatemala was the most beautiful country we visited, and we spent time in the reconstructed old city of Antigua. The crowds of maimed and famished people that attended us wherever we went made our son Magnus almost physically sick with horror. Guatemala was a country of preposterous riches and abject poverty and it had been wrecked by a ferocious war, prosecuted for 15 months by General Rios Montt before he was deposed for not being as corrupt as he was brutal. Montt had a mixed reputation as equally ferocious in putting down rebels and putting down corruption. He was exceptional in more than one way, because he belonged to a neo-Pentecostal group called El Verbo, with American connections, and also came from the old elite. I tried to interview him but he was suddenly called away on business. That hardly mattered, because his church was clearly one of the mega-churches appealing to the Guatemalan urban middle class. In the countryside we found Pentecostals making rapid progress among the majority 'Indian' population. Even in remote Petén, which we visited in a rickety plane to reconnoitre Mayan monuments long lost in the forest at Tikal, you could see numerous poor dwellings with biblical texts displayed on the exterior.

There were signs of a massive religious upheaval all over Guatemala. As we travelled in a coach with a party of academics we could see dozens of little house churches of every kind of denomination, and buses announcing 'Jesus is coming'. Our guide mentioned that Guatemala was a country whose population was 66 per cent Catholic. Not a single academic asked about the religion of the other 34 per cent, such was the power of prior perceptions. Mere observation through the coach window counted for nothing.

My first visit to Brazil was a disaster, because I ignored the advice of those who knew the country well and warned me to stay in a really good hotel. On arrival at the airport in Rio it seemed no hotel had been booked for me so I set out with a Mauritian to locate one, only to find myself in a remarkable hell-hole. It was the New Year Festival and everybody was walking into the sea in honour of the Immaculate Conception. I took the Mauritian out for a meal, only to find later that he had stolen my camera and used my credit card number to finance a £500 journey to New York. I shifted as soon as I could to a hotel in Ipanema and found that taxis did not stop at crossroads since the risk of an accident was less worrying than the risk of being robbed.

The second visit was properly organized under the kindly aegis of Paul Freston, my co-researcher, and it involved Bernice as well. In Brazil we observed a religious upheaval in a country about the size of the USA. The Protestant population, a majority of them Pentecostal, already numbered 20 to 25 million, and is now 40 million, or 22 per cent of the population, a three-fold increase in few decades. Pastors outnumbered priests. We visited middle-class house churches and went to religious gatherings in converted cinemas, in particular a riotous gathering at the Universal Church of the Kingdom of God at which people were liberated from their demons once the pastors had determined the name of the relevant demon. Bernice went to a God is Love church where the young pastor proposed liberating her from what he took to be long-standing demonic infestation. Warily, and not wanting to be tossed in the air as part of a ritual exorcism, she explained she had lived with these spirits on familiar terms for some while and that their loss might be followed by the arrival of yet more ferocious demons, as indicated in the Gospels. The most aston-ishing occasion during our visit involved a Two Choirs Festival in a newly built Pentecostal church in Campinas, a city a few miles from São Paulo. It was conducted by a young woman and concluded with a rendering of the Hallelujah Chorus which stimulated thunderous cries of 'Gloria' from a mainly black congregation of maybe two thou-sand. It was a predictable surprise. Here were marginalized blacks in Brazil singing what begrimed miners in Wales and mill-workers in industrial Yorkshire had sung. There are many ways to find your voice and to announce a presence, and jubilant mass singing is one of them.

Interim closure: a day in Chile, 22 November 1991

'In my end is my beginning', and this account of a single day in Rengo, Chile, a small town in the Central Valley 75 miles south of Santiago, looks back to the early experiences of childhood and early adolescence. My purpose in coming to Rengo as a sociologist was not understood and I found myself having to play the part of a charis-matic evangelist if the research were not to collapse, at least in Rengo. I had with me members of the Pontifical University and the novel-ist and political scientist Arturo Fontaine, my host at the Santiago Centre for Political Studies. In the course of a totally exhausting day, 22 November 1991, I had to reconcile two different personae.

At its conclusion I broke down in hysterical laughter and had to rest on the bed for a day until I recovered. I spent the day gently reading a book in Spanish, *He Did Not Die* (*El no ha Muerto*), by one of the pastors we had met; the book was about how his son died and was raised from the dead. The son had fallen seriously ill and for several hours had been given up for dead. Already the candles burnt beside his body while the despairing parents wept in another room. But then a brother evangelist who was also a paramedic arrived and learnt of their grief. Together they prayed and the evangelist received a word from the Lord that he should inject the child with penicillin. Full of wonderment he replied he had never heard of injecting the dead, but nevertheless did as the Lord had commanded him. To their amazement and joy the son sat up and began to talk. From that moment he was healed. 'No se olvide que al "que cree, todo es posible". Boundless belief that everything is possible if only you have faith and hope sustains people no matter how often disappointed.

The Central Valley lies in the narrow strip of lowland stretching for hundreds of miles between the sea and the snow-clad Andes. It is very green, traversed by lines of trees and veined by rivers which shift from side to side of their shallow courses and occasionally inundate the surrounding countryside. Arturo Fontaine explained that a few fine old buildings were relics of a time when this rich farmland had been carved up into great estates, until land reform had broken them up into plots taken over by *campesinos*. But many of the plots had broken down or proved unworkable, and had been bought up by large agribusinesses. So the *campesinos* had passed from exploitative patriarchal relationships to brief independence, and then to the industrial relationships of modern scientific agriculture. Apart from the toilsome business of picking the fruit, their human skills were now replaced by machines, and when fruit was not in season they cut wood, using a truck if they were lucky enough to acquire one. The truck offers mobility for all of them, and for Evangelicals, a minority of about 3,000 in a town of 45,000, it offers a chance to spread the Word in Santiago, rather like my father in his taxi in London. They occupy a social space such as my grandfather occupied in rural Dorset, not quite the same because he had the opportunity for honourable work in a market, but they like him could at least express their spiritual independence in running their own religious business.

We meet our host, Pastor Arnaldo Umaña, author of *He Did Not Die*, in a lorry drivers' restaurant outside town. The temperature is in the high eighties and exotic gold and green birds flash their wings behind wire mesh as the ceiling fans whirr and the electronic equipment beats out 'Chitty Chitty Bang Bang'. Pastor Umaña shows himself part of what I call a 'buried intelligentsia', again a bit like my grandfather. He and his father were miners in northern Chile and, like both my maternal uncles, members of the Communist Party, followers of Carlos Marx. When Arnaldo's father contracted emphysema, his mother called in a Pentecostal healer and he recovered. As usual the believing woman takes the initiative on behalf of her sceptical and rumbustious man. Her rumbustious son thought this all mere suggestibility, and was tempted to test out this God in a series of dramatic gambles. But the time came when he too needed and found healing power, and the whole family became united as members of the Methodist Pentecostal church. Father and son were then expelled from the party, which proved no bad thing, because when they were questioned as possible subversives their names had been crossed off the membership roll.

Pastor Umaña is sixty-ish, about five feet tall, with a flat face, lined and darkish brown like the caked earth in the nearby watercourses. He is probably Aymara, one of the indigenous Andean peoples highly responsive to Evangelical Christianity. He is curious, sagacious and ready to push his nose into anything of interest or profit. He is also a flyweight boxer and sneaks up like a cunning little fox to demonstrate how to manage a quick foul with the elbow while the referee is watching your head. Asked about turning the other cheek, he explains that you also need 'measure for measure'. Did not the Lord himself say, 'It is better to give than to receive'?

Hearing my wife and I are Anglicans, he says he knows Anglicanism is a famously moderate religion: two minutes for greeting, three for praying, four for reading and ten for preaching. When I ask about the order of this evening's service, he hands me an alarming piece of paper on which I am advertised as the speaker. Sensing crisis ahead, I offer to give a greeting, five minutes or so, but this is not what he has in mind. It occurs to me if I am asking local Pentecostals for their family stories of faith and work, I ought to set an example and tell my own family story. After all, Pentecostalism is a narrative faith, telling the 'old, old story'. It is testimony and life experience, and in recounting my family story I falsify nothing. I am worried about what my bearded colleagues at the Pontifical University are going to make of an English sociologist taking a typically uproarious Evangelical service, but in the event they are sympathetically engaged and even say they have 'at last seen the soul of the Chilean people'.

As architect and builder, Pastor Umaña had to put up his own church. That is normal, and we have today seen two of his colleagues deep in mud digging the latrines of their future churches. The local congregation of 11 thought their tiny buildings quite adequate, but Umaña had his own vision and shamed them into cooperation by employing his own children. He was also helped by miracles. If anyone knows how to make a miracle fall off the back of a lorry or to badger a sluggish Providence into action, it is Umaña. First, a well-dressed man appeared at his door and mysteriously changed into working clothes. He had arrived at the Lord's bidding and had brought his tools with him. Then it came to pass that Umaña was walking past a building site and noticed the workers had put up a badly curved wall. This meant they had to knock it down again, and he saw a chance to ask for the spoiled bricks. It also happened that Providence led him to pass by as workers were about to bury a cracked beam in a trench. Not only did the construction firm let him retrieve the beam but it lent him a vehicle to take it away. With such manifest blessing the flagging faith of the brothers was replenished and their zeal increased.

Adjacent to his church is a half-completed building and a space for a new school. The building is ready to be divided up, with bathrooms and an area for Umaña's new acupuncture clinic. Umaña strongly approves of science, especially practical and useful science as compared to humanist learning. Indeed he approves of whatever works, and a Korean lady evangelist, who is also a doctor, has shown him the benefits of acupuncture. She will practise here for a while till Umaña has learnt how to use the needles and take over. Arturo Fontaine mutters he would not want to be the first patient.

During the day we talk to some of the other pastors and their wives, one of whom weeps as her husband recounts the details of his unregenerate life. And then, after due passage of Chilean time, largely determined by when people came in from the fields, things begin to happen. We hear in the distance the sounds of a straggling procession of people coming into the village and singing 'Onward, Christian Soldiers'. Two friendly demonstrations occur. Another pastor's daughter comes up to me, falls on my shoulder and begins to sob uncontrollably. I become rather worried and recollect the story of Mary Magdalene in the Gospels. This woman has only once before in her life seen a *gringo* and I am like a visitor from another world. Then a bus arrives with more members of Pastor Umaña's congregation, and a crowd of children, perhaps members of his children's choir, runs towards us for me to pick them up and bless them. Then we walk with the pastors into the church through a side door to take our places on chairs of honour on the platform. We watch the congregation process into the church and the men of the orchestra with their banjos, accordions and guitars make their way to the choir stalls. Behind us is a mural of the Good Shepherd rescuing lost sheep from a ravine. They have been caught in barbed wire and are covered in blood. Some realistic sheep on the other side remain safe in the fold.

Singing, praising and praying begins, with clapping and raising of hands. Prayer is a spontaneous outburst from everyone present, lasting about a minute. Pastor Umaña introduces us and the programme for the evening. Another hymn. More prayer. Pastor Umaña gathers his children's choir together in a half circle and gives them their notes in three parts. First they sing 'Stand up, stand up for Jesus' (just as I used to in Sunday School) and then a folksy Latin American song. According to Umaña the choir includes an eight-year-old tenor – actually an alto – and one of the pieces is sung by a boy soloist. Much popular enthusiasm follows. Another pastor then addresses the congregation with great authority and reminds those present of Umaña's forthcoming Saturday seminar on the Antichrist and other future events. I am introduced as from Great Britain and as a professor from Oxford University. It hardly seems the moment to insert a pedantic correction. I rise to speak.

Gloria a Dios! Amen!

It is a very great privilege to speak to you tonight because I feel there is more real life here among you than in the whole University of Oxford. And there is more true music in your hearts than in the best choirs in the world.

This morning in Santiago I was talking to a reporter from the great newspaper *El Mercurio* about the spread of the gospel among the Chilean people and he asked me what makes the Evangelical people different. I told him that all believers are able to tell their own story, the story of their lives and difficulties, and of what God has done for them. I have already heard many marvellous stories. Your pastors have told me theirs. But all of you have a story of what God has done in your lives and how he has helped you to a better life.

You know, there is something that makes me sad. My grandfather and my father had great stories, but I never sat down and asked for them as I am asking you. But let me tell you what I know. The story begins not very far from London. My grandmother could not read or write and when she got married she made a mark on her marriage certificate, like this +. My grandfather worked on the farm of the big house and looked after the prize bulls. Gradually he began to treat her as if he did not love her any more. He would come in late at night and hit her, and when he was angry he took off this (pointing to my belt) and beat my father with it. Yet one day he heard the gospel and all that changed. Amen. *Gloria a Dios.* He became a new man. He had one of these (I walk over to the players with their accordions) –

and he stood on the street corner playing and singing 'Stand up, stand up for Jesus'. (I then sing the first two lines myself.) Amen. Amen.

Then one day something terrible happened. A horse reared up and kicked him and he died.

They are now absolutely silent and supportive at this recollection, so close to their own experiences, and one cries out, 'He is in Abraham's bosom.'

Let me tell you about my father, too. He worked in the stables of the great house, looking after the horses. He left school early and went to London looking for work. First of all he found work in the stables of the Archbishop of Canterbury. But then came the car: a beautiful shining car called the Delaunay-Belleville. He drove that car. And it became his life's ambition to work until he had a car of his own. When he left the Archbishop's place, the Archbishop's wife said, 'Fred, you have been a good worker. Here is a New Testament for you.' He read that New Testament, but still he was not converted. He became a chauffeur, first to the Chancellor of the Exchequer, then for the Prime Minister. That experience gave him his idea of heaven. He told me, 'Heaven is like when all the traffic lights turn green.'

Then one day he heard a famous evangelist on the radio, which was just a little machine with a whisker. The evangelist was a gypsy, Gypsy Smith, and he spoke to my father's heart so that he became converted. *Gloria a Dios*. Amen!

After many years of hard work, the dream of his life came true. He bought his own taxi. He used his taxi to spread the gospel and would often stop for an hour in Hyde Park, which is just like the centre of Santiago, and preach. My mother would smile gently when he had been preaching and would say, 'Fred, what have you being doing today?' Just before my father died my eldest son looked at him and said, 'Grandad, what has given you this confidence all your life?' And then he said, 'I know. It is your faith, isn't it?' Amen! Amen!

But what about me? The Word speaks to us all one way or another. One night I was returning to the Army after a weekend spent at home. As the train went hour after hour into the night I opened the Bible and read the New Testament. The words that specially spoke to me were 'God so loved the world that he gave his only begotten son' and 'I am persuaded that neither height nor depth, nor death nor life, nor any other creature, can separate me from the love of God which is in Christ Jesus, our Lord.' This is my story. Tell me yours!

I come from another country, a distant one, England, but we are all one people, God's people.

I speak another language, English, but we have one tongue in the Spirit, and in the music we have sung together. *Gloria a Dios.*

Finally I would like you to remember three sayings. They are by John Wesley, an English evangelist, who began this great movement of the Spirit.

'Is your heart as my heart? Then give me your hand.'

I point to my heart and open my hands as if to walk towards them.

'I am a man of one book and that book is the Bible.'

I hold up the Bible.

And then, holding up his hand just before he died, he cried: 'The best of all is, God is with us.'

I hold my hands above my head.

Amen! Amen!

As I finish, Pastor Umaña tells them one or two things about John Wesley and asks Bernice to give them a Christian greeting. There follows a long testimony from a young farmer who works on Rengo radio and has travelled down from Santiago in a (distinctly expensive) car. As his testimony concerns adultery, there is an initial reluctance to come forward in response to his appeal to repent, but soon some pick up courage, and weep and tremble as they kneel or prostrate themselves on the platform steps.

Then everyone breaks out singing. One woman who earlier told us of how her feet had been marvellously healed after prayer prostrates herself and begins gracefully to dance. She holds her arms forward in a gesture of offering as though she were the Virgin of the Annunciation. Her arms stay modestly spread, her palms upward, her eyes closed and her head slightly to one side. With no movement of her hips, she rocks forward and back as if making fresh gestures of offering. Her back stays slightly bent. Having danced to the front she retires again, and as she completes her dance another woman tenderly and supportively attends her back to her seat.

As the blessing concludes, the congregation flows onto the platform all around us, greeting us and praying for us. One man stands with hands above my head and calls down repeated blessings in the name of the Father, the Son and the Spirit. The service has lasted two and a half hours and as we get into our car for the journey back to Santiago, hands are stretched through the open window just to touch us.

215

As I lay on the bed recovering, Bernice said the occasion had brought a closure in my relationship with my father. The tiny Chilean chapel was not the Albert Hall of his imagination, and maybe he had never heard of Chile, but Bernice was right. In the course of the long 'education of David Martin' many mistakes and mishaps remain beyond correction, and many follies beyond expiation, but on 22 November 1991, my father might have seen the travail of his soul and been satisfied.

Retrospect: losses and recoveries of faith and further reflections on violence

⎯⎯•⎯•⎯•⎯⎯

Here I revisit in retrospect, and with a more analytic eye, what I canvassed in prospect in my Introduction. This memoir has been about losses and recoveries of faith that have animated my education and motivated my engagement, first with theology and then with sociology. Most of us have at some time undergone losses and recoveries of faith. My faiths have been as much political and social as religious, partly because I think all three spheres intimately overlap without being coincident, and partly because *all* our major life choices, religious, political, social (and, of course, intimately personal), are acts of faith, equally subject to doubt and to those breaches of faith we call faithlessness.

Ernest Gellner, an LSE colleague I admired in spite of our differences, once lampooned his fellow philosopher Alisdair MacIntyre for starting off an Anglican, becoming a Marxist and ending up a Catholic. He said, 'To lose one faith is understandable, to lose two looks like carelessness.' I laughed, but he was wrong. To lose a faith is a sign of carefulness, unlike breaches of faith which really are signs of carelessness. To lose only one faith is to be pretty unadventurous, and in this I was a virtuoso. I have described how I began life in an Evangelical home based on belief in the Bible, and how my father expected me to make a profession of faith through a conversion experience at a definite moment. I needed to witness publicly to that moment when I was 'born again', 'a brand plucked from the eternal fire'. Hell was a reality in which my father frequently and implausibly said he believed, and there was a book on our shelves, illustrating what divine justice might have in store for the heedless, called *The Great Assize*. But if my heavenly father was as good as my earthly father, the threat could be discounted. Love would find a way.

David Martin, FBA, 2007

I have explained how my education began when I lost faith in the Bible. I had no conversion experience, at least not one my father could recognize. But if you extend the meaning of conversion, I had several of them, like the moment of release from obligatory beliefs I experienced on the train to Cardiff as I read Karl Popper. Secular beliefs, like all other beliefs, derive much of their power from the authority of a group to which you defer. When they lose that power, it is not so much because an idea finally sticks in your throat but because another authority absolves you from the need to subscribe. I just gave up all authorities in favour of what I found authoritative, whatever its provenance. I was as much exhilarated by my vertiginous knowledge of intellectual freedom as one 'born again' is exhilarated by the forgiveness of sins. Happily my loss of secular faith did not require me to attest my scepticism. My exit could be silent and unheralded. I went quietly.

I had begun my silent exodus from my father's faith by trawling those parts of the Bible I found appealing, like the peaceable kingdom of God 'within us' proclaimed in the Sermon on the Mount. I then translated the Sermon into Tolstoyan pacifism, the Brotherhood of Man and liberal socialism. Many Nonconformist Christians did precisely that from the 1870s on and it seems a bigger shift than it really is, because revivalists like my father read their Bibles through benevolent filters. We revivalist Christians might read in Scripture that 'the Lord is a man of war', but the warrior god lurking behind the text was filtered out. Literalism is in practice morally selective, judging Scripture by Scripture supplemented by common decency, common sense and Christian benevolence.

Our filter was even powerful enough to prevent us asking whether 'Gentle Jesus, meek and mild' gave a full account of the prophet of Nazareth. After all, the Lord excoriated the Pharisees for hypocrisy and said with characteristic hyperbole that whoever 'offended against a little child' might be better off in the world to come with a millstone placed round his neck and 'cast into the depths of the sea'. What my church, especially my Sunday School, really inculcated was *niceness*, even politeness. Christians should keep their noses clean and keep smiling when other people treated them badly. In spite of believing that grace was 'sufficient to cover all our sins', and dismissing the prescriptions of the law as 'mere morality', a doctrine of holiness lay in the background which we scaled down to good behaviour, decency and niceness.

When I embraced Tolstoyan pacifism, I not only felt a genuine horror of war and violence. I was acquiring 'advanced' opinions. Tolstoy was a great literary genius, and for an adolescent of literary inclinations his pacifism carried intellectual credentials. Yet in practice it was yet more niceness, this time extended from personal relations, where it might work up to a point, to relations between nations fighting over supremacy, resources and *Lebensraum*, where it could be downright dangerous. I no more questioned whether Tolstoy's views made political sense than my father questioned whether the Bible was 'true from cover to cover' or whether 'Gentle Jesus' was really 'meek and mild'. We all claim we think for ourselves, when we all imbibe our opinions from people regarded as authoritative by those we know. Cutting free from the simple faith held by someone like my father, who left school at 11, is a prescribed rite of passage and attracts applause as proof of maturity. Ditching the faiths required of you by a confident middle class is existential grind, and attracts serious sanctions.

Alan Yentob, a clever media man, presented a BBC TV programme on Tolstoy in 2011 in which he endorsed his views on peace and war as prophetic. Yentob did not discuss how a man so nasty in his personal relations could confidently recommend the gospel of niceness when it came to international relations, as he would have done had Tolstoy been a conventional evangelist. That matters, because each of us knows our predilection for nice opinions is no guarantee of moral action. Each of us *ought* to know that the spiralling amorality of violence in international relations is mirrored in personal relations, and vice versa. Yet we prefer to believe that the personal sphere is one of relative freedom and the international sphere one of relative constriction. Appalling costs are exacted in both alike: realignments for better net advantage, secret diplomacy, vengeance for loss of face, broken treaties, shows of force, exemplary maiming, rituals of humiliation, and the ultimate arbitration of violence.

It was not the modest trauma of surreptitiously translating my father's faith into an intellectually acceptable version of being nice that drove my semi-conscious programme of self-education. It was my loss of faith in my revised version and an accelerating doubt about the Tolstoyan ethic and utopian liberal socialism. When I first adopted that revised version in my mid-teens, I felt a free spirit when I mostly wanted to be accounted politically righteous. No wonder in my late twenties I turned to sociology, a subject which rehearses the evidence for political righteousness and documents what the high-minded already believe. For someone brought up in an Evangelical atmosphere, sociology conferred intellectual respectability on what had previously been mere morality. No wonder it appeals to ministers of religion anxious to take off their collars.

In Britain and North America, sociology has roots in the Christian social gospel and the Enlightenment. In England the sociological tradition not only traces its origins to the Lunar Society and the social Darwinism of Herbert Spencer, but also to the social philosophers T. H. Green and L. T. Hobhouse, both of them 'children of the vicarage'. In the late nineteenth century Green and Hobhouse gave the Evangelical and Nonconformist conscience a consuming interest in liberal reform through the state. The politics of conscience worked itself out in social statistics and sociological reflection, and this intellectual genealogy placed me in the sociological mainstream till 1950. But it was marginal from the 1960s on. I have remained marginal and have often had to find my interlocutors in other disciplines.

My second loss of faith was not quite the familiar reversion to an earlier conservatism after a bout of youthful radicalism. I still believed in a translation of Christianity into social liberalism as a moral and political position. To this day I believe in the obligations imposed upon us by the common good. It was just that I no longer accepted the liberal account of the way the world works and the way it is bound to go, for example the liberal triumphalism of Francis Fukuyama. The world cannot be easily divided up into progressives and reactionaries, or good and bad, or those destined to win and those destined to lose.

The survival of liberalism depends on recognizing the way the world *is*, rather than constructing the world and assimilating the future in a liberal image. *Morally* we need to contain, constrain and interdict the struggle for survival, and *practically* that requires us to understand a political reality where children and dictators, small tribes and expansive empires, struggle for living room. For years my automatic liberalism camouflaged and provided cover for my distaste and horror of things as they really are. No one wants to abandon a happy combination of being right and nice. It is easier to believe that the world revealed as it ought to be, whether in the Sermon on the Mount or under the bo tree, unlocks the door to human betterment and corresponds to the grain of the universe. The truth about the world is hard to take, but in the end it proves liberating because senseless evil now makes its own kind of sense.

If the moralization of our social relations is against the social and biological grain, then the key question is not why the Israelites smote the Amalekites hip and thigh. That is merely the default position of humankind. The key question is why Jesus said we should love our enemies and why Christianity lacks an honour code. Once I realized the world resisted moralization, I found myself mired in a chronic moral ambiguity which was psychologically distressing. I was distressed by a personal and political reality where the actors wore different masks at different times, sometimes admirable, sometimes not, according to situation and circumstance.

My attitude to social Darwinism and Machiavellianism was the reverse of my attitude to social liberalism. As a moral perspective the struggle for survival is repugnant. But as an account of the world it codes profoundly shocking features of political and personal life, and of the public and the intimate spheres. To set up and applaud dog fights is very bad, but our moral repugnance does not license us to forget that dogs really do eat dogs. Given the findings of socio-biology and evolutionary psychology, it is not in the least surprising that religion, along with all the other sources of social bonding, codes violence. What surprises and needs explaining is the existence of non-violent manifestos like the New Testament completely contrary to the ubiquitous honour codes of human history. To that extent the philosopher John Gray is right to characterize human animals as *Straw Dogs*. In the struggle for survival, bonding and competing go together, simultaneously uniting and dividing, with erotic charges passing between the negative and the positive poles. These things are the stuff of literature and myth and they inform the subterranean codes of religion.

Sociology, especially Durkheim, gave me permission to respond to a Burkean conservatism understood as conservation, as tradition and continuity, as the power of signs and symbols to sustain our membership one of another, and as the solidarity of the generations over time. I became *more* liberal because I now recognized the complementarity as well as the opposition of the great traditions of political thinking. There was something to be said for realism *and* for idealism. There was a case for promoting change, and a case for maintaining continuity, and a case for traditions of continuous change. It was through reading the theologian Reinhold Niebuhr's *The Children of Light and the Children of Darkness* (1944) that I understood the complementarities and oppositions of political thinking. It was through Niebuhr I learnt that, as times and circumstances change, it is not all that easy to separate the children of light from the denizens of darkness. The wheat and the tares grow together until harvest, even though from time to time we are in clear and present danger from manifest evil and need to make a stand.

Sociology too easily provides documentation for the attitudes of 'right-thinking' people. I came to see sociology more as a way of understanding the power and depth of the image, the sign and the story, in sustaining our collective and personal existence and our identity over time. Faith is realized in the density of the image. It is not waiting to receive a philosophical translation into principles. What is condensed in the image is not an obscure apprehension, one day to be clarified at the touch of pure reason. When it comes to the issues of life and death, reason is far from pure. Faith enacts the stories and realizes the signs that bind us together in a communion over time, and probes the depths of grace and judgement. Faith exposes for all to see and understand the true costs of our losses, our hopes and our redemption. It placards what Pascal called our glory and our wretchedness and asks, 'O all you who pass by in the way, is it nothing to you?' The risky throwing forward that defines faith is not an interim condition or stage of development, but inherent in what constitutes us as human.

When you move from Evangelicalism to the philosophical and reformist translation provided by Green and Hobhouse, you are still chronically prone to divide the world into the good and the bad. Those who proclaim the importance of being non-judgemental only rotate the criteria of judgement. When I left Evangelicalism behind and adopted left-liberalism, the cast lists of the good and the bad might be different but I still knew how to apportion moral praise and blame. I was 'politically correct' *avant la lettre*. I was merely equipped to applaud and condemn the actors in the moral drama with a nicer discrimination. Yet this revised version of the parable of the sheep and the goats is only half the story. Just because it is an affair of the mind with no sense of the judgement and forgiveness of God, it extends no grace to those who do not know which selection of boxes to tick or how to secure an acceptable test profile. There is something more important than knowing you are intellectually correct: you need to know that your sins 'though they be as scarlet are washed whiter than snow' and that you cannot perform this absolution for yourself. Absolution rests in the judging and compassionate hands of higher powers than yours.

Social science ought to lead to compassionate understanding but too often encourages political righteousness. That paradox illustrates how impossible it is to release discourse about human affairs from moral saturation. The crass scientism which supposes we can render phenomena bare and unambiguous through metrics and propositions misunderstands the nature of human science. The human sciences are embedded in cultural, linguistic and therefore moral categories. Of course, we have to stand back to adopt a more objective standpoint, but we still frame our response within the moral and religious domains of judgement governed by compassion. In the end you have to know what it is to stand in the place of the judged as well as the place of the adjudicator. You have no other ground of appeal than Luther's 'A sinner but justified'. That is why judgement and compassion are linked so intimately with the Christian story of the Passion and of a 'Disposer Supreme' who is violently disposed of by a flawed judicial process. There is no more concentrated summation of the human condition or of the genesis of injustice and violence than this. This is where a faith in atonement makes sense. The inbuilt resistance to moralization we identify as the obduracy of sin works itself out in the entrapment of incarnate love. It is exposed for all to see in the spectacle of a suffering innocence that when reviled refuses to revile, and forgives those 'who know not what they do'. The atonement is not a dogma but an existential trans-action whereby as a matter of universal experience the costs of sin are visited elsewhere, and its power is misrepresented and rendered immoral when construed as the active transference by God of his righteous anger from the guilty to the innocent. To redeem is to pay the price of buying back our experience and entering it in the column of our gains rather than our losses. It forgives our debts in full. It is a story that tells the untold cost of love.[13]

I have been very slow to realize that what seems obvious to a social scientist, and therefore barely worth articulating, is far from obvious to the educated public. The logic and the methods of the social sciences remain opaque, no matter how often appeal is made to their data and conclusions and no matter how far causal connections appear to displace moral judgements. It is still difficult to discuss the ways in which religion and secular ideology are *alike* implicated both in solidarity and the struggle for survival, because according to a narrative derived from the *Philosophes*, religion remains the preferred scapegoat. We come together in solidarity and we maintain that solidarity by separating those within from those without, and by struggling against those without.

One reason why it is so difficult to displace this distorted narrative lies in the identification of science with natural science, and another lies in the polemical debasement of the debate by those who pretend to a scientific attitude, and even claim to represent it. There are natural scientists who misuse the authority rightly accorded them on account of their specific expertise to maraud at will and pronounce dogmatically in areas far beyond their competence. The issues of religion and war that have most concerned me in the course of my education, and have so often driven it forward, need to be treated with scientific caution and courtesy. We need to recognize our interim findings are always provisional and not be bemused and amused by celebrities strutting from media event to media event, beating their chests, denouncing opponents as evil and stupid, and announcing their moral and intellectual supremacy. Speaking daggers in this way is an intimate similitude of warfare inappropriate to the courtesies of shared inquiry. It approximates the expressions of contempt characteristic of jousting in a tournament or joshing in a pub.

Every rule of serious scientific engagement is broken when the representatives of the 'New Atheism' assume what is to be proved, point crudely to historical instances out of context rather than seek patiently to understand them in context, load the net consequences of multitudinous factors onto religion treated as a moral scapegoat for everything else (as when Christopher Hitchens claimed 'religion poisons everything'), manipulate the boundaries of concepts and entities to deliver conclusions by definitional fiat, elect opportunistically to determine what is essential and what accidental, and engage in the rhetorical judo of taking the part for the whole.

My own interim conclusion would be that when human beings seek to justify actions driven by the dynamic of the struggle for power, wealth and status, they may appeal to religion, or secular ideology, or the 'natural human right' of self-determination against a background history of oppression, but the justifications obscure much of the dynamic. The Christian Doge of Venice sets forth on crusade, but sacking Christian Byzantium en route provides a more lucrative motive for action. In defiance of a mandatory superstition, I suspect that religion itself, if you can even think of religion as a coherent and self-contained category, is neither here nor there, and certainly not *the* roadblock in the path of progress.

The beneficent and critical pressure exercised by the universal and the transcendent, at least since the Axial Age, whether expressed in ideals of harmony or of peace and non-violence, will be partly confiscated by more local loyalties in the very act of appropriation. All such loyalties are Janus-faced. Blaming something called religion for 'all the trouble we are in' is (like religion itself) as much the problem as the answer. It is intellectual laziness. It is a triumph of self-righteousness over the shared pursuit of truth. It is also a triumph of impact over content that illustrates only too shamefully and shamelessly what has happened in our universities, where the humanities and the social sciences have been subjected to criteria alien to the kinds of truth they represent. It seeks to solve a complex problem through a moral and empirical short-cut which is more than likely to stimulate yet more oppression and conflict in order to root the wretched thing out.

Humans are inclined to believe what they need to believe given their interests and circumstances. That not only colours how they create and read their sacred texts, but shapes how they frame and interpret their secular opinions. I have been particularly exercised by the high-mindedness of secular middle-class opinion in a Britain sheltered from the icy blasts that blow elsewhere by the exercise of imperial power operating from a sheltered island (or by American power). The 'bloodlands' of Eastern Europe are easily dismissed as illustrating the nasty instincts of people 'over there'. Up to 1914 the English middle class was morally privileged by relative safety and it never lost the knack. In the thirties and again in the sixties we capitalized on our moral advantage to lecture the world on good behaviour, as though that gave us the right intermittently to intervene elsewhere and proclaim our actions had nothing to do with our interests and everything to do with the good of humankind. To utilize a formulation from my 1965 book, *Pacifism*, we are either liberal pacifists or liberal imperialists. We elide the moral ambiguity and even obliquity of actions dictated by short-term political necessity, from the brutal suppression of Mau Mau in Kenya to the uncertain calculus of ends and means in Iraq. All this I painfully discovered over decades of self-education that put me at odds with intellectual peers and cherished friends. The engine for this empirical exposure of inherent dilemmas and the abyss of evil lying below the civilized surface was precisely the imaginative resources supplied by a Christianity that placed them at the heart of its redemptive narrative.

We remain reluctant to believe that children and dictators, small tribes and expansive empires, may need to be restrained, and that the least costly form of restraint *might* in certain circumstances be a pre-emptive strike before they are out of their minds and out of control. You may have to endure moral obloquy from the 'unco' guid' for getting your retaliation in first before you are totally justified, but that seems better than holding back till you are morally in the clear and your chance of avoiding a prolonged and costly war vastly impaired. I do not see what is so admirable about ensuring millions have to die to keep your scruples intact and your conscience clear.

The biggest moral problem arises not when issues of 'great pith and moment' are at stake but when men and women are willing, or at any rate expected, in the service of the *polis* to sacrifice themselves for the twists and turns of policy based on the unstable mixture of interests, loyalties, alliances and ideals that are unavoidable aspects of the political game. To fight in a dirty war against Mau Mau in Kenya in one of the last stands of discredited empire imposes almost impossible strains and attracts no elegiac commemoration or commendation on what used to be known in Britain as Armistice Day. At the same time the logic of international relations, like the logic of personal relations, minimally requires each and all to set limits beyond which we will not be pushed. Whether in the nursery or at the conference table we are obliged to mark out boundaries and circumscribe outrageous demands, or rue the consequences. Non-violence is vastly preferable to automatic mayhem, but there are limits to its application: Gandhi faced a British Empire with intermittent moral inhibitions and a critical mass of moral opposition at home in Britain; the Armenians did not have the same advantages. I have listened to 'Turks' apologizing in Istanbul, but they were Kurds waiting and waiting for an apology like the Armenians.

Working all this out had little to do with my formal schooling. I recollect writing a sixth-form essay on Bismarck where I commented on his moral obliquity and the fact that he was in some sense a Christian, adding with a flourish 'but then some of the greatest blackguards in history have been Christians'. Mr Bacon, my history teacher, wrote in the margin, 'Please keep this kind of abuse out of your essays.' So I did learn something at school, many things in fact from a quite small group of genuinely stimulating masters. Mostly I did not shine and did not work. Though I have many criticisms of the 'progressive' nostrums that replaced the tramlines laid down by that kind of schooling, I was not suited to it and I might well have flourished under a less prescriptive and more wide-ranging regime.

At any rate my formal education was a mess, in part because my reading was mostly off the syllabus. No sooner was a book prescribed than I left it on the shelf. Like a modern Pilgrim, the burden strapped on my back by my Evangelical childhood pushed me to undertake a very different kind of personal schooling, motivated by the need to get straight what was still 'true' about Christianity once you had worked your way through modern critical thinking about the Bible and modern science. I put the word 'true' in inverted commas not because I harbour post-modern doubts about the notion of truth but because truths are not all of a kind. The temperature at which water boils is a truth different in kind from a claim to *be* the Way, the Truth and the Life, or all that is conveyed by Titian's final Pietà or his *Noli me tangere*. Unlike Bunyan's Pilgrim, the burden of my quest never quite rolled away, though there were Delectable Mountains as well as Sloughs of Despond and prolonged periods in the dungeon of Giant Despair.

A good soaking in the Bible is the perfect goad to self-education, because it poses all the big questions and all the major life choices in narrative and poetic forms that bring them home to the imagination. It does not make you moral: that is more likely to come when you observe your own bad behaviour mirrored in other people. The Bible, understood as a contorted geological record of superimposed layers of human inquiry into first things, does at least push you to work out on the pulses why most of the answers offered in Scripture are problematic. The miseries of Job raise the problem of suffering and God responds with a revelation of a glory that passes all human understanding. The revelation may be magnificent but it is not an answer. The Bible is not an answer to a puzzle. It is a *tale* of two cities, an earthly city wrapped in 'the old miasmal mist', and a heavenly city where, after much travail, humanity comes together to drink freely of the water of life. It is a picture imagined by Blake not a theoretical scheme devised by Newton. The drama of the Passion codes the irreducible dilemmas of the human situation and the always imminent danger of descent into radical evil, *not* the incremental realization of progress under the auspices of optimistic scientific guides and philosopher kings acting as the privileged agents of some ultimately benevolent secular *telos*. There is, of course, a religious analogue of this, according to which God is an immanent *telos* ensuring that the net consequences of mayhem will in the end be for the best in the more or less best of all possible worlds.

From the problems and dilemmas of international relations to contentious debates over what is to count as knowledge in educational curricula, the Blakean imagination has to be defended against the encroachment of an attitude to problems that sees them as a form of Sudoku, and elevates reason as a solution rather than an indispensable tool. Too many 'secular humanists' are fixated on critical thinking as *the* basis of education and forget that you educate yourself and gain new perspectives by the disciplines of hard experience, imagination and the nurture of empathy. What looks like the direct route to moral thinking intellectually is the long way round experientially. Moral education is more properly pursued by the kind of pilgrimage detailed here than through training in rational inference from abstract principles. Almost anyone of modest intelligence can find a way through the strictly limited game rules of moral philosophy, and knowing how to play the game has scant connection with quality of moral performance. It is more likely to lead to sophisticated modes of exculpation in which we are all of us expert by sheer necessity. Morality is not a subject like geometry because it is about the experience of the human *subject*. It is a picture we paint about our place in the world rather than a diagram we construct by working to rule. We are too easily fooled and seduced by the elegance of the diagram. You experience the game vicariously through stories written on the fleshly tablets of the heart not through playing logical games in your own solitary head. The sovereign arbitrament of reason breeds as many subtle schools as the sole authority of the Bible breeds subtle sects. The house of Reason divides against itself. In popular imagination, Christianity is an alternative version of causal thinking rather than an imaginative understanding of the human condition. The imaginative and the imaginary are poles apart.

That is the main problem lying behind the education of David Martin. Getting straight what was profound in Christianity meant serious intellectual work which I pursued because I needed to know. Alongside very modest progress in jumping through the standard hoops of formal schooling, I forged ahead with my real education, not realizing that this unmarked and unassessed extra-mural struggle was the real thing. Helped by the accidents described in this memoir, I took up sociology in my spare time to help resolve the nagging problems of faith, violence and non-violence. There were 15 intellectually strenuous years between my appearance before a tribunal as a conscientious objector in 1948 and the moment I lost faith in pacifism on a day in 1963 halfway through a doctoral thesis at LSE on the interwar period. In the years between 1948 and 1963, as I said in my Introduction, I moved to my intense surprise, and with a great deal of trauma, from a failed musician and a would-be 'writer' teaching in primary schools, to a post in the sociology department of the LSE and then in 1971 to the chair of the department. Would-be writers need something other than 'the self' to 'express' and write about. I needed some objective problem about which I cared, and in the event what had been the meagrely stocked field of the sociology of religion provided enough subject matter for a lifetime. I did not become the writer of my romantic imagination, pouring out selfhood, but I did become a writer of sorts, judged by the content of what I argued. To write well mattered, but like happiness it came indirectly as an uncovenanted grace.

I was, of course, invited to be confirmed and accepted as a full member in the Temple of Reason, with its separate niches set aside for devotions to patron saints from August Comte to Noam Chomsky. In 1970 I read a book by Hazel Barnes in The New Thinker's Library entitled *The University as the New Church* which anticipated Alain de Botton's idea of a secular cathedral. In my solitary pilgrim's progress I briefly enrolled as a novice in this New Church, not yet fully aware of all its internal sects of reason and unreason. My correspondence course in sociology provided no map of the dominant ideologies demanded of neophytes. My parents had revered martyrs for the Protestant faith like Ridley and Cranmer. That narrative has been in recession for some decades, as you can see from the ignorance about its history induced in the schools or the indifference of passers-by to the statues of major Protestant figures like William Tyndale and Robert Raikes on the Thames Embankment. On belatedly reaching university, I was offered associate membership in an academic congregation that worshipped intellectual heroes like Bertrand Russell. For an influential section of the middle class, Russell was celebrated as a paragon of disinterested rationality. Slowly I realized that, when it came to life choices and the great problems of society, in particular violence, Russell's mixture of abstract logic and sentimentality carried no more authority than the prophetic pronouncements of Tolstoy.

The views and influence of Russell illustrate what happens when eminence in one field is applied to issues in other fields where its modes of inference are irrelevant if not downright misleading. Russell even suggested that issues in international relations should be approached like problems in symbolic logic. It is rather like trying to operate international money markets solely by computer programs. I reluctantly surmised that the confident pronouncements of philosophers and scientists outside their intellectual remit were just so much unfounded opinion.

The debate over foreign policy (and the Campaign for Nuclear Disarmament, CND) in the sixties caused my oldest school friends to fear I was making off in the wrong direction, and they blamed my exposure to sociology. They were only half right, because I was being educated out of some of my previous prejudices by the plain implications of the subject, not by the predictable opinions of its practitioners. I discovered that what I implicitly believed about the importance of empathic subjective 'understanding' of speech, sign and text in cultural context, and about the delusion of *pure* objectivity, had been articulated by Michael Polanyi in his 1958 book *Personal Knowledge*, and in the philosophy of Wilhelm Dilthey. Anglo-Saxon positivism and the scientism associated with it represented thin gruel, morally and methodologically. It represented a truncated humanism alien to the vagaries and imaginative leaps native to humanity. There were thinkers like Polanyi and Dilthey who articulated a hermeneutic approach consonant with Christian understandings.

After my 'conversion' I no longer had an instinct for what I 'ought' to think or say, and preferred nourishing my friendships over the large area where agreement was still possible to airing my opinions where it was not. It was a serious moment when I lost my automatic bearings and mistrusted all authorities. I realized that abject humility in these matters before what even then were the established sources of correct opinion was just the academic version of the 'deference' academics so despised in people of my social background. Like St Joan, adjured for arrogance by the inquisitor in Bernard Shaw's play, I came to the disturbing conclusion that the only source of judgement I possessed was my own. There is no alternative to making up our own minds even though we also need sounding boards. The loss is serious when your echo-box no longer lets you hear yourself played back by cherished friends, but it has to be borne.

I had no desire to come on all embattled, and I do not want to sound embattled now. My exits have been mostly reluctant, silent and unconfessed. I did not spread it around that I had joined discussions at Windsor and Cumberland Lodge, Windsor Great Park, under the aegis (I think) of Martin Charteris, the Queen's Private Secretary, to keep the bomb and counter the influence of the disarmers. I agreed with the disarmers that we had entered a new era with the advent of the bomb, but there was no way back, and a muddled and partial attempt to re-enter the past before the bomb would introduce dis-equilibria that might prove fatal. Unilateral disarmament as pursued in Britain was irresponsible and unrealistic. It offloaded the moral onus on the USA in order to allow us on our 'tight little island' the moral luxury and imperial hubris of 'setting an example to the world', while in practice saving money. There might well be a plausible case for saving money and cutting our cloth to suit our purse, but it hardly needed elaborate moral dressing up. Unilateral disarmament whereby 'the bomb' really was banned returned us to a world of wars between whole populations, mobilized on an industrial scale. It made that kind of war all the more likely, just like the Peace Pledge Union in the thirties, and I was passionately anti-war. Frank Parkin wrote an analysis of the ideology and personnel of CND as a movement of *middle-class* morality.

Moreover this morality came in job lots about any number of logically unrelated things, as became all too clear when I attended a peace conference in Helsinki and heard the (then) CND leader, Monsignor Bruce Kent, abusing the 'so-called loyalists' in Ulster. I held no brief for loyalists, but they and their opponents alike were mired in historical entanglements and confined in scripts they did not know how to alter without losing their sense of who they were and where they were coming from. In Northern Ireland the baleful processions of the past walked onto the stage of the present. That should exempt them and their Republican opponents from mere abuse. When I had made my statement of conscientious objection to the Fulham tribunal in 1948, I believed that all its disparate parts hung together, including the anarchist aestheticism, the Tolstoyan reading of the Gospels, the liberal objection to mass conscription, and the socialist objection to preparing to fight our erstwhile ally the Soviet Union. By the time I had finished my book on pacifism between the wars, these very different streams of thought and feeling had been traced back to quite distinct religious and ideological sources. The only link that had held them together was me and my horror of war.

It was precisely my Bible-embedded upbringing that schooled me in doubt and inoculated me against the shibboleths of the university. I refused to profess secular vows and might well have been 'excommunicated'. Put under pressure at LSE, particularly by the experience of student revolution, my hitherto silent exit became explicit. My inaugural lecture at the LSE in 1972 entitled 'Order and Rule' was my statement of disaffiliation from the faiths required of the sociologist. I now thought the Enlightened ideology and utilitarian ethics written into much of the sociological catechism pretty dubious. I was not only critical of Enlightened expectations about secularization, but of the pre-eminent role the Enlightenment assigned itself in the process of modernization. An elite ideology assigned a pre-eminent role to the Enlightened elite in the process of modernization, whereas religion was dismissed either as backward or as an irrelevant backwater. Meanwhile I had moved to the theology of St Augustine, in particular as expounded by Reinhold Niebuhr in *Moral Man and Immoral Society* (1934). There is a profound resistance to the peaceful kingdom of God proclaimed in the Gospels and redemption begins in acknowledging wretchedness and accepting the divine gift of grace embodied in the self-giving of the Saviour. That kind of interest ensured I was always marginal to mainstream sociology and its concerns.

For some of my colleagues, politics was the ultimate arena of the real and the rational, and therefore pursued with appropriate dedication and passion. For me, politics was the necessary bulwark of such fragile civility as might be possible in a fallen world. Politics pursued as an arena of displaced and misplaced hopes of utopia and fears of secular apocalypse is a dangerous delusion, and one that undermines

Habermas's notion of the public sphere as the privileged space of reason's reign. Politics is corrupted by the dynamics of power and at the same time it is the necessary bulwark of our solidarity one with another. Politics is one useful launching pad among others for the pursuit of betterment and welfare. Corruption is a standard part of the lexicon of political science, but it is also a theological category we bracket at our peril. Henry Adams wrote *The Education of Henry Adams* (published in 1918) late in life, and he concluded that 'politics as a practice, whatever its professions, has always been the systematic organization of hatreds'.

With only a slight risk of over-interpretation, I suspect that a Bible-embedded upbringing meant I could and would never see myself as practising a discrete and bounded sub-discipline called the sociology of religion. Instead I approached religion and politics as intimately related modes of human activity governed by the dynamic of varied kinds of power, material and spiritual combined. That is why I consciously used the same vocabulary in analysing both, for example sect and excommunication, subscription and creed, and it is why I found the same dilemmas inherent in both, like the conflict between sincerity and hypocrisy, prophetic critic and priestly practitioner, denunciation and annunciation. The increasing demand for sincerity and inwardness in the course of biblical revelation (or critical and cumulative discovery), from Jeremiah to Jesus and Augustine to Anselm, drove my interest in the criticism of politics, and my concern over a growing scepticism about politics on grounds of the hypocrisy of politicians. Though I believed in sincerity as one of the virtues, I thought it created problems, especially in politics where saying what you sincerely think can be disastrous for everybody and for the good causes to which you are committed. It is a cardinal sin in politics to speak sincerely but out of turn.

So I built up a critique of spontaneity and sincerity, which later I found I shared with a Jewish friend, Adam Baruch Seligman, who had come to similar conclusions by another route. Of course, he had the advantage of me, because encouraged by a religion that had no doubt about the importance of adhering to statute and loving the ordinances of the law. I by contrast was schooled in William Blake and inclined to be self-interested in, and attracted by, the idea that those who control their passions have passions susceptible to control. In my work on peace and war, quietism and violence, I have argued that embracing the pacifism of the Radical Reformation easily leads to some version of the antinomian heresy, dating from the origins of Christianity, that you can 'love God and do as you like'. That misreading of Augustine was understandably popular in the student revolution.

The Bible and Evangelicalism, taken together, ensured I would be drawn to the problems of politics and of sincerity, including sincerity in the power plays of politics, but also in the power plays of intimate personal relations where 'Each man kills the thing he loves . . . The coward does it with a kiss,/The brave man with a sword'. Evangelicalism demands sincerity as part of 'the good confession' and as I grew older I found the demand irksome, which was one good reason for eventually moving to the Church of England. To lose faith in sincerity as an unfailing guide to conduct in all things and all circumstances poses more difficulties than you might think, and I took a great deal of time and trouble over it. Sincerity is both an obvious virtue and a virtue that needs to be practised with care and consideration. To think hard about just when and where sincerity is appropriate is the beginning of wisdom, and you need to be very careful *what* you are sincere about, as there is nothing admirable about being sincerely greedy. A nuanced account of sincerity is difficult to come by, and at different times in my academic life I tried to give such accounts of the problems and the high demands and risks associated with the virtues of sincerity, spontaneity, creativity and niceness.

Discretion suggests it is not very discreet to describe in any detail how you acquired it, if indeed I ever did. Beyond the dangers of indiscretion lies another problem. Once you confess to a loss of faith in sincerity, people are disinclined to believe you, and accuse you of being hypocritical and putting on an act. It is almost as dangerous to disavow sincerity as it is to confess sincerely that you have scant 'respect' for at least some aspects of other faiths, even when you cover yourself by saying quite sincerely that you have scant respect for aspects of your own faith. The excellent virtue of sincerity has to be understood and analysed at every level from the international to the intimate, and once you do that it becomes clear that sociology is the modern form of Adam Smith's *Theory of Moral Sentiments*.

In analysing how politicians negotiate the affairs of nations, as in analysing how people negotiate the intimate sphere, one has to understand the roles played by sincerity and hypocrisy and the roles played by victimage and invincibility, and all in the context of the opportunity costs of strictly limited alternative courses of action. When it comes to the moral sentiments and to the moral dilemmas of everyday life, sociology is ready enough to analyse (say) friendship, or honour and shame, but rarely inquires into (say) the subtler modes of coercion, corruption and power. Stalin's random alternation of raising up and casting down finds its analogues at every level of existence from oriental despots to the autocrats of the breakfast table.

Politics arouses scepticism from those who have been schooled to expect too much, but politics is as much the precondition of any kind of civilized existence as authority, and though vast evil can be perpetrated in the name of both, nothing good is possible in their absence. Anarchy is effectively chaos governed only by the war of all against all. I have found it difficult to make that obvious point and well remember the murmurs of disapprobation about 'authoritarianism' that went up from some colleagues at Lancaster University when I made it. I managed to arouse a similar shudder of chill avoidance when I experimented with dropping the word 'duty' into an otherwise civil conversation with an LSE colleague. In the rhetoric of the time, words like 'authority', 'authoritarian' and 'duty' played a key role in defining who you were socially, and what you were presumed to stand for. It was not that I offered any kind of example of how to exercise authority or perform duties. I was simply interested in reiterating the obvious, and in the negative response elicited by words that denoted processes and virtues central to anything one might call 'civilization'. 'Civilization' was itself a word only the foolhardy or the ignorant dared to use. The contemporary edition of the Index Librorum Prohibitorum is continuously augmented and includes words that must not be used, ideas that must not be discussed, as well as views that may not be held.

The heart of the matter lies in accountability and responsibility, especially as realized in the prophetic critic and the 'priestly' practising politician. Gradually, in the course of embracing a pacifist faith and then losing it, I had acquired a close familiarity with the rhetoric of prophetic denunciation and with the rhetoric of established religious and secular power. I did more than watch the incumbents of prophetic and priestly roles walk the walk; it was just as important to listen to how they talked the talk. Having begun by excoriating those in the political role from what I regarded as a prophetic antiwar position, I began to see the roles of critic and practitioner as complementary, and to sympathize with hard-pressed practitioners. Political practitioners exemplify hypocrisy to an exceptional degree because the art of politics is a masked ball with knives at the ready should survival demand it.

Politicians know the score quite as well as their critics and inquisitors in the commentariat. Contemporary inquisitors on radio and television enjoy the right to demand unequivocal answers, and to evade questions about their own preferred solutions, by hiding behind their critical role. They shoot from the safety of a hideout that only a few seek out to destroy. As incumbents of an important democratic role, they are allowed and expected to be finger-wagging moralists *and* exempt from moral responsibility. Far more than ministers of religion, they occupy the coward's castle of a pulpit above contradiction and beyond a demand to choose between alternatives. Their pulpit is uniquely privileged. Politicians by contrast enjoy the consolations of power and ministerial cars, but they are the prisoners of responsibility, unable to lay bare all the facts relevant to their defence, or freely to speak their minds, or make the optimum choices, or enjoy the pleasures of consistency. Unlike commentators, politicians are inhibited by voters who insist on incompatible policies, who desert the moment the going gets difficult, and by their volatility restrict even the options that to the onlooker in the stands appear available.

Politicians confront their inquisitors in the media with one hand tied behind their backs. As a spectator too horrified by the reality I descried to act, I was always fascinated by the confrontation between commentators and political actors and wrote on the complementary roles played by the Christian 'prophet', the secular commentator and the practising politician. Of course, commentators also have to accept the kind of constriction inherent in acting out their prescribed role. The British television interviewer Jeremy Paxman best performs his role when he pretends to understand less than he really does about the exigencies of politics and pretends to be less intelligent than he really is. He plays by turns the part of the amazed, or obtuse or indignant onlooker in the stands. He is the sophisticated barrister employed and highly remunerated by 'society' to represent the bemused onlooker. Unlike a real fool he feigns naïveté, and unlike a genuine prophet he acts out ersatz anger.

As not much of an actor, and only intermittently adopting the role of observer, I gravitated to the tertiary role of one who observes the interaction between those who act and those who observe. I became fascinated with the role played by hypocrisy and by the masquerade both in political commentary and in political action, and with the different rhetorical tricks deployed in the game of critic and questioner versus practitioner. I came to regard the study of rhetoric as a major key to understanding the masks of power and the nature of political action. The language used by politicians provides a coded index of the nature of moral contestation in the political arena. Language under strain tells you where the cracks and stresses lie, beginning with the request for sympathetic understanding implied by the ubiquitous use of 'You know'.

I put this fascination with hypocrisy and dissimulation down to the moral itches and dilemmas set up by a Bible-embedded childhood. Christianity is about the demand for righteousness and the seeds of corruption, about repentance and acceptance, about priestly mediation and prophetic denunciation. All that is in play in transmogrified form in the confrontations of critic and practitioner. It lies latent in the luxury enjoyed by the commentator and the strict constraints experienced by whoever accepts responsibility, whether to govern a country or run a university.

You find it in the contrast between the demand for probity, integrity and consistency, and the shifts and stratagems required by events you cannot hope to anticipate. It lies behind the choice politicians make between insisting for the sake of party reputation that they acted in good faith, and weighing up the costs for yourself and the party of apologizing and repenting in public. It lies behind the choice between accepting at least some of the blame, and arguing blind that the mess was created by your opponents or by persons known or unknown elsewhere. That is the home territory of religion, yet many of my colleagues considered religion an evanescent sideshow. For me religion was simply life itself. It enacts the fundamental scenario in which the Son of Man is betrayed by a kiss and in which the one who tells the truth is arrested at night by a posse 'with swords and with staves', and hustled away to be confronted by false witnesses. Religion is about the general conditions of politics and shares in them intimately. It is the prologue to the political play and the cheering and keening chorus to the action. I do not believe 'the political' is the beginning and end of life, let alone that it offers 'final solutions'. My head of department lamented the delay in the arrival of *the* revolution. I lacked a secular apocalyptic.

The human condition had been given a progressive and potentially violent gloss by the Enlightenment. Enlightenment generates frustration and self-congratulation that you are not as benighted as other men are. Christianity by contrast reveals as much about the sad folly of humanity as about the goodness of God, and in the end the attempt to root out faith and grace as *the* source, or even a main source, of our troubles is inhumane folly on the grandest scale. Enlightened St Petersburg, Paris and Washington are as much built on pyramids of skulls as Christian Rome and Byzantium – or Muslim Isfahan. Thomas Hardy was right: 'If way to the better there be it exacts a full look at the worst.' And the worst is to be found across the board, including the religion of love and the secular ideology of the 'Party of Humanity'.

I discovered sin and the ravages of radical evil, and I found 'the worst' placarded for all to see at Golgotha and Auschwitz, Katyn and Rwanda. This was inscribed in literature over and over again, all the way from the humiliation of the body of Hector by Achilles to the murder of the wife and children of Macduff. But in literature, and in great swathes of human history, 'senseless' violence lies within the malignant reciprocities demanded by the rule of honour and power, rather than the free exchange of love. Christianity had reversed all that by making the mark of humiliation the sign of triumph. Christianity had transferred honour and power, glory and might, from the vengeful act of humiliation to the humiliated body itself. It is the body with the marks of the nails and the wound in the side that rose triumphant from the dead.

I had moved from the utopian vision propagated by the Radical Reformation to the realistic approach accepted by the Magisterial Reformation looking back to Augustine. There is a Big Issue latent here. Dr Martyn Lloyd Jones, preaching to us Evangelical Christians for a full hour at Westminster Chapel, spoke as though our individual sickness, and what you might even call our depravity, was the infection burrowing away in the heart of the rose. Social scientists on the other hand are preachers of quite another kind. They suppose that corruption, a word they use indifferent to its theological roots, is an infection of the social system. In fact it is a two-way traffic between the personal and the social. There is an endemic war between the necessary constraints of solidarity and the human longing to be free of them. There is war and aggression; there is cooperation and sympathy; there is cooperation and solidarity for the purposes of war; and there is individual protest and collective persecution. All of them are written in, socially and biologically, at *every* level of human interaction.

What we took for granted

This exercise in memory has rarely made explicit what remains 'obvious' to most in our generation, because it lies implicit in what we write, how we write and how we speak. Younger people notice the way we speak in complete sentences, but they are less conscious of the kinds of contemporary demotic we avoid. We know the difference and reflect on it, but they have no special need either to know or reflect on what comes naturally to them. In conclusion I evoke what

David Martin at home in his garden, 2008

'we' took for granted before the 'Present . . . latched its postern against my tremulous stay'. In particular I evoke the kind of Christian socialization that was available up to the 1960s and was then systematically wiped out, so that most people born after 1950 have little access to the background of this memoir.

We were marked as a historical generation by the time between appeasement in 1938 and the moral outrage of Anglo-French action in Suez in 1956. Like Günter Grass on the 'other side' in his autobiography *Peeling the Onion* (2007), we learnt geography following with hope and alarm the progress and regress of the war. We became intimately familiar with places on the North African front like Sidi Barrani, Mersa Matruh, and Tobruk, or ports on the Atlantic as far apart as Montevideo and Narvik, or bombed cities like Coventry and Rotterdam, Dresden and Nagasaki, or obliterated villages like Oradour and Lidice. We were mesmerized by Dunkirk, the loss of Singapore and the sinking of the *Repulse*, the *Prince of Wales* – and the *Bismarck*. Some of us were corralled to sing patriotic songs in (say) the Frederick Wigan Hall, Mortlake, like A. P. Herbert's *Song of Liberty*, 'March to liberty with me' or 'Non nobis, Domine' or 'This royal throne of kings . . . this fortress built by nature for herself against infection and the hand of war'. We heard the anthems of the

Allies every night before Big Ben struck nine for us to listen together to the news.

Most of us had our schooling disrupted up to a point, but my classmate Justham told us a tale of being torpedoed in the Atlantic as he returned from the safety of Canada in 1943. We played on bomb sites. General Dobbie, who commanded the garrison in the defence of Malta, came to our church in 1942. Like General Wingate of the Burma campaign, he was a Plymouth Brother, and when he signed my autograph book it was the same solitary signature that had confirmed the order to cease fire in 1918. Laurence Olivier's film of *Henry the Fifth*, which I saw at a Marble Arch cinema in 1944, hit the solar plexus when it included 'Our king went forth to *Normandy*' and concluded with a poignant speech of mutual reconciliation by the Duke of Burgundy shot against lambent horizons of ruined landscapes. I was part of the surging crowd in Whitehall that waited for hours for Churchill to come out and speak on VE night. I could not then imagine meeting a German airman in 2011 who on that very day was (as he said with a smile) making his first land trip to England on the Isle of Wight, prior to three years in America as a prisoner of war. What he and I had in common is a recollection that is now uncommon almost to the point of extinction. Perhaps that is as good a reason as any for having written about my education.

People of our generation were relatively well disposed to Christian faith and certainly not inclined to abuse Christians as psychologically inadequate, ignorant, evil-doing, and, according to A. C. Grayling, stupidly cherishing notions that had befuddled the heads of 'ignorant goatherds'. Maybe there was a partial pause in the tradition of rationalist superiority represented by Thomas Huxley when he dismissed my father's faith as 'corybantic'. This tradition has been recently revived, exploiting the moral credit line extended by September 11, 2001, without enquiring too closely just where in the interstices of international *Realpolitik* that appalling bonfire was fuelled. I became aware of friendliness to faith on visits to Europe during the years when people recognized the threat from the East. They had not yet relaxed into a safety guaranteed by the Americans that allowed them to become moral freeloaders, letting the Americans be the moral load bearers, before blaming them for the Cold War and promoting a moral equivalence between East and West. Of course, the Americans were as imperialist as we, the French and the British, had been when we had scope and opportunity, but given a choice of imperialisms they were better than the post-war alternatives.

We shared a Christian socialization which, however haphazard and superficial, has now largely disappeared in England apart from those church schools that keep alive, against a background of captious criticism, an older moral and intellectual ethos, including some introduction to Christianity beyond the kind of religious education that mechanically rehearses what adherents of the major world religions are supposed to believe. Up to 1960 most children in England acquired some very modest sense of Christian identity as something to do with being ready to forgive as the Prodigal Son was forgiven, being a Good Samaritan to those on the other side of the tracks who needed help, and loving your neighbour as yourself. They had a repertoire of well-known hymns, like 'The Lord's my shepherd, I'll not want' and 'O God, our help in ages past'. They probably had some vague recollection of the more dramatic Bible stories from Joseph and his brethren, and David and Saul, to the coming of the shepherds and the three Wise Men, and the narrative of the Passion. They knew that of the three great virtues of faith, hope and charity, the greatest of these was charity. The Student Christian Movement still flourished, and educated young people read Dietrich Bonhoeffer, Simone Weil and C. S. Lewis, even though the long-term feminization of the Church meant that males treated confirmation as licence to abandon unmanly pursuits. That often left the Church to young people like myself with passionate interests in music and poetry, or people like Alan Bennett who was just the kind of introverted youth his parish priest was not anxious to have at early morning communion.

The disruptions of the 1960s involved the promotion of an ethos of self-expression, including spirituality, rooted in what Charles Taylor has called 'the turn to the self', and it sought freedom from the institutional forms that in practice made the achievement of selfhood possible. Callum Brown attributes the rapid decline of institutional attachment from the 1960s to the entirely proper pursuit of female emancipation, but the changes have a wider provenance than this allows, not least the Church's own loss of faith in the continued relevance of settled habits, liturgical enactments and rites of passage. After 1960 Christian formation became the preserve of a minority who had received a public school education or who had attended schools, often under Church aegis, where the older moral and intellectual ethos was fostered and nourished. These schools were and are much sought after. Christianity became increasingly identified with gathered churches on the Evangelical model and appealed to people who wanted a relatively safe environment for themselves and their children. The Alpha Course to some extent made up for the absence of a taken-for-granted Christian socialization, while the charismatic movement offered some of the emotional satisfactions of intimacy and the overt expressions of fellow-feeling promoted by the cultural changes of the sixties.

Yet the Church of England as my generation experienced it offered a musical, architectural and liturgical presence that spoke with plangent urgency to the aesthetic and intellectual imagination. Although the parish system is currently under financial and organizational pressure, it remains the only possible carrier of a serious liturgical tradition summoning up the diurnal sequence of the Christian narrative. The occasional offices remain the one entry point through which this sense of place, time and meaning can be offered to those who stand in the vestibule of the Church seeking its benediction on their lives but very far from having the time or inclination to make long-term commitments. What marks the contemporary scene, whether in religion or in politics, or indeed in personal life, is wariness about long-term commitments and the responsibilities they entail. However much people of my generation failed to fulfil those commitments, they knew what they were and acknowledged their authority.

The shift to a mixture of the expressive, the utilitarian and the short-term was the legacy of the sixties as I and others experienced it, and it means that those, like my daughter Jessica, who now take up the parish ministry find themselves either servicing the dying or having to start all over again with such Christian socialization of the young as is possible. It is through activities for children that parents are brought into some contact with what the Church has to offer by way of community and mutual support. Many parish priests, men and increasingly women, are drawn from just those highly educated sectors of society in which the Church is either cherished or roundly abused. They know the score and they know the odds they are up against, whether financial or demographic, but the quality of their commitment to the Church in a place and the Church for the sake of the whole community is as high as, or higher than, it ever was in the past. It is a project of recuperation which should inform the concerns of those who direct the mission of the Church. This memoir has itself offered an account of a socialization of a taken-for-granted kind that no longer exists and of a recuperation of imaginative resources in a cold climate.

Notes

1. In the 1901 census he is listed as aged 22, a 'stationary engine driver', living at Prospect Place, Elwell St., Upwey, as a boarder. My mother, Miriam Rhoda, was born in 1904.
2. In the 1990s I gave the Assize sermon in Winchester Cathedral to open the proceedings of the Western Circuit, and afterwards incautiously recollected to an urbane judge the judicial ferocity of Jeffreys, only to be reminded that 'after all, they were traitors, you know'.
3. I think I was invited to meet the Queen because I had made some comments on the royal family in a radio broadcast following a physical attack on Princess Anne in the Mall. A conversation with the Queen is private but some of the other conversations surprised me. Sir Edward Ford wanted to know how many men I had under me at the LSE, and when I said the famous LSE library was less than a century old he confessed that in his view it was impossible to build up a decent library in less than four hundred years. Another courtier wanted to know whether I knew Sir Anthony Wagner, Garter Principal King of Arms. I had to admit I had not had the pleasure, greatly to his surprise. 'I thought everybody knew Anthony, a German family you know, came over with the Hanoverians.' He went on to ask me what I thought of Ramsey, and when I said I did not know much about football explained that he 'was not talking about Sir Alf Ramsey but about Michael Ramsey, the Archbishop'. I replied he was 'a brilliant man if a bit fluffy behind the ears'. I was then asked, 'What shall we do about this slot at York? How about Runcie?' I ventured a brief character reference of Robert Runcie which somehow seemed not quite enough when the archbishopric of York was under consideration. He persisted, 'Is he for example the kind of chap who would write a commentary on the Second Epistle to the Galatians?' Confronted by this esoteric addition to the New Testament, I felt confident in assuring him that Runcie would not do a thing like that, indeed that he was incapable of it.
4. The papers of Gerda Seligsohn and her father, the philosopher Richard Kroner, are held at the Leo Baeck Institute, New York, and chronicle an extraordinary family history.
5. Published as *Forbidden Revolutions: Pentecostalism in Latin America and Catholicism in Eastern Europe* (London: SPCK, 1996).

6   Her daughter Ruth Gipps was a distinguished anti-modernist composer and the subject of a study by Jill Halstead.

7   Throughout these latter sections of the chapter I am drawing selectively on my memorial address for him, published by LSE, which I gave alongside other addresses by Julius Gould and Terence Morris in March 1998.

8   Hugh McLeod, *The Religious Crisis of the 1960s*, Oxford: Oxford University Press, 2008.

9   In these sections I draw occasionally on my memorial address for him, given in the chapel of All Souls in February 2005, and later printed by the College.

10 David Martin (Charles Sisson) 'Polity and Religion', *Poetry Nation Review* 39, Vol. 1 No. 11, 1984.

11 Along with the historian John Shelton Reed and the sociologist Richard Fenn, both close family friends, and the controversialist Peter Mullen.

12 No. 17 in David Martin, *Sacred History and Sacred Geography*, Vancouver: Regent College Publishing, 2008.

13 There are many issues encapsulated here, some related to doctrines of substitutionary atonement as expressed in Wesley's hymns and the Book of Common Prayer. If you respond to the words, as my father did and I do, and nevertheless reject the idea of Christ sacrificed to placate an angry God (rather than being driven to death as a consequence of 'the evil that is in man'), then one has recourse to Paul's 'God was in Christ reconciling the world to himself' and Wesley's '(He) emptied himself of all but love'. One responds to the free gift of the broken body and receives the body and blood in the Eucharist under the forms of bread and wine as realized signs of the divine dwelling among us and in us, and vulnerable to all that besets humanity, including death and desolation.

Bibliography

Three significant early articles by David Martin

1962   'The Denomination', *British Journal of Sociology*, Vol. XIII No. 1

1965   'Towards Eliminating the Concept of Secularization', *Penguin Survey of the Social Sciences 1965*, edited by Julius Gould (Penguin)

1969   'Towards a General Theory of Secularization', *European Journal of Sociology*, Vol. X, December

Books by David Martin

1965   *Pacifism: A Historical and Sociological Study* (Routledge and Kegan Paul)

1967   *A Sociology of English Religion* (SCM Press)

1969   *The Religious and the Secular* (Routledge and Kegan Paul)

1973   *Tracts against the Times* (Lutterworth)

1978   *The Dilemmas of Contemporary Religion* (Blackwell)

1978   *A General Theory of Secularization* (Blackwell)

1980   *The Breaking of the Image: A Sociology of Christian Theory and Practice* (Blackwell)

1990   *Tongues of Fire: The Explosion of Protestantism in Latin America* (Blackwell)

1996   *Forbidden Revolutions: Pentecostalism in Latin America and Catholicism in Eastern Europe* (SPCK)

1997   *Reflections on Sociology and Theology* (Clarendon)

1997   *Does Christianity Cause War?* (Clarendon)

2002   *Christian Language and its Mutations: Essays in Sociological Understanding* (Ashgate)

2002   *Pentecostalism. The World their Parish* (Blackwell)

2005   *On Secularization: Towards a Revised General Theory* (Ashgate)

2011   *The Future of Christianity: Reflections on Violence and Democracy, Religion and Secularization* (Ashgate)

2014   *Religion and Power: No Logos without Mythos* (forthcoming)

Festschrift for David Martin

2001   *Restoring the Image: Essays on Religion and Society in Honour of David Martin*, edited by Andrew Walker and Martyn Percy (Sheffield Academic)

Books of sermons by David Martin

1989   *Divinity in a Grain of Bread* (Foreword by Robert Runcie) (Lutterworth)

2002   *Christian Language in the Secular City* (Foreword by Rowan Williams) (Ashgate)

2008   *Sacred History and Sacred Geography: Spiritual Journeys in Time and Space* (Regent College)

David Martin as guest editor

1979   *Crisis for Cranmer and King James: Poetry Nation Review* 13, Vol. 6 No. 5

Selected books edited by David Martin

1969   *Anarchy and Culture: The Problem of the Contemporary University* (Routledge and Kegan Paul)

1980   *Sociology and Theology: Alliance and Conflict*, edited with John Orme Mills OP and W. S. F. Pickering (Harvester)

Index

Printed in Great Britain
by Amazon.co.uk, Ltd.,
Marston Gate.